D1742050

1 MONTH OF
FREE
READING

at

www.ForgottenBooks.com

By purchasing this book you are eligible for one month membership to ForgottenBooks.com, giving you unlimited access to our entire collection of over 1,000,000 titles via our web site and mobile apps.

To claim your free month visit:
www.forgottenbooks.com/free921224

ISBN 978-0-266-99970-6
PIBN 10921224

ACTS AND RESOLVES

PASSED BY THE

GENERAL ASSEMBLY

OF THE

STATE OF VERMONT,

AT THE

THIRD BIENNIAL SESSION, 1874.

PUBLISHED BY AUTHORITY.

MONTPELIER:

FREEMAN STEAM PRINTING HOUSE AND BINDERY.

1874.

NEW YORK
PUBLIC
LIBRARY

LAWS OF VERMONT.

A. D. 1874.

PUBLIC ACTS.

No. 1.—AN ACT RELATING TO INSURANCE.

It is hereby enacted by the General Assembly of the State of Vermont:

SEC. 1. All mutual fire insurance companies in this state shall be responsible for the acts and neglect of the several agents appointed by them, as between the said companies and the applicants for insurance therein, or the assured, while in the performance of their duties as the agents of said companies.

SEC. 2. All fire insurance companies, other than those chartered by the general assembly of this state, are prohibited from taking insurance in this state, unless such company or companies shall be responsible by the laws of the state in which such company or companies are situated, or by the act incorporating such company or companies, or by a proviso to that effect inserted in their policies of insurance, for the acts and neglect of their agents as between said companies and the assured, and as between said companies and the applicants for insurance therein.

SEC. 3. If any person shall take any application or make any survey intending to effect insurance on any property in this state, in any fire insurance company not chartered by the legislature of this state, said company not being liable for the acts and neglects of such persons, as specified in the preceding section, said person shall, upon conviction before any court proper to try the same, forfeit and pay a sum not less than seven dollars for every such offense; one half of such penalty shall go to the person prosecuting the same, and the other half to the treasury of the town where such offense shall have been committed.

Sec. 4. Whenever application for fire insurance shall be taken or transmitted by or through a local or traveling agent of any fire insurance company, it shall in law be deemed to be the act of the said company; and such agent shall not therein be deemed to be the agent of the applicant or insured, and in all questions arising as to the facts stated in such application, the said agent shall be taken and deemed to be the agent of the insurers, and not of the insured.

Sec. 5. There is hereby established a distinct bureau, to be known as the insurance bureau, which shall be charged with the execution of the laws of this state in relation to insurance.

Sec. 6. The secretary and treasurer of this state are hereby declared *ex-officio* insurance commissioners.

Sec. 7. That no joint stock insurance company, not organized under the laws of this state, shall be permitted or allowed to transact the business of such company in this state, unless it shall have a *bona fide* paid up capital, invested in securities readily convertible into cash, of at least one hundred thousand dollars; not less than one half of which shall be invested in cash securities, other than mortgages of real estate, nor unless such company shall have, in addition to such capital, assets equal in amount to all its outstanding liabilities, reckoning fifty per cent

of premiums on outstanding fire risks, the whole amount
of premium on marine risks, and tho premium reserve on
life risks, based on tho actuaries' table of mortality, with
interest at four per cent, as a liability ; provided, that the
insurance commissioners may, at their discretion, license
any company to do business in this state whoso impair-
ment of capital doos not exceed twenty per cent of the
above rule; nor shall any mutual fire or life insurance
company or co-operative insurance company, association
or society, not organized under the laws of this state, be
permitted or allowed to transact the business of such
company in this state unless it possesses assets amounting
to ono hundred thousand dollars, invested in securities
readily convertible into cash, not less than one half of
which shall be invested in cash securities other than mortgages of real estate, nor unless it possesses such assets
equal to all its outstanding liabilities (including re-
insurance, to bo estimated as in the case of joint stock
insurance companies above named, and including the
amount of guarantee capital as a liability) ; nor until all
the laws relating to insurance companies of other states,
enacted by this state, shall have been complied with.
And further provided, that nothing herein shall be so
construed as to require any mutual fire insurance company to keep on hand any cash re-insurance reserve or
funds invested in securities other than their premium
notes, when said premium notes amount in gross to three
per centum of the amount of risk by said company.

SEC. 8. No insurance company, not organized under
the laws of this state, shall do business in this state until
it has filed with the secretary of this state a written stipulation, agreeing that any legal process affecting the com-

pany, served on either of the insurance commissioners, shall have the same effect as if served personally on the company within this state. So long as any liabilities of the stipulating company to any resident of this state continue, such stipulation cannot be revoked or modified. Service of process according to the stipulation aforesaid shall be sufficient service on the company; a copy of such stipulation, certified by either of the commissioners, and his certificate that process has been served on him, shall be sufficient evidence thereof. When process against or affecting an insurance company is served on the insurance commissioners, or either of them, it shall be served by duplicate copies, and they or he shall immediately forward by mail one copy of the same to the company at its home office, or to any person whom such company shall designate.

SEC. 9. It shall not be lawful for any insurance company embraced in section seven to transact any insurance business in this state, unless such company shall first obtain license of the insurance commissioners, authorizing the company so to do. Before receiving such license, the company shall file with the secretary of state a certified copy of its charter and by-laws, and a full statement, under oath of its president and secretary, showing the financial condition and standing of the company, in accordance with blanks furnished by him. Upon receiving such copies and statements, if the commissioners are satisfied with the same, and that the company meets the requirements of section seven, and has complied with the requirements of section eight of this act, they shall grant such license, authorizing such company to do insurance . business by authorized agents, subject to the laws of this state, until the first day of April thereafter; and annually thereafter, on the first day of April such license may be renewed, so long as such company shall comply with the requirements aforesaid, and the commissioners shall regard the company as safe, reliable, and entitled to public confidence. For each license or renewal, as above, the company shall pay to the insurance commissioners the sum of five dollars.

Sec. 10. No person shall act as agent of any insurance company aforesaid, not organized under the laws of this state, until he shall have filed with the secretary of state a certificate from the company or its authorized general agent, authorizing him to act as such agent, and obtained license thereon from the commissioners so to do. Upon filing the certificate aforesaid, the commissioners shall issue a license to such person to act as an insurance agent in this state; provided, the company for which such person proposes to procure or solicit applications for insurance therein shall be authorized to do insurance business in this state, which license shall continue until the first day of April thereafter, unless, for cause, revoked in the meantime. And upon filing a certificate as aforesaid, such license may be renewed on said first day of April, and annually thereafter, and for such license and each subsequent renewal the person receiving the same shall pay to the commissioners the sum of one dollar. If any person shall solicit or receive any risk or application for insurance, or receive money or value therefor for any insurance company or agent, without such license from the commissioners, he shall be punished for each offense by fine not exceeding one hundred dollars; one half to the use of the prosecutor. But any policy issued on an application thus procured, shall bind the company, if otherwise valid; provided, however, that this section shall not apply to any person who only acts as clerk to any insurance company or agent.

SEC. 11. Any person may be licensed by the commissioners as insurance broker to negotiate contracts of insurance, and to effect insurance for others than himself for a compensation; and by virtue thereof he may place risks or effect insurance with any insurance company of this state, or with the agents of any insurance company who have been licensed to do an insurance business in this state, but with no other. For such license he shall pay the sum of ten dollars, which shall authorize him thus to act until the first day of April then next; and on payment of the same fee, his license may be renewed from year to year afterwards, ending annually on the first day of April. Any person without such license, assuming to act as such broker, shall forfeit not less than fifty dollars; one half of which forfeiture shall go to the complainant, and the other half to the state treasury; provided, that any authorized insurance agent, whose payments for certificates of authority shall amount to ten dollars per annum, may act as such broker without further charge for license, and any such agents whose payments for such certificates shall have been less than ten dollars may have such license as a broker on paying such sum as will, with the sum already paid for certificates, make the sum of ten dollars.

SEC. 12. The insurance commissioners shall be authorized at any time to examine into the condition and affairs of any insurance company not organized under the laws of this state, doing business or proposing to do business therein, or cause such examination to be made by some person appointed by them, not interested in such company; and may in like manner examine into the business transacted by any agent of such company in this state, and may require such company or agent to produce all books or papers relating to such company or agency, and to answer in writing, under oath, all reasonable questions relating thereto; and if, in their opinion, the affairs of such company are in an unsound or failing condition, they shall revoke any license that may have been granted to such company, and all licenses that may have been granted to agents of such company, by written notice to the company, and publication of the same by six consecutive insertions in one daily or weekly newspaper in each county where such company may have had authorized agent or agents.

Sec. 13. Every fire insurance company not organized under the laws of this state, but doing business therein, on or before the first day of February in each year, and every life insurance company not organized under the laws of this state, but doing business therein, on or before the first day of March in each year, shall transmit to the insurance commissioners a statement, under oath of its president and secretary, of the whole amount of premiums received in money, or in the form of notes, credits, loans or any other substitute for money, by or on account of said company, during the year ending on the 31st day of the preceding December, for any insurance made by it on persons or property, in this state; also exhibiting its assets, liabilities, amount of capital stock actually paid in, the amount of outstanding risks, and the business, standing and affairs of the company generally, in accordance with blanks, to be furnished by the commissioners, adapted to the business of such company, which statement shall be filed in the office of the secretary of state; and shall pay to the commissioners, upon filing such statement, the sum of twenty dollars, which shall be paid by said commissioners to the state treasurer. And for the purpose of the above statement the commissioners shall prepare suitable blanks, proposing such interrogatories as may be necessary to ascertain the business, standing and affairs of such company, and forward duplicates of the same in the month of December in each year, to every such company; and the commissioners may demand a like statement of its standing and affairs at any other time when, in their opinion, the same may be necessary for the safety of the public.

SEC. 14. When by the laws of any other state or nation any taxes, fines, penalties, licenses, fees, deposits of money or of securities, or other obligations or prohibitions are or would be imposed on life insurance companies of this state doing business in such other state or nation, or upon their agents therein so long as such laws continue in force, the same obligations and prohibitions, of whatever kind, shall be imposed upon all life insurance companies of such other states or nations doing business within this state, and their agents herein.

SEC. 15. When by the laws of any other state or nation any taxes, fines, penalties, licenses, or fees, would be required to be paid to, or a deposit of money or of securities made with, the treasurer of such other state by life insurance companies of this state, doing business in such other state or nation, so long as such laws shall continue in force, the same taxes, fines, penalties, licenses, or fees shall be paid to, and deposits of money or of securities made with, the treasurer of this state, by the life insurance companies of such other state or nation doing business in this state.

SEC. 16.   Unless any judgment rendered in this state against any insurance company shall be paid within thirty days after demand made upon any agent of such company, and notice thereof given to the insurance commissioners by the officer holding the execution, the insurance commissioners may suspend the power of the company to do business in this state until it shall be paid; and if the company, or any agent therefor, shall, after notice of such suspension, issue any policy in this state during such suspension, said company and agent shall each forfeit a sum not exceeding two hundred dollars.   But any policy so granted shall be valid and binding against the company.

SEC. 17.   Any insurance agent doing business in this state, who shall appropriate to his own use any money or substitute for money received by him as such agent, and refuse or neglect to pay over such money or substitute for money to the company or other party entitled to receive the same, for the space of thirty days after notice to make such payment, shall be deemed guilty of larceny, and upon conviction, shall be punished therefor in accordance with the laws of this state.

SEC. 18.   All copies of charters, by-laws, certificates, appointments, and all copies of other papers required by law to be filed in the office of the secretary of this state, made and certified by either of the insurance commissioners, shall in all cases be competent evidence in the courts of this state.

SEC. 19. Whenever the insurance commissioners shall have reason to believe that any insurance company embraced in section seven of this act, or any insurance company organized under the laws of this state, or any officer or agent of any of the aforesaid insurance companies, or any other person, shall have violated any law of this state, relating to such companies, officers or agents, or the business of insurance, or fail to comply with any requisition of the laws of this state relating to such companies, officers or agents, or the business of insurance, they shall forthwith report the fact with any information they may have relating thereto, to any state's attorney in this state, who shall, if in his judgment it is advisable so to do, prosecute every such company, officer, agent or other person therefor; and any such company, officer, agent or other person, upon conviction, shall be liable for each offense to a fine not exceeding two thousand dollars and costs of prosecution.

SEC. 20. The insurance commissioners shall biennially, on or before the first day of October, cause to be printed and laid before the legislature an abstract of the annual statements made to them by insurance companies of other states for the two years next preceding, with such statistics, general information and suggestions relating to the subject of insurance as they may think proper to insert in such report, giving the name and location of every such company; and the secretary of state shall keep on file the charters of all such companies, and all certificates relating to the means or authority of such companies, and the name and residence of every agent licensed to do insurance business in this state, together with the certificate of the company, or general agent of such company, upon which such agents have been licensed; and they may appoint a deputy to assist them in carrying the provisions of this chapter into effect, for whose acts they shall be responsible; and the fees from agents and companies for licenses and examinations hereinbefore provided for, together with any fees they may receive for copies furnished by them, shall be in full compensation for their services as commissioners.

SEC. 21.   Sections one, two, three and four of chapter eighty-seven of the general statutes, and all acts and parts of acts inconsistent with this act, are hereby repealed.

Approved, November 24, 1874.

No. 2.—AN ACT TO ENABLE INSURANCE COMPANIES TO COMPLY WITH THE LAWS OF OTHER STATES OR COUNTRIES.

It is hereby enacted by the General Assembly of the State of Vermont:

SEC. 1.   It shall be lawful for any life insurance company chartered in this state to deposit with the treasurer of this state, or the comptroller or chief financial officer of another state, any funds or securities of such companies which the laws of any other state or country may require, to enable the company or companies of this state to establish agencies and prosecute the business of insurance within such other states or countries.

SEC. 2.   It shall be the duty of the treasurer of this state to safely keep said securities for the benefit of all the policy holders of such company; but companies so depositing shall at all times have the right to receive the interest or dividends upon such mortgages or stocks, or to exchange them for others of equal value.

Sec. 3. This act shall take effect from its passage.

Approved, November 12, 1874.

No. 3.—AN ACT AUTHORIZING THE COMPILATION OF THE LAWS RELATING TO THE GRAND LIST.

Section	Section
1. Governor to appoint person to compile grand list laws.	procure the p inting of and distribute said compilation.
2. Secretary of state directed to	

It is hereby enacted by the General Assembly of the State of Vermont:

Sec. 1. The governor is hereby authorized and required to appoint some suitable person to compile all the laws relating to the grand list that may be in force at the close of the present session of the general assembly.

Sec. 2. The secretary of state shall, as soon as conveniently may be done, procure twelve hundred copies of such compilation to be printed and bound in paper, in the same style as the session laws are printed, and distribute the same in the following manner : Four copies to each organized town and city in the state. And it shall be the duty of each of the town and city clerks in the state to keep the same in some suitable place in their respective offices for the use of the inhabitants thereof;

provided, that three of said copies shall be for the use of the listers while engaged in the duties of their office as listers:

Approved, November 24, 1874.

No. 4.—AN ACT TO ASSESS AND TAX THE REAL ESTATE OF RAILROADS IN THIS STATE.

SECTION
1. Real estate of railroad companies to be set in the grand list; railroad bed and track, &c., to be considered real estate.
2. Road bed and track not to be valued at more than two thousand dollars per mile of main line.

SECTION
3. Exemption from taxation for ten years from beginning of traffic operations.
4. Constables in default of payment of tax may levy on personal property.
5. Certain laws repealed.
6. To take effect.

It is hereby enacted by the General Assembly of the State of Vermont:

SEC. 1. The listers of the several towns and cities in this state shall appraise and set in the grand lists of their respective towns and cities all the real estate situated in such towns or cities, which shall be owned or occupied by any railroad corporation, or which shall be owned, leased, possessed or operated by any persons, company or corporation whose title, right, interest or possession shall have been derived in any manner from such railroad corporation; and the road-bed and track of any railway, and all land taken and used for railroad purposes, shall be considered real estate for the purposes of this act; and all said real estate shall be set in the list to such corporations, owners, occupants and possessors, and shall be subject to the general provisions relating to the assessment and taxation of real estate, except as herein otherwise provided.

SEC. 2.   No road-bed and track shall be assessed by the listers of any town or city at a valuation exceeding two thousand dollars for every mile of the main line of the road in such town or city.

SEC. 3.   The real estate of any railroad shall be exempt from taxation for a period of ten years from the time when regular trains for public traffic and accommodation shall have commenced running over the entire length of said road within this state ; and it shall be the duty of the clerk of any railroad company, upon request, to report such time in writing, under oath, to the listers of any town or city through or into which the railroad of such company extends.

SEC. 4.   The several constables and collectors of taxes in this state shall have power, in default of payment of any tax assessed under and by virtue of this act, to collect the same out of the goods and chattels of the corporation, company or persons owning, leasing, operating or possessing the property upon which such tax is assessed; and any engine, car or other article in use on said road by the corporation or persons managing or running said road, and which has at any time been owned by said corporation or persons, shall be deemed to be the property of such corporation or persons for the purpose of satisfying said tax ; and the same may be taken and sold by virtue of said constable's or collector's warrant, in the same manner as personal property is now taken and sold for the collection of taxes.

2

Sec. 5. Section seventeen of chapter eighty-three, and sections eighty-eight, eighty-nine, ninety, ninety-one and ninety-two of chapter twenty-eight of the general stattutes, are hereby repealed.

Sec. 6. This act shall take effect from its passage.

Approved, November 24, 1874.

No. 5.—AN ACT RELATING TO THE DUTIES OF LISTERS.

It is hereby enacted by the General Assembly of the State of Vermont:

Sec. 1. Whenever from any cause there shall be occasion for the appraisal of real estate, not included in the next preceding quadrennial appraisal of real estate, it shall be the duty of the listers to appraise such real estate and set the same in the grand list of the town in which such real estate is situated, according to the provisions of law relating to the grand list.

Approved, November 24, 1874.

No. 6.—AN ACT IN AMENDMENT OF THE SECOND
CLAUSE OF SECTION FOURTEEN OF CHAPTER
EIGHTY-THREE OF THE GENERAL STATUTES,
ENTITLED "OF THE GRAND LIST."

SECTION	SECTION
1. Machinery to be assessed; in assessing stockholders for	stock, value of machinery to be deducted.
	2. To take effect.

*It is hereby enacted by the General Assembly of the State
of Vermont:*

SEC. 1.   The second clause of section fourteen of chapter eighty-three ef the general statutes is hereby amended so as to read as follows:

Second.   All machinery employed in any branch of
manufacture, and belonging to any corporation or company, shall be assessed to such corporation or company in
the town where such machinery may be situated or
employed; and in assessing such stockholders for the
stock in any manufacturing corporation or company, there
shall first be deducted from the value thereof, the value
of the machinery and real estate belonging to such corporation or company, and the value of any other property
belonging to such corporation or company, and represented by such stock, which may be situated in any other
state or country, and which shall be liable to and shall be
taxed by such other state or country; provided, that in
no case the value of property outside the state be offset
against the visible property of such corporation within
the state, which may be set in the list under the provision
of this section.

SEC. 2.   This act shall take effect from its passage.

Approved, November 24, 1874.

No. 7.—AN ACT RELATING TO THE ASSESSMENT AND COLLECTION OF TAXES.

SECTION
1. Omission by mistake, to set polls or ratable property in the grand list, such omission may be supplied by with approval of selectmen or aldermen; such additions shall be reported to secretary of state.

SECTION
2. Upon such supplemental list taxes may be assessed same as upon the original list, such supplemental tax may be collected same as if assessed upon the original list.
3. To take effect.

It is hereby enacted by the General Assembly of the State of Vermont :

SEC. 1. When the listers in any town or city in this state, after completing the grand list, discover that they have by mistake omitted any polls or any real or personal estate liable to taxation, they may, on or before the first day of July, with the approval of the selectmen or mayor and aldermen of such town or city, supplement such polls and real or personal estate to the valuation and grand list, certifying that they were omitted by mistake, and all assessments thereon shall be valid notwithstanding that by such supplement the whole exceeds the sum to be assessed or alters the proportion of the tax allowed by law ; provided, no such addition shall be made to any list after the return of the abstract of said list to the office of the secretary of state, as required by law, which said addition shall be included in said abstract.

SEC. 2. There may be assessed on such supplemental list its proportion of all such taxes as have been or may be imposed on the original grand list, according to the principle on which such assessments have been or may be made, stating that said supplemental list was omitted by mistake; and such supplemental tax shall be committed to the collector stating that the power in the previous warrant, naming the date of it, is extended thereto, and the collector shall have the same power and be under the same obligation to collect said tax as if it had been contained in the original list.

Sec. 3. This act shall take effect from the first day of April, 1875.

Approved, November 24, 1874.

No. 8.—AN ACT IN AMENDMENT OF SECTION FORTY-SEVEN OF CHAPTER EIGHTY-THREE OF THE GENERAL STATUTES.

It is hereby enacted by the General Assembly of the State of Vermont:

Sec. 1. Section forty-seven of chapter eighty-three of the general statutes is hereby amended so as to read as follows:

If the clerk of any company, treasurer of any savings bank, or the cashier of any bank or other corporation, mentioned in this chapter, shall neglect to make the returns required of them by this chapter, he shall be liable to a fine not exceeding five hundred dollars, to be recovered in an action on the case in the name and for the benefit of the town where such report should have been made.

Approved, November 24, 1874.

No. 9.—AN ACT TO AMEND AN ACT APPROVED NOVEMBER 26, 1872, RELATING TO THE GRAND LIST.

It is hereby enacted by the General Assembly of the State of Vermont:

SEC. 1. Section two of an act approved November 26, 1872, relating to the grand list, shall be amended to read as follows:

Any person or persons feeling aggrieved by the appraisal of real estate by the listers may, within three days after the fifteenth day of June, as heretofore provided, appeal to the board of civil authority in the town or city where such real estate is situated; and such appellant shall give immediate notice to one or more of the selectmen or aldermen, and to one or more of the listers of such town or city; and the town or city clerk, upon application of any member of the board of civil authority, shall immediately call a meeting of the civil authority, by posting notices in three public places not less than six nor more than ten days prior to the time of such meeting; and a decision of a majority of said board shall be final. It shall be the duty of the listers, on or before the first Tuesday in July, to meet to revise and perfect the grand list, and at such meeting to appoint one of their number to meet at the place now required by law in each county to equalize the grand list of their respective counties.

SEC. 2.   This act shall take effect from its passage.

Approved, November 5, 1874.

No. 10.—AN ACT IN AMENDMENT OF AN ACT ENTITLED "AN ACT RELATING TO THE GRAND LIST," APPROVED NOVEMBER 26, 1872.

It is hereby enacted by the General Assembly of the State of Vermont:

SEC. 1.   Section four of an act relating to the grand list, approved November 26, 1872, is hereby amended by adding the following words:

And in view of any vacancy that may exist in the state equalizing board, by reason of inability of the member to attend, or from any other cause, there shall be a substitute member to supply said vacancy, elected at the same time, and subject to the same conditions of eligibility as are prescribed for members thereof, and said substitute members shall have the same power when acting with said board, as is delegated to the principal members.

Approved, November 17, 1874.

No. 11.—AN ACT IN RELATION TO THE COLLECTION OF TAXES.

It is hereby enacted by the General Assembly of the State of Vermont:

SEC. 1. Every collector of town taxes shall, when requested so to do by notice in writing signed by a majority of the selectmen of such town, pay into the town treasury all moneys belonging to such town by him collected up to that time, and submit his tax-book and list to said town treasurer for inspection and computation.

SEC. 2. All collectors of school district taxes shall, on request in writing signed by one or more of the prudential committee of such school district, pay to the treasurer of such school district all moneys belonging to the same by him collected up to that time, and submit his tax-book and list to said treasurer for inspection and computation.

SEC. 3. Any collector neglecting or refusing for the space of ten days to perform the duties required by sections one and two of this act shall be liable to a fine of one hundred dollars for each neglect or refusal; and such fine may be recovered in an action upon this statute in favor of such town or district.

SEC. 4. This act shall take effect from its passage.

Approved, November 24, 1874.

No. 12.—AN ACT IN AMENDMENT OF SECTION SIXTY-SEVEN OF CHAPTER EIGHTY-FOUR OF THE GENERAL STATUTES, ENTITLED "OF THE COLLECTION OF TAXES."

SECTION
1. Grand list completed May 15, to be list on which all school district taxes, voted on March 1, or after, shall be assessed.

SECTION
2. Act approved November 7, 1872, repealed.
3 To take effect.

It is hereby enacted by the General Assembly of the Sta of Vermont :

SEC. 1. Section sixty-seven of chapter eighty-four of the general statutes shall be so amended as to read as follows :

The grand list to be completed on the 15th day of May for the assessment of town and highway taxes, shall be the list on which all school district and village taxes voted on the first day of March, or at any time thereafter within one year, shall be assessed.

SEC. 2. An act approved November 7, 1872, entitled "An act in amendment of section sixty-seven of chapter eighty-four of the general statutes," is hereby repealed.

SEC. 3. This act shall take effect from its passage.

Approved, October 22, 1874.

No. 13.—AN ACT RELATING TO THE COLLECTION OF NON-RESIDENT TAXES.

SECTION
1. Section twenty-two, chapter eighty-four, general statutes, amended by inserting the word "January" in place of "August."
2. Lands of non-residents may

SECTION
be sold for taxes between 25th of February, and 1st of June.
3. Constable commencing sale of lands for taxes shall continue therein notwithstanding expiration of term of office.
4. To take effect.

It is hereby enacted by the General Assembly of the State of Vermont:

SEC. 1: Section twenty-two of chapter eighty-four of the general statutes is hereby amended by striking out the word August wherever it now occurs in said section twenty-two, and inserting in lieu thereof the word January.

SEC. 2. Number twenty-two of the public acts approved November 15th, 1869, which is an amendment to section thirty-three of chapter eighty-four of the general statutes, is hereby amended so as to read as follows:

Sale of lands of non-residents for taxes, may be made at any time between the twenty-fifth day of February and the first day of June following.

SEC. 3. Whenever the first constable of any town in this state shall have commenced a sale of lands for the collection of taxes under said section twenty-two of chapter eighty-four, he shall be the officer to complete the sale thereof although his term of office as such constable, may have expired.

SEC. 4. This act shall take effect from its passage.

Approved, November 24, 1874.

No. 14.—AN ACT RELATING TO THE COLLECTION OF SCHOOL DISTRICT TAXES.

SECTION
1. Collector to make such deductions from taxes of tax payers as fixed by vote of school district.
2. Collector to give notice when

SECTION
  and where he will receive taxes.
3. Refusal to pay tax as thus provided not to entitle tax payer to said reduction.

It is hereby enacted by the General Assembly of the State of Vermont :

SEC. 1.   Whenever any school district shall raise a tax, such school district may, by vote passed at the same meeting, direct the collector of taxes to deduct such per cent as shall be fixed by said vote from the tax of every tax payer who shall pay his or her tax, by a day fixed by said vote.

SEC. 2.   The collector of taxes shall notify the tax payers of such school district at what time and place he will attend to receive taxes so voted, and allow such deduction by posting notice thereof in three public places in said district, and by causing the same to be published in each newspaper that may be printed in said district, at least ten days before the time named in such notice.

SEC. 3.   Every tax payer who shall neglect to pay his or her tax on or before the day named in such vote, shall not be entitled to such deduction, and the collector shall collect the whole tax of such delinquent tax payer in the manner now by law provided.

Approved, November 5, 1874.

No. 15.—AN ACT REGULATING THE CAPTURE OF FISH AND GAME.

It is hereby enacted by the General Assembly of the State of Vermont:

SEC. 1. Whoever takes or catches any salmon in any of the waters of this state, or has in his or her possession any such fish captured within the limits of this state, for five years from the passage of this act, shall forfeit and pay a fine not to exceed ten dollars or each and every salmon so taken, captured or possessed, to be recovered on indictment of any grand juror, before any justice court within the town or county where such offense was committed.

SEC. 2. Whoever takes or catches any trout, land-locked salmon, salmon trout or longe in any of the public waters of this state, or has in his or her possession any such fish captured within the limits of this state, between the

first day of September of one year and the first day of
May of the next year, shall forfeit and pay a fine not to exceed ten dollars for each and every fish aforesaid, so taken,
captured or possessed, to be recovered on indictment of
any grand juror before any justice court within the town
or county where such offense was committed.

SEC. 3. Whoever takes or catches any black bass in any
of the public waters of this state, or has in his or her possession any such fish, captured within the limits of this
state, between the first day of June and the first day of
August in any year, shall forfeit and pay a fine not to exceed five dollars for each fish so taken, had or possessed,
to be recovered on indictment or otherwise, before any justice of the peace within the town or county where such
offense was committed; one half of said fine to go to the
person who made the complaint, and the other half to go to
the state.

SEC. 4. Whoever takes or catches any white fish or lake
shad in any of the public waters of this state, or has in his
or her possession any such fish taken within the limits of
this state, between the first day of October and the first
day of December in any year, shall forfeit and pay a fine
not to exceed ten dollars for each fish so taken, had or possessed, to be recovered on indictment or otherwise, before
any justice of the peace within the town or county, where
such offense was committed; one half of said fine to go to
the person who makes the complaint, and the other half to
the state.

SEC. 5. Whoever takes or catches any wall-eyed pike
or pike perch in any public water of this state, or has in
his or her possession any such fish taken within the limits

of this state, between the first day of April and the first day of June of any year, shall forfeit and pay a fine not to exceed five dollars for each and every fish so taken, to be recovered on indictment or otherwise, before any justice of the peace within the town or county where such offense was committed; one half of said fine to go to the person who makes the complaint and the other half to the state.

SEC. 6. No person shall be allowed to capture any trout, land-locked salmon, salmon, salmon trout, or longe, in any of the public waters of this state, except by hook and line in the ordinary way, with bait, fly or troll, under a penalty of twenty dollars for each violation of this act; provided, always, that the fish commissioners may be allowed to take fish in any season of the year for stocking ponds, lakes and rivers, and for maintaining and cultivating fish artificially, and for no other purpose—and may also grant permits in writing for other persons to capture fish for artificial propagation and maintenance in private ponds.

SEC. 7. Any person legally engaged in the artificial culture and maintenance of fish may take them in his own waters, how and when he pleases, or take them in the public streams for breeding purposes; provided, he gets the written permit of the commissioners of fisheries to do so, or the permit of the selectmen of any town where he so takes them, but shall not sell them for food at seasons when their capture is prohibited by this act.

SEC. 8. All pound-net or trap-net fishing in the public waters of this state are hereby prohibited; and any person or persons who shall be found fishing with any such pound or trap nets within the limits of this state, shall be punished by a fine of one hundred dollars for each offense, and forfeit his net or nets to the use of the state by any officer making the arrest.

SEC. 9. It shall not be lawful for any person to fish for white fish or lake shad with a net whose meshes are less than two inches in extension, knot to knot, nor less than one and one quarter inches in extension, knot to knot, for the capture of wall-eyed pike or pike-perch, under a penalty of twenty-five dollars for each offense so committed, to be recovered by indictment, with confiscation of the net or nets, before any justice of the peace or city court within the town, city or county where such offense was committed; and one half of said fine shall go to the person who makes the complaint, and the other half to the state.

SEC. 10. It shall not be lawful for any person or persons to engage in stocking any of the public waters in this state with pickerel. And any person or persons violating this section shall be guilty of a misdemeanor, and upon conviction, shall be punished by a fine of one hundred dollars, or six months imprisonment in the county jail, or both, in the discretion of the court.

SEC. 11. It shall not be lawful for any person in this state to catch, kill or destroy any fish in the private ponds, preserves or streams when the same are being bred artificially, and cultivated or maintained, without the consent of the owner or owners thereof, under a penalty of five dollars for each fish so caught, killed or destroyed, to be recovered in the same manner as in sections one and two of this act.

SEC. 12. Any person or corporation of persons who engage in the culture of fish in private enclosures within this state, shall put up notices at convenient places on their premises, wherein they shall indicate that no fishing is permitted on said premises. And if, after such notice is publicly given, any person shall enter upon said premises and catch any fish, or in any manner foul the water thereof by any substance deleterious to the life and growth of said fishes, or shall break or destroy any dam, reservoir or embankment, or divert the water, or do any damage whatever to said premises, he shall be liable to a fine of one hundred dollars or imprisonment in the county jail not more than six months, and shall be likewise liable to the owner or owners thereof, in a civil suit for the damages occasioned, in any court within the town or county where such offense was committed.

SEC. 13. No person shall pursue, kill or destroy any wild deer, buck, fawn or elk within the limits of this state, save through the months of September, October, November and December in any year, nor shall any person kill, catch or destroy any mink, beaver, fisher, or otter between the first day of April and the first day of October in any year, under a penalty of twenty dollars for each offense, to be recovered on indictment or otherwise before any justice of the peace within the town or county where such offense was committed; and one half of said fine shall go to the person who makes said complaint, and the other half to the state.

SEC. 14. No person shall kill any of the wild animals mentioned in section thirteen of this act by poison, and any person convicted of such offense shall upon conviction thereof, be liable to a fine of not less than ten dollars for each animal so poisoned and destroyed.

SEC. 15. This act shall take effect from its passage.

Approved. November 24, 1874.

No. 16.—AN ACT FOR THE PROTECTION OF GAME BIRDS IN THE STATE OF VERMONT.

It is hereby enacted by the General Assembly of the State of Vermont :

SEC. 1. No person shall take, kill, or have in his possession within this state, any woodcock between the first day of March and the first day of August in any year, nor any ruffled grouse, commonly called partridge, between the first day of March and the first day of September in any year, nor any wild goose or wild duck between the first day of May and the first day of September in any year, nor shall any person at any time within this state take, or destroy, or have in his possession any eggs of either of the birds in this section mentioned, or take or kill any such bird by means of any snare, net or trap ; provided, that nothing in this act shall be construed to prevent any person from hunting upon his own lands except during the times hereinbefore named.

SEC. 2. No person within this state shall engage in hunting, shooting, or the pursuit, taking or killing in any way of any wild game, or other birds or animals, nor discharge any firearms for such purpose, nor for any purpose except the just defense of person or property, or in the cause of proper military or police duty, on the first day of the week, commonly called Sunday.

SEC. 3. Any person who shall violate either of the provisions of the foregoing sections of this act, shall, on conviction thereof, forfeit and pay for each and every such offense the sum of ten dollars to the use of the state ; and such person may be prosecuted for such offense by any state's attorney or town grand juror, by complaint in common and simple form, before any justice of the peace, in the manner and subject to the regulations provided by the general laws of the state for the prosecution of offenses punishable by fine and cognizable by justices of the peace.

SEC. 4. Whenever any penalty shall be collected and paid into the treasury of this state, by any prosecution for violations of the provisions of sections one and two of this act, it shall be the duty of the state treasurer, upon the certificate of the officer, who prosecuted such case that the conviction therein was obtained upon the information of any person voluntarily furnished, to pay to such person one half of such penalty.

Approved, November 18, 1874.

No. 17.—AN ACT DEFINING PUBLIC WATERS IN THIS STATE.

It is hereby enacted by the General Assembly of the State of Vermont:

SEC. 1. All natural ponds of water in this state covering a superficial area of seventy-five acres or more, not private property, shall be considered public waters, into which the commissioners of fisheries may introduce choice varieties of fish.

SEC. 2. This act shall take effect from its passage.

Approved, November 18, 1874.

No. 18.—AN ACT RELATING TO DITCHES AND
WATER COURSES.

It is hereby enacted by the General Assembly of the State of Vermont:

SEC. 1. Whenever the public good or the necessity or convenience of individuals shall require the opening of a ditch or water course for the purpose of draining low or swamp lands, in order to enable owners or occupants thereof to cultivate and improve the same, such owners or occupants of the land, through which said ditch or water course is required, shall open a just and fair proportion of such ditch or water course according to their several interests.

SEC. 2. If the parties herein named cannot agree what proportion each shall make of said ditch or water course, the selectmen that shall be annually elected in the several towns of this state, shall decide all disputes between the owners or occupants of adjoining lands in their respective towns, respecting the opening, making or paying for ditches and water courses, as provided in this act.

SEC. 3. Every decision or award of selectmen, as provided in this act, shall be in writing, signed by a majority of the whole board, and they shall lodge the same, or a certified copy thereof, in the town clerk's office of the town where the decision or award is made, and the clerk shall keep the same on file ; and they shall also deliver a copy of the same to the parties interested, and such decision or award shall be binding on all of the parties.

SEC. 4. When there is a dispute as to the opening of a ditch or water course, or the part, width, depth or extent that any person shall open or make, either party may, by writing, notify the selectmen of the town in which said lands are located of the dispute, asking for an investigation, and naming in the notice for the investigation thereof the time and place of meeting, and shall also notify the other party or parties in the same manner, which notice shall be at least ten days before the time set for hearing.

SEC. 5. On receiving such notice the selectmen shall attend at the time and place named, and after being satisfied that the other party or parties have been duly notified, they shall examine the premises and hear the parties and their witnesses, if demanded, on the subject matter of the reference, and shall divide or apportion the ditch or water course among the several parties, having due regard to the interest of each party in the opening thereof, and shall fully determine the matters in dispute.

SEC. 6. On any reference requiring the opening or making of any ditch or water course, the selectmen shall decide what length of time each of the parties shall have to open the share of the ditch or water course which the selectmen decide that each of such parties shall open or make, and if it appears to the selectmen that any of the owners or occupiers of any tract of land, are not sufficiently interested in the opening of said ditch or water course to make said owner or occupant perform or pay any part thereof, and at the same time it shall appear necessary for the other party or parties, that such ditch or water course should be constructed across such tract or piece of land, they may award the same to be done at the expense of such other party or parties proportionately to the benefits each may receive, and after such award the party or parties interested, and in whose favor said award is made, may open the ditch or water course across such tract of land at his or their own expense without being trespassers.

SEC. 7. All ditches or water courses opened under the provisions of this act shall be kept cleansed and rendered fit for the passage of all water into the same, and any person failing to do his or her proportionate share of cleaning or repairing said ditch or water course, the same proceedings may be had and all disputes in reference to the same settled in the same way and by the same board, as is herein provided for opening ditches or water courses.

SEC. 8. The owner of any land higher than that of his neighbor, shall not be required to make or assist in making a water course or ditch, through his said neighbor's land, of any greater depth than is necessary for draining his own land.

SEC. 9. All expenses under this act shall be paid by the party or parties interested in opening and making such ditches or water courses, in such proportion as the selectmen who try the cases respectively, shall order, and the selectmen shall receive the same amount of compensation as other town officers in the towns where they shall act under this law.

SEC. 10. If any party or parties shall fail to open any ditch or water course, or any share or proportion thereof, in accordance with the order of the selectmen as aforesaid, and within the time limited by such order, any person interested who was a party of record in said proceedings may open said ditch or water course and collect pay for the same of the party or parties who were to do the same by said order of said selectmen.

SEC. 11. If any owner of land through which a drain is to be constructed shall claim damages or compensation therefor, the selectmen shall hear the parties interested therein, and may award such damages to the owner of such land as they shall judge reasonable to be paid by the parties benefited thereby, in such proportions as such selectmen shall deem just; and in estimating the damages which may be sustained by any person owning or interested in lands through which said ditch or water course is to be laid, the benefits which said person may receive thereby shall be taken into consideration.

SEC. 12. Any person owning land through which a drain or water course is to be laid, may appeal from the decision or award of the selectmen to the next stated term of the county court, in which said land is situated, by entering into a recognizance with good and sufficient sureties, before said board of selectmen, in such sum as said selectmen may require; conditioned, that said appellant shall prosecute said appeal to effect and pay all intervening damages and cost in case said decision or award is affirmed. And upon said appeal being entered in county court by the report of the decision or award of said selectmen in writing, and with the recognizances aforesaid, the county court may, in their discretion, upon hearing, accept or reject said report, or may appoint a commission consisting of three disinterested freeholders of the vicinity, who shall make an examination of the premises, and after due hearing, upon notice to all parties interested as aforesaid, make report thereof to the next stated term of said court.

SEC. 13. The county court shall make all necessary orders, judgments and decrees to carry out the decisions upon the report of said selectmen or commissioners, and tax cost as may seem right and proper.

SEC. 14. A certified copy of the report of the selectmen or commissioners, finally accepted by the county court, together with the orders, judgments and decrees in said court, shall be recorded in the town clerk's office where said lands are situated.

Sec. 15. All ditches and water courses opened under the provisions of this act may be discontinued by the same proceedings and under the same regulations provided for opening the same.

Sec. 16. The authority establishing water courses or ditches under this act, may, in their discretion, direct any part of the same to be covered in such manner as they shall direct.

Sec. 17. All acts and parts of acts inconsistent with this are hereby repealed.

Approved, November 24, 1874.

No. 19.—AN ACT IN AMENDMENT OF SECTION TWO OF AN ACT ENTITLED " AN ACT RELAT- ING TO PRIVATE CORPORATIONS BY VOLUN- TARY ASSOCIATION," APPROVED NOVEMBER 23, 1870.

It is hereby enacted by the General Assembly of the State of Vermont:

Sec. 1. Section two of an act entitled " An act relat- ing to private corporations by voluntary association," ap- proved November 23, 1870, is hereby amended by inserting the words "music, lecture and other public halls," after the word "hotels" in the sixth line of said section.

Sec. 2. This act shall take effect from its passage.

Approved, November 24, 1874.

No. 20.—AN ACT RELATING TO PRIVATE COR-PORATIONS.

It is hereby enacted by the General Assembly of the State of Vermont:

Sec. 1. Before any private corporation hereafter organized, whether under special charter or the general laws of the state, shall commence business, the president and directors thereof shall make a certificate, which shall be verified by their oaths or affirmation, which certificate shall state the amount of capital actually paid in; and shall also make a similar certificate upon any increase of the capital stock; which certificates shall be filed in the office of the secretary of state.

Sec. 2. This act shall take effect from its passage.

Approved, November 12, 1874.

No. 21.—AN ACT IN AMENDMENT OF SECTION ONE OF CHAPTER NINETY OF THE GENERAL STATUTES, RELATING TO THE FORMATION OF CERTAIN ASSOCIATIONS WITH CORPORATE POWERS.

It is hereby enacted by the General Assembly of the State of Vermont:

SEC. 1. The seventh subdivision of section one of chapter ninety of the general statutes is hereby amended by adding thereto the following:

Or for the cutting, storage and sale of ice.

SEC. 2. The eighth subdivision of section one of chapter ninety of the general statutes is hereby amended by adding thereto the following:

To establish and maintain bands of music, or other societies for musical purposes, or associations for the purpose of breeding or propagating fish or game.

SEC. 3. This act shall take effect from its passage.

Approved, November 20, 1874.

No. 22.—AN ACT IN AMENDMENT OF AN ACT ENTITLED "AN ACT RELATING TO PRIVATE CORPORATIONS BY VOLUNTARY ASSOCIATION," APPROVED NOVEMBER 23, 1870.

It is hereby enacted by the General Assembly of the State Vermont :

SEC. 1. Section two of an act relating to private corporations by voluntary association, approved November 23, 1870, is hereby amended by adding thereto the following:

"And provided further, that such name shall indicate that it is a corporation."

SEC. 2. Section fourteen of said act is hereby amended so as to read as follows:

The articles of agreement provided in section two of this act shall be in substance as follows: "We, the subscribers, hereby associate ourselves together as a corporation, under the laws of the state of Vermont, to be known by the name of   , for the purpose of   at   in the county of   , in said state, with a capital stock of   dollars, divided into   shares of   dollars each.

Dated at   , this   day of   A. D.

Which articles of agreement, duly filled out and signed by the corporators, shall be transmitted to the secretary of state, who shall thereupon, if such articles are duly filled out and executed in compliance with law, record the same in a book kept by him for that purpose, and return to said corporators a certified copy thereof, which record and certified copy shall have the force and effect of a special charter. Before such corporation shall commence business it shall cause such certified copy of its articles of agreement to be published at length in one newspaper printed in the county where such corporation is located, if such there be ; and if not, in an adjoining county. Whenever such corporation shall desire to increase its capital stock, a certificate of such increase, signed by the president and directors, shall be filed with the secretary of state and recorded by him, and a certified copy returned and published in the same manner as prescribed in the case of the original articles of association.

SEC. 3. Sections seventeen and twenty-three of said act of 1870 are hereby repealed.

SEC. 4. This act shall take effect from its passage.

Approved, November 12, 1874.

No. 23.—AN ACT TO AMEND SECTION FIVE OF AN ACT ENTITLED " AN ACT TO ENABLE TOWNS AND CITIES TO AID IN THE CONSTRUCTION OF RAILROADS," APPROVED NOVEMBER 26, A. D. 1872.

SECTION
1. Commissioners to carry into effect the vote of the town or city; powers of commissioners; their votes and acts to be binding on said town or city; subscriptions.
2. To take effect.

It is hereby enacted by the General Assembly of the State of Vermont :

SEC. 1.   Sections five of an act entitled " An act to enable towns and cities to aid in the construction of railroads," approved November 26, A. D. 1872, shall be altered and amended so as to read as follows :

Sec. 5.   The commissioners, selectmen or aldermen aforesaid, as soon as the assent is given and recorded as aforesaid, shall proceed to carry into effect the vote of said town or city, according to the terms and conditions thereof, and shall have power to vote and act for said town or city on all proper occasions to carry into effect the vote aforesaid, and their votes and acts shall be binding on said town or city ; and in case any town or city shall vote or shall have voted to subscribe to the capital stock in such railroad, such subscriptions may be made prior to the fil'ng of the articles of association of such road with the secretary of state, as provided by section two of an act entitled · " An act to authorize the formation of railroad corporations and to regulate the same," approved November 20, A. D. 1872, and such subscription may form a portion of the amount required to be subscribed before said articles of association may be filed as provided by said section two of said act.

SEC. 2.   This act shall take effect from its passage.

Approved, November 23, 1874.

No. 24.—AN ACT TO AMEND SECTION ONE OF AN
ACT ENTITLED "AN ACT TO AUTHORIZE THE
FORMATION OF RAILROAD CORPORATIONS, AND
TO REGULATE THE SAME," APPROVED NOVEM-
BER 20, A. D. 1872.

SECTION	SECTION
1. Company may be formed; purpose; may make and sign articles of association; provisions of same; capital stock; shares; with proviso that any reasonable change of route may be made ; which shall not invalidate articles of association; but such change	must not violate conditions of votes of towns; duties of subscribers to said articles; articles to be filed with secretary of state; he to record the same; said association then to be considered a corporation; powers, rights and privileges; bylaws; subject to general laws.

*It is hereby enacted by the General Assembly of the State
of Vermont:*

SEC. 1.   Section one of an act entitled " An act to authorize the formation of railroad corporations, and to
regulate the same," approved November 20, A. D. 1872,
shall be altered and amended to read as follows :

Sec. 1.   Any number of persons not less than twenty-
five, a majority of them being inhabitants of this state,
may form a company for the purpose of constructing,
maintaining and operating a railroad for public use in conveyance of persons and property ; and for that purpose
may make and sign articles of association in which shall
be stated the name of the company, the places from and to
which the road is to be constructed or maintained and operated, the length of such road as near as may be, and
the name of each city, town and county in this state
through or into which it is made, or intended to be made ;

the amount of the capital stock of the company, which shall be divided into shares of one hundred dollars each, and shall not be less than ten thousand dollars for every mile of road constructed or proposed to be constructed, and the number of shares of which said capital stock shall consist, and the names and places of residence of the directors of the company, who shall be chosen from and by the persons subscribing to said articles of association, and shall manage its affairs for the first year and until others are chosen in their places; provided, however, that in the final location of such railroad any necessary or reasonable variation or change of line may be made, although by such change or variation the line may pass into town or towns, or a city not named in the articles of association, or not touch or pass through some of those named in such articles, while the general route and direction and the terminal points mentioned are observed, and the description of route made on any preliminary survey for such railroad, notwithstanding such necessary and reasonable change of line in the final location, shall be deemed a sufficient compliance with this act; and such change or variation of line shall in no wise invalidate the articles of association of any company formed under this act for the construction of such railroad. And such change and variation in the line may be made at the option of such company, unless the same shall violate the condition or conditions of the vote of any town or city, or of some subscription to render aid in the construction of such railroad; in which case the assent of such town or of the party making such condition or subscription shall be first had and obtained; and the route, as changed, shall be filed with the secretary of state as an amendment of the original articles of association filed in his office. Each subscriber to such articles of association shall subscribe thereto his name, place of residence and number of shares of stock he agrees to take in said company; but no subscriber shall be bound to pay beyond ten per centum of the amount of his subscription until a corporation is duly established under the provisions of this act. On compliance with the provisions of section two of this act, said articles of association, may be filed in the office of the secretary of state, who shall endorse thereon the day when the same was so filed, and shall record the same in a book to be provided and kept by him in his office for that purpose; and thereupon the persons who have so subscribed such articles of association, and all persons who shall become stockholders in such company, shall be a corporation in fact and in name, by the name specified in such articles of association, which name shall be one not in use by any other railroad corporation in this state; and as such shall have power to have succession by such corporate name for the period limited in such articles of association, or perpetually if no period is limited in such articles; to sue and be sued, complain and defend in any court of law or equity; to make and use a common seal, and alter the same at pleasure; to lay out, construct and maintain, for public use in the conveyance of persons and property, a railroad on the line or route designated or defined in such articles of association; to take, hold, purchase, use and convey such real and personal estate as may be necessary for the construction, maintenance and accommodations of such railroad, and the stations and other accommodations necessary to accomplish the objects of their incorporation, and as the purposes of the corporation shall require, not exceeding the amount, if any, which]may be limited in such articles of association or by-laws; to take and convey persons and property on such railroad by the power or force of steam or of animals, or by any mechanical power, and to receive compensation therefor, subject to such regulations as are or may be provided by law; to erect and maintain all necessary and convenient buildings, stations, fixtures and machinery for the accommodation and use of the passengers, freights and business on or over such railroads; to regulate the time and manner in which said passengers and property shall be transported on such railroad, subject to any regulations which are or may be provided by law; to appoint such subordinate officers and agents as the business of the corporation shall require, and to allow them a suitable compensation; and make by-laws, not inconsistent with any existing law, for the management of the property of the corporation, the regulation of its affairs, and the transfer of its stock, and for all purposes shall be deemed to be a railroad company or corporation, duly incorporated under the authority of this state, and as such shall also have all the powers, rights, franchises, and privileges granted to or vested in railroad companies or corporations by chapter twenty-eight of the general statutes, and any act or acts passed or to be passed in addition thereto or in amendment thereof; and shall be subject to all the duties, liabilities and provisions contained in said chapter, or in any law of this state, which may affect or be applicable to railroad companies or corporations.

Approved, November 18, 1874.

No. 25.—AN ACT IN ADDITION TO CHAPTER NINE-TY-FOUR OF THE GENERAL STATUTES.

It is hereby enacted by the General Assembly of the State of Vermont:

SEC. 1.　Any person within the state of Vermont, who shall act as the agent of any other person or persons, firm or firms, for the sale of spirituous or intoxicating liquors, or who shall travel from place to place within the state, selling, furnishing, disposing of or giving away spirituous or intoxicating liquors, for any other person or persons, firm or firms, or who shall take any order or orders for any other person or persons, firm or firms, or who shall be instrumental in any way, in causing any order or orders to be sent to any other person or persons, firm or firms, other than a lawfully authorized and appointed agent in this state for the sale of liquors, for any kind of spirituous or intoxicating liquors, or who shall in any way, directly or indirectly, aid, abet or assist any other person or persons, firm or firms, to sell, furnish or give away, or in any manner dispose of any spirituous or intoxicating liquors within this state, or who shall carry or exhibit, or cause to be exhibited, any sample or samples of any spirituous or intoxicating liquors, or give, state, show or in any way indicate the price or prices of the same, with a view to induce any person or persons to purchase said liquors, or such liquors, as said sample or samples represent, shall be adjudged guilty of an offense against chapter ninety-four of the general statutes, and shall forfeit and pay for each offense, to the treasurer of the state upon the first conviction, one hundred dollars and costs of prosecution; on the second conviction, he shall forfeit and pay for each offense as aforesaid, three hundred dollars and the costs of prosecution; and on the third and all subsequent convictions, he shall forfeit and pay for each offense, as aforesaid, five hundred dollars and the costs, and shall also be imprisoned in the county jail for a term not exceeding six months; provided, that nothing in this act be construed to prevent the selectmen of any town in this state, from purchasing intoxicating liquors for the purposes set forth in said chapter ninety-four.

SEC. 2. The prosecutions under this act shall be in accordance with and shall conform to the provisions of chapter ninety-four of the general statutes.

SEC. 3. This act shall take effect from its passage.

Approved, November 24, 1874.

No. 26.—AN ACT IN AMENDMENT OF AND IN ADDITION TO SECTION TWENTY-TWO OF CHAPTER NINETY-FOUR OF THE GENERAL STATUTES, ENTITLED " OF THE TRAFFIC IN INTOXICATING DRINKS."

It is hereby enacted by the General Assembly of the State of Vermont:

SEC. 1. In any town where there is no regularly appointed agent, any liquor seized under the provisions of this chapter, and adjudged forfeited to the use of the town, shall be delivered to the selectmen of said town, who shall have the same power now conferred upon the agent by said section twenty-two of chapter ninety-four of the general statutes, to dispose of and to examine the same; and in case it is found unfit for medical, chemical or mechanical purposes, to make certificate to that effect upon the warrant, in the same manner as agents are empowered by law to do.

SEC. 2. This act shall take effect from its passage.

Approved, November 5, 1874.

No. 27.—AN ACT IN AMENDMENT OF AN ACT ENTITLED "AN ACT IN AMENDMENT OF AND IN ADDITION TO CHAPTER NINETY-FOUR OF THE GENERAL STATUTES, ENTITLED 'OF THE TRAFFIC IN INTOXICATING DRINKS,'" APPROVED NOVEMBER 16, 1869.

SECTION
1. Penalty to seller for damages inflicted by intoxicated persons; how recovered; parties may be joined in same action; in case of death of injured party; all damages may be recovered from seller or fur-

SECTION
nisher; coverture or infancy no bar to proceedings under this act; marriage relation not to be a disqualification for witnesses.
2. To take effect.

It is hereby enacted by the General Assembly of the State of Vermont:

SEC. 1. Section three of an act in amendment of and in addition to chapter ninety-four of the general statutes, entitled "Of the traffic in intoxicating drinks," approved November 16, 1869, is hereby amended so as to read as follows:

Whenever any person, by reason of intoxication, shall commit or cause any injury upon the person or property of any other individual, any person who by himself, his clerk, or servant, shall have unlawfully sold or furnished any part of the liquor causing such intoxication, shall be liable to the party injured for all damage occasioned by the injury so done, to be recovered in the same form of action as such intoxicated person would be liable to; and both such parties may be joined in the same action, and in case of the death or disablity of any person, either from the injury received as herein specified, or in consequence of intoxication from the use of liquors unlawfully furnished as aforesaid, any person who shall be in any manner dependent on such injured person for means of support, or any party on whom such injured person may be dependent, may recover from the person unlawfully selling or furnishing any such liquor as aforesaid, all damage or loss sustained in consequence of such injury, in any court having jurisdiction in such cases; and coverture or infancy shall be no bar to proceedings for recovery in any case arising under this act, and no person shall be disqualified as a witness, by reason of the marriage relation in any proceeding under this act.

Sec. 2.   This act shall take effect from its passage.

Approved, November 23, 1874.

No: 28.—AN ACT IN ADDITION TO SECTION THIRTY-THREE OF CHAPTER NINETY-FOUR OF THE GENERAL STATUTES.

It is hereby enacted by the General Assembly of the State of Vermont:

Sec. 1. It shall be the duty of the officer arresting any intoxicated person under and by virtue of section thirty-three of chapter ninety-four of the general statutes,. to immediately give notice of such arrest, and of the taking of the disclosure of such intoxicated person to a grand juror or city attorney of the town or city in which such intoxicated person shall be found so intoxicated, or the state's attorney of the county in which such town or city lies; and thereupon it shall be the duty of such grand juror, or such city attorney or state's attorney, to attend at the taking of such disclosure; and if said justice shall issue his warrant under. and by virtue of said section, it shall be the duty of such grand juror, city attorney or said state's attorney to appear and prosecute said cause in the same manner as if such grand juror, city attorney or said state's attorney had been complainant in the same. And if said officer so making the arrest as aforesaid, or said magistrate, grand juror, city attorney or state's attorney shall refuse or neglect to do and perform according to the terms of this act, they shall be severally liable to the penalties prescribed by section forty-two of chapter ninety-four aforesaid.

Sec. 2. This act shall take effect from its passage.

Approved, November 24, 1874.

No. 29.—AN ACT RELATING TO THE MANUFAC-TURE AND SALE OF DOMESTIC WINES.

It is hereby enacted by the General Assembly of the State of Vermont:

SEC. 1.   The several provisions of chapter ninety-four of the general statutes, relating to the manufacture, sale and use of cider, shall apply to the manufacture, sale and use of wine which is made in this state, from grapes or other fruits, the growth of this state, and which is without the admixture of alcohol or spirituous liquor; provided, that such sale and use be for medical purposes only.

SEC. 2.   This act shall take effect from its passage.

Approved, November 12, 1874.

No. 30.—AN ACT TO AMEND SECTION TWO OF AN ACT ENTITLED "AN ACT RELATING TO WIT-NESSES IN PROSECUTIONS FOR SELLING OR FURNISHING INTOXICATING LIQUORS," AP-PROVED NOVEMBER 27, 1872.

It is hereby enacted by the General Assembly of the State of Vermont:

SEC. 1.   The second section of an act entitled "An act relating to witnesses in prosecutions for selling or furnishing intoxicating liquors," approved November 27,

1872, is hereby amended by inserting in the second line thereof, after the word "shall," the word *not*.

SEC. 2. This act shall take effect from its passage.

Approved, November 5, 1874.

No. 31.—AN ACT RELATING TO THE REGISTRY OF MARRIAGES AND BIRTHS.

SECTION

1. Bridegroom to deposit certificate within sixty days with town or city clerk, when married without the state; penalty for neglecting or refusing so to do.
2. Heads of families becoming permanent residents, may deposit certificate of marriage with town or city clerk, with names of children, if any; but such records not to be returned to secretary of state.
3. Town and city clerks to make record; fees therefor.
4. To take effect.

It is hereby enacted by the General Assembly of the State of Vermont:

SEC. 1. Whenever any male resident of this state shall be married without the state, he shall within sixty days thereafter deposit with the clerk of the city or town where he shall so reside, a certificate embracing all the statistics now required by law in marriage certificates; and in case of neglect or refusal to comply with the provisions of this section, the person so neglecting or refusing shall be liable to the same penalty, to be recovered in like manner, as may now be imposed for neglect to return certificates of marriages solemnized in the state.

SEC. 2. The head of any family, who shall hereafter become a permanent resident of this state, may cause to be recorded in the office of the town or city clerk, where such residence may be, a certificate of the marriage of such head of family, which certificate shall embrace as nearly as possible all the statistics now required by law in similar certificates; and may also cause to be recorded in such town or city clerk's office, the birth of any child or children belonging to such head of family, which may have been born without this state, and such record shall embrace all the statistics relating to births now required by law, and such head of family shall make oath to the correctness of such statistics; but the records provided for in this section shall not be returned to the secretary of state.

SEC. 3. It shall be the duty of any town or city clerk to properly record all the matters of record herein provided for, and shall receive therefor the same fees as are now provided by law for similar records.

SEC. 4. This act shall take effect from its passage.

Approved, November 17, 1874.

No. 32.—AN ACT IN RELATION TO. PUBLIC LANDS.

It is hereby enacted by the General Assembly of the State of Vermont:

SEC. 1. The words " public worship," in section one of an act entitled " An act in amendment of an act entitled an act in amendment of an act approved November 15, A. D. 1869, entitled of public lands," approved November 10, A. D. 1870, shall be construed to mean public worship and preaching, conducted by a regularly authorized minister of the gospel according to the rules of the several religious societies respectively, and no other religious exercises whatever.

SEC. 2. This act shall take effect from its passage.

Approved, November 23, 1874.

No. 33.—AN ACT TO ABOLISH THE BOARD OF EDUCATION AND TO CREATE THE OFFICE OF STATE SUPERINTENDENT OF EDUCATION.

SECTION
1. Sections repealed.
2. Joint assembly to elect state superintendent of education; duties of.
3. May hold one annual institute on application of twenty-five teachers; may employ assistants; limitation of expense.
4. Said superintendent to prescribe forms and blanks; and to procure and furnish registers.
5. Duties of town superintendent.

SECTION
6. Duties of academies and graded schools.
7. Superintendent to make biennial report to legislature; to print and distribute same; to whom.
8. Vacancy in office of, how filled.
9. Section nine of chapter twenty-two amended.
10. Salary of state superintendent.
11. Acts inconsistent herewith repealed.
12. To take effect.

It is hereby enacted by the General Assembly of the State of Vermont:

SEC. 1. Sections one, two, three, four, five, six, seven, eight, one hundred nine, one hundred twelve, and one hundred thirteen of chapter twenty-two of the general statutes, and all acts and parts of acts amendatory of and in addition thereto, are hereby repealed.

SEC. 2. The joint assembly shall elect at each biennial session of the legislature, a state superintendent of education, who shall faithfully devote his whole time in promoting the highest educational interests of the state, and visit every part thereof during each year, deliver lectures upon the subject of education, confer with town superintendents, visit schools in connection with them, and furnish each of them blank forms for collecting school statistics.

SEC. 3. He shall annually, upon a written application of twenty-five teachers in any county —except Grand Isle and Essex counties, in which the number may be fifteen teachers—for that purpose, hold one teachers' institute in such county, at a time when the common schools are not in session as far as practicable, not to exceed three days each. Said state superintendent may employ assistants to give efficiency and interest to such institutes as he may be required to hold, and a sum not exceeding thirty dollars per day actually paid by said state superintendent for such services, and for advertising and other necessary expenses thereof, shall be paid to said state superintendent by the state treasurer, on the allowance and order of the auditor of accounts.

SEC. 4. Said state superintendent is hereby required to prescribe blank forms for a school register, conveniently arranged for keeping a daily record of the attendance of children upon the school, and containing printed interrogatories addressed to teachers and to district clerks, for the procurement of such statistical information as he may seek to obtain in each year, and such information as will enable the selectmen of towns to divide the public money according to law; and in the month of January in each year the state superintendent shall procure and furnish to every town superintendent in this state a sufficient number of such registers to supply all the district clerks in

each town with one register for every school for the ensuing year. Any town superintendent receiving such
registers shall immediately forward his receipt therefor to
the state superintendent; and on failure to receive such
registers by the first day of February in each year, the town
superintendent shall immediately notify the state superintendent thereof, who shall supply the deficiency forthwith. Each district clerk shall annually, on or before the
first week in March, procure of the town clerk a register
for each school in his district, and be responsible for the
safe keeping thereof.

SEC. 5. Town superintendents of schools shall annually,
on or before the tenth day of April, make out and return
to the state superintendent, the statistics of the schools
in each district in their respective towns, in accordance
with the forms prescribed by said state superintendent,
agreeably to law. The state superintendent, upon the
receipt of such returns, shall forward a certificate thereof
to the town superintendent making the return.

SEC. 6. It shall be the duty of the trustees of the
academies and grammar schools which have been incorporated by the legislature of the state of Vermont, to
cause their principals to return to the said state superintendent, on or before the first day of April in each year,
true and correct answers to such statistical inquiries as
may have been addressed to them by the state superintendent in the month of January previous.

SEC. 7. The state superintendent of education shall
prepare and present to the legislature, on the first day of
each biennial session thereof, a report of his official
doings for the preceding two years, and a statement of

the condition of the schools in the state, of the expenditure of the school money therein, with such suggestions for information and improvement relative to the various schools in the state, as he may deem proper. He shall cause to be printed not more than three thousand and five hundred copies of his biennial report, and have the same ready for distribution on the assembling of the legislature, and shall distribute the same as follows, viz., one copy to each member of the legislature; one copy to each town superintendent, for the use of him and his successor in office; one copy to each district clerk; and one copy to the principal of each graded, union, or high school in the state; and any remaining copies shall be deposited in the state library for future reference, exchange or sale. The said state superintendent shall forward the necessary copies for distribution, except for members of the legislature, to the various town clerks, which shall be by them distributed in the same manner as the laws are distributed.

SEC. 8. The governor shall have power to appoint any suitable person to fill any vacancy that may occur in the office of state superintendent; and the person so appointed shall have the same power and perform the same duties as if elected agreeably to the provisions of section two of this act.

SEC. 9. Section nine of chapter twenty-two of the general statutes is hereby amended by striking out in line twenty-three of said section, the words "secretary of the board," and inserting in lieu thereof the words *state superintendent of education.*

SEC. 10. The state superintendent shall receive the sum of fifteen hundred dollars per year and his actual traveling expenses while in the performance of the duties of his office, and the expense of procuring blank forms, and postage, which allowances shall be paid by the treasurer on the acceptance and order of the auditor of accounts.

SEC. 11.   All acts and parts of acts inconsistent with this act are hereby repealed.

SEC. 12.   This act shall take effect from its passage.

Approved, November 18, 1874.

No. 34.—AN ACT TO AMEND AN ACT APPROVED NOVEMBER 22, 1870, ENTITLED "AN ACT TO EXTEND THE PROVISIONS OF AN ACT ENTITLED 'AN ACT TO ESTABLISH A STATE NORMAL SCHOOL,' APPROVED NOVEMBER 17, 1866."

It is hereby enacted by the General Assembly of the State of Vermont:

SEC. 1.   The provisions of an act approved November 22, 1870, entitled " An act to extend the provisions of an act entitled ' an act to establish a state normal school,' approved November 17, 1866," and the existence of the state normal schools extended and continued under the provisions of said act, are hereby extended and continued until August 1, 1880.

SEC. 2.   All acts and parts of acts inconsistent with this act are hereby repealed.

SEC. 3.   This act shall take effect from its passage.

Approved, November 23, 1874.

No. 35.—AN ACT RELATING TO NORMAL SCHOOLS.

It is hereby enacted by the General Assembly of the State of Vermont:

SEC. 1. It shall be the duty of the state superintendent of education to nominate and approve a principal teacher and a first assistant teacher for each of the normal schools of this state established by law, and to withdraw such approval whenever the interests of the school demand; and no person not so nominated, or the approval of whom shall have been withdrawn by the said state superintendent, shall be employed as such principal or first assistant; but the said principal shall be allowed to select his other assistants, and to provide for the discipline of the school.

SEC. 2. The governor shall annually appoint one practical teacher from each congressional district, whose duty it shall be, together with the state superintendent of education, and the principal of the normal school in each district, to attend and assist in the examination for graduation at the normal school in the district for which he is appointed, and such officers shall constitute a board to grant certificates of graduation, and shall have power to revoke the same upon cause shown; and for services rendered by such person so appointed, he shall receive the sum of four dollars per day, for time actually occupied by him under such appointment, and in addition thereto, his traveling expenses while in the discharge of such duties.

SEC. 3. The trustees of each normal school in the state, in conjunction with the state superintendent of education, shall arrange two courses of study for said schools, and shall wholly control the examination for admission. One course of study shall include all the branches required by law to be taught in the common schools of Vermont; the other course shall include all contained in the first course and higher branches, and shall require for its completion at least one full year of study, and certificates of graduation shall be granted to all who pass the required examination in the first course, or in both courses. The certificates of graduation from the lower course shall have the effect of licenses to teach in the common schools of the state for five years from the date thereof, and certificates of graduation from the higher course shall have the effect of licenses to teach in said schools for ten years from the date thereof.

SEC. 4. The sums now annually appropriated for each normal school in the state shall be expended as follows, namely:

Five hundred dollars to be expended by the trustees of each of said schools, with the concurrence and under the direction of the state superintendent of education, in aiding and assisting each of said schools, and the remaining one thousand dollars for the purpose of assisting those young men and women, inhabitants of this state, who may desire to more perfectly qualify themselves for teaching by attending the normal schools aforesaid, and who shall give satisfactory assurances to the state superintendent of education, that they will hold themselves in readiness to teach in the common schools of this state at least two years subsequent to their graduation.

SEC. 5. The several counties in each congressional district shall be entitled to their share of the free scholarships, according to their population; and in case applicants for such scholarships from any such county equal to the number assigned to such county, shall not present themselves on the first day of each term, the scholarships thus remaining vacant may be assigned by the principal of each school to applicants from some other county in this state ; provided, no town shall receive more than ten scholarships.

SEC. 6. The assignments of scholarships to the several counties in each congressional district, shall be made annually in the last week of June, by the state superintendent of education, and the trustees of each normal school. Applicants for scholarships must be at least fifteen years of age, and be recommended by the town superintendent of the town in which he or she may reside.

SEC. 7. All acts and parts of acts inconsistent with this act are hereby repealed.

SEC. 8. This act shall take effect from its passage.

Approved, November 24, 1874.

No. 36.—AN ACT RELATING TO THE DUTIES OF TOWN SUPERINTENDENTS OF COMMON SCHOOLS.

It is hereby enacted by the General Assembly of the State of Vermont:

SEC. 1.   It is hereby made the duty of the town superintendents of common schools in each county to meet annually on the third Tuesday of March, at ten o'clock A. M., in each year, at the county court house in each county—except that in Bennington county the said meeting shall be holden at the town house in Arlington—for the purpose:

First, of agreeing upon a set of questions to be used throughout the county in the written examination of teachers.

Second, of fixing the standard of qualification of teachers for the ensuing year.

SEC. 2.   The town superintendents of common schools, when assembled as mentioned in section one of this act, may annually elect from their number a president to preside at said meeting, and a secretary, whose duty it shall be to keep a correct record of the proceedings of such meeting, and procure to be printed and distribute to the several superintendents in such county the lists of questions agreed upon at such meeting; and the expense of such printing and distribution shall be paid by the state treasurer on the allowance of the state auditor.

SEC. 3. Sections three, four and five of an act entitled "An act relating to the duties of town superintendents," approved November 22, 1870, are hereby repealed.

SEC. 4. Sections one and six of an act entitled "An act relating to the duties and compensation of town superintendents of schools," approved November 27, 1872, are hereby amended by substituting the words *state superintendent of education*, for the words "secretary of the board of education," wherever they occur in said sections, and in said section one all is stricken out after the words "for necessary travel," and in lieu thereof the words *in attending the annual county meeting of town superintendents*, as provided in this act, are inserted.

Approved, November 24, 1874.

No. 37.—AN ACT RELATING TO THE DUTIES OF PRINCIPALS OF GRADED AND UNION SCHOOLS.

SECTION
1. Principals of union or graded schools not required to procure certificates from town superintendents.

SECTION
2. School districts may establish evening schools.
3. To take effect.

It is hereby enacted by the General Assembly of the State of Vermont:

SEC. 1. The principals of graded and union schools shall not be required to procure any certificate of qualification from the town superintendent or any other officer;

and all contracts for teaching hereafter made between the trustees of any graded school district, or prudential committee of any union school district, and their principal teacher, shall be valid without such certificate of qualifications.   ;

SEC. 2.   Any school district may, by vote at a meeting duly warned and holden for that purpose, authorize the prudential committee or trustees of such district to establish an evening school or schools in such district, and make all necessary arrangements and provisions therefor, in the same manner as day schools are now sustained; and each session of such evening school shall be treated and considered as a half-day session of a public school.

SEC. 3.   This act shall take effect from its passage.

Approved, November 23, 1874.

No. 38.—AN ACT REPEALING AN ACT REGULATING THE ATTENDANCE OF TEACHERS UPON TEACHERS' INSTITUTES.

It is hereby enacted by the General Assembly of the State of Vermont:

SEC. 1.   An act entitled "An act regulating the attendance of teachers upon teachers' institutes," and approved November 13, 1869, is hereby repealed.

Approved, November 23, 1874.

No. 39.—AN ACT TO AMEND SECTION THIRTY-SEVEN OF CHAPTER TWENTY-TWO OF THE GENERAL STATUTES.

It is hereby enacted by the General Assembly of the State of Vermont:

SEC. 1. Section thirty-seven of chapter twenty-two of the general statutes is hereby amended to read as follows:

It shall be the duty of the clerk of each school district in this state to keep a fair record of all votes and proceedings of school meetings in their respective districts, and to certify the same when required; and every district clerk, and every prudential committee discharging the duties of a district clerk, who shall willfully violate the provisions of this section, shall be subject to the penalty imposed in section fifty-eight of this chapter.

SEC. 2. This act shall take effect from its passage.

Approved, November 24, 1874.

No. 40.—AN ACT RELATING TO THE DIVISION OF PUBLIC MONEY AMONG SCHOOL DISTRICTS, AND IN AMENDMENT OF SECTIONS EIGHTY-THREE AND EIGHTY-SIX OF CHAPTER TWENTY-TWO OF THE GENERAL STATUTES.

SECTION
1. One half of public money to be divided equally; the other half to be divided in proportion to aggregate attendance; mode of computing aggregate attendance.

SECTION
2. Division of public money in fractional districts, how made.
3. Acts inconsistent herewith repealed.
4. To take effect.

It is hereby enacted by the General Assembly of the State of Vermont:

SEC. 1. Section eighty-three of chapter twenty-two of the general statutes is hereby amended so as to read as follows:

The one half part of the proceeds of the tax assessed by the selectmen, with the income of any town appropriated to the use of schools, and all sums raised by vote of the town for such use, shall annually, on the Friday next preceding the last Tuesday of March, be divided by the selectmen of such town between the several common school districts in such town equally, without regard to the number of scholars such district may contain; and the remaining one half shall be divided between such districts, including also any union district, in proportion to the aggregate attendance of the scholars of such district, between the ages of five and twenty years, upon the common schools in such district, during the preceding school year; such aggregate attendance to be ascertained from the record thereof, to be kept in the registers of such schools, by adding together the number of days of actual attendance of each legal scholar, as shown by the register. And the same shall be paid over, under the direction of the selectmen, to the several treasurers of such districts; provided, that no union district, nor district for the support of common schools, shall receive any share of such moneys unless there shall, during the year next preceding such distribution, have been kept in such district a school for two full terms of ten weeks each, or their equivalent; provided, also that nothing herein shall affect the powers of the Montpelier union district, under the act entitled "An act to enlarge the powers of such district," approved November 21, 1859.

SEC. 2. The last clause after the word "second" of section eighty-six of chapter twenty-two of the general statutes is amended so as to read as follows:

Of that part of the public money which is required to be divided among the districts in proportion to the aggregate attendance of the scholars of such districts, between the ages of five and twenty years, each district shall receive such sum as will be in proportion to the whole sum to be divided in such towns, which the aggregate attendance of the whole number of children in such district, residing in such town, bears to the aggregate attendance of the whole number of children in such town. And the clerk of such district shall make returns to the town superintendent of schools in each town, specifying the number of children in the district between the ages of five and twenty years, and the number residing in each of the towns composing such district, and the aggregate attendance of children in such district residing in each town, and also the aggregate attendance of the whole number of children between the ages of five and twenty years, in such district.

SEC. 3. All acts inconsistent with the provisions of this act are hereby repealed.

SEC. 4. This act shall take effect from its passage.

Approved, November 24, 1874.

No. 41.—AN ACT AUTHORIZING THE COMPILATION OF THE SCHOOL LAWS.

SECTION	SECTION
1. Governor authorized to appoint a compiler of school laws now in force.	2. Three thousand copies to be printed and distributed under direction of secretary of state.

It is hereby enacted by the General Assembly of the State of Vermont:

SEC. 1. The governor is hereby authorized and required to appoint some suitable person to compile all school laws of this state that may be in force at the close of the present session of the general assembly, and annex thereto a concise digest of the decisions of the supreme court of this state having reference to the schools and schools laws of this state, and also forms for the use of school district officers; provided that the expense thereof shall not exceed two hundred dollars.

SEC. 2. The secretary of state shall, as soon as conveniently may be done, procure three thousand copies of such compilation, digest and forms to be printed and bound in paper, in the same style the session laws are printed, and distribute the same in the following manner:

To each organized town and city in this state, one copy, to be deposited in the clerk's office, and one copy for each school district in such town or city one copy, to each superintendent of schools, for the use of him and his successors in office, and the balance shall be deposited in the state library for distribution under the direction of the state librarian.

Approved, November 23, 1874.

No. 42.—AN ACT IN RELATION TO CITY, TOWN AND PRIVATE TELEGRAPH LINES.

It is hereby enacted by the General Assembly of the State of Vermont:

SEC. 1. Cities and towns may construct for their own use lines of electric telegraph upon and along the highways and public roads within their respective limits, subject to the provisions of chapter eighty-eight of the general statutes, so far as the same are applicable.

SEC. 2. The board of aldermen of cities and the selectmen of towns may authorize any persons, upon such terms and conditions as they may prescribe, and subject to the provisions of chapter eighty-eight of the general statutes, as far as applicable, to construct for private use a line of electric telegraph upon and along the highways and public roads of the city or town. After the erection of such line the posts and structures thereof, within the location of such highways and roads, shall be subject to the regulation and control of the board of aldermen or selectmen, who may at any time require alterations in the location or erection of such posts and structures to be made by the parties using the same, and may order the removal thereof, having first given such parties notice and an opportunity to be heard. And the city or town may at any time attach wires for its own use to such posts and structures, under such terms and conditions as they shall deem just and reasonable.

SEC. 3.   The provisions of section six of chapter eighty-eight of the general statutes, respecting penalties for injuries to telegraph lines therein referred to, shall apply to similar injuries to telegraph lines, or any of the structures thereof, which may be erected under the authority of this act.

SEC. 4.   This act shall take effect from its passage.

Approved, November 5, 1874.

No. 43.—AN ACT TO PROVIDE FOR THE PAYMENT OF INTEREST ON TOWN AND CITY BONDS OR NOTES, TO IMPROVE THE CREDIT OF THE SAME, AND TO LAY A TAX FOR THE PAYMENT OF THE SAME.

SECTION
1. When bonds are issued, town or city treasurer to preserve registration of same
2. In default of payment of interest, treasurer to deliver tax-bill to collector; tax, how

SECTION
collected; money thus raised to be applied to payment of said interest and expenses—without vote of town or city.
3. To take effect.

It is hereby enacted by the General Assembly of the State of Vermont:

SEC. 1.   Whenever any city or town in this state shall hereafter issue its notes or bonds for the payment of any sum of money, with interest coupons attached, payable semi-annually, annually, or otherwise, it shall be the duty of the treasurer of such city or town to make and keep in a proper book for that purpose, an accurate registration of the number and amount of such bonds or notes, with all other necessary particulars of dates and description.

SEC. 2. In case any town or city shall neglect to make seasonable provision for the payment of the interest on said obligations as the same shall become due, it shall be the duty of any such town or city treasurer to seasonably make out and deliver to the collector of taxes in any such town or city, a tax-bill on the list of the inhabitants of such town or city, and he shall therewith issue to said collector his warrant, substantially in form as now provided for to be issued by a justice of the peace for the collection of town or other taxes, directing the collection and payment of said tax to said town or city treasurer within sixty days from the time of such delivery, in amount sufficient to seasonably and promptly pay, with all proper charges for collection, the interest due, or the payment of which is to be provided for on the notes or bonds of such town or city. And such tax shall be collected and paid to such town or city treasurer promptly, according to warrant; and the money so collected and paid to such town or city treasurer shall be specially held, appropriated and used for the payment of such interest, and for no other purpose, save the incidental expenses of assessing and collecting such tax. And it is hereby made the duty of such town or city treasurer to provide for and promptly pay such interest, without any vote therefor of such town or city; and such tax-bill shall have all the force and authority, in every respect, of a tax-bill for a tax voted at any regular meeting of such town or city.

SEC. 3. This act shall take effect from its passage.

Approved, November 24, 1874.

No. 44.—AN ACT FIXING THE TIME OF HOLDING THE COUNTY COURT IN THE COUNTY OF CHITTENDEN.

It is hereby enacted by the General Assembly of the State of Vermont:

SEC. 1.   The stated terms of the county court in the county of Chittenden shall hereafter be held as follows :

On the first Tuesday in April and the third Tuesday in September in each year.

Approved, November 24, 1874.

No. 45.—AN ACT TO CHANGE THE TIME OF HOLDING THE SUPREME COURT IN THE COUNTY OF FRANKLIN.

It is hereby enacted by the General Assembly of the State of Vermont:

SEC. 1.   The stated term of the supreme court in the county of Franklin shall hereafter be held on the first Thursday after the second Tuesday of January in each year.

SEC. 2.   This act shall take effect from its passage.

Approved, November 24, 1874.

No. 46—AN ACT TO CHANGE THE TIME OF HOLDING THE SUPREME COURT IN THE COUNTY OF GRAND ISLE.

It is hereby enacted by th: General Assembly of the State of Vermont :

SEC. 1. The stated term of the supreme court in the county of Grand Isle shall hereafter be held on the third Tuesday of January in each year.

SEC. 2. This act shall take effect from its passage.

Approved, November 24, 1874.

No. 47—AN ACT TO CHANGE THE TIME OF HOLDING THE COUNTY COURT IN GRAND ISLE COUNTY.

SECTION	SECTION
1. Change of time for holding court.	2. All processes to be returnable to term herein fixed.
	3. To take effect.

It is hereby enacted by the General Assembly of the State of Vermont:

SEC. 1. So much of section twenty-six of chapter thirty of the general statutes, as relates to the time of holding the county court in Grand Isle county, is so amended as to read as follows :

In the county of Grand Isle on the last Tuesday of August and the last Tuesday but one in February.

SEC. 2.   All processes returnable to the February term of said court on the last Tuesday of February shall be returned to said term to be holden on the last Tuesday but one in February, the same as though made returnable at said last mentioned time.

SEC. 3.   This act shall take effect from its passage.

Approved, November 24, 1874.

No. 48—AN ACT IN RELATION TO THE TIME OF HOLDING THE SUPREME COURT IN THE COUNTY OF RUTLAND, AND IN AMENDMENT OF SECTION SEVEN OF CHAPTER THIRTY OF THE GENERAL STATUTES.

SECTION	SECTION
1. Change of time for holding court.	2. Suits pending not prejudiced by change.
	3. To take effect.

It is hereby enacted by the General Assembly of the State of Vermont:

SEC. 1.   So much of section seven of chapter thirty of the general statutes, as relates to the time of holding the supreme court in the county of Rutland, is hereby amended so as to read as follows:

In the county of Rutland on the first Thursday after the fourth Tuesday in January.

SEC. 2.   All suits, petitions, motions, bills of exceptions or processes pending in or returnable to said court shall be returned to, heard and tried in said court at the term commencing as provided in the first section of this act.

SEC. 3. This act shall take effect from its passage.

Approved, November 24, 1874.

No. 49.—AN ACT TO AMEND AN ACT TO ESTAB-LISH A MUNICIPAL COURT IN AND FOR THE VILLAGE OF RUTLAND, IN THE COUNTY OF RUTLAND, APPROVED NOVEMBER 26, 1872.

SECTION
1. Jurisdiction of municipal court established.
2. Cause may be removed to county court, under certain conditions.
3. Laws relating to pleadings and practices in county courts applicable in this court.

SECTION
4. New trials may be granted by this court, and also by supreme court, of cases heard in this court
5. Section seven of chapter thirty-eight and rules of law applicable to judgments rendered by this court.
6. Costs, how taxed.

It is hereby enacted by the General Assembly of the State of Vermont:

SEC. 1. The jurisdiction of the municipal court within and for the village of Rutland is hereby enlarged so that said court shall have jurisdiction of all actions of a civil nature, if either party resides in the town of Rutland at the time of the commencement of the action, within the limits and subject to the provisions and exceptions provided in section one of number three of the public acts of A. D. 1872, to which this section is in addition.

SEC. 2. In all cases where the judge of said municipal court is disqualified to act, or where it shall be made to appear to said court that a fair and impartial trial cannot be had in said municipal court, upon motion by either party, made before any trial shall be commenced therein, the cause may be removed into the county court for the county of Rutland at the next term thereof; and the process, pleadings, said motion and order of removal, being certified to said county court, the case shall be proceeded with the same as it would be if originally commenced in said county court or properly brought up by appeal.

SEC. 3. The statutes of this state in reference to pleadings and practice in the several county courts and passing causes to the supreme court shall, so far as applicable, be applied to and govern the proceedings of said municipal court.

SEC. 4. Said municipal court may grant new trials in cases determined in said court agreeably to the usages of law, on petition ¡brought for that purpose within twenty days after the rendition of said judgment, and the supreme court may grant new trials in cases tried before said municipal court upon the same terms and under the same regulations as in cases tried in any county court.

SEC. 5. Section seven of chapter thirty-eight of the general statutes, and the rules of law on the same subject, shall apply to judgments of said municipal court, the same as to judgments rendered by a justice of the peace.

SEC. 6. Writs returnable before said municipal court shall be taxed and allowed at the same as in justice court, and the court fees taxed and allowed in any action or prosecution shall be double the fees now allowed in the courts of a justice of the peace; provided, however, that if the plaintiff shall not recover a greater sum than four dollars in debt or damages, he shall not recover a greater sum than four dollars costs; and in other cases he shall recover no more costs than damage, except costs in the supreme court, in cases carried up by the defendant when the judgment is affirmed, or costs arising from continuances granted on motion of the defendant.

Approved, November 24, 1874.

No. 50.—AN ACT IN AMENDMENT OF AND IN ADDITION TO AN ACT TO ESTABLISH A MUNICIPAL COURT FOR THE VILLAGE OF ST. ALBANS, APPROVED NOVEMBER 26, 1872.

SECTION
1. Exceptions to decisions of court upon questions of law made appealable to supreme court, under regulations pro-

SECTION
vided for exceptions from county courts.
2. Fees and costs.
3. To take effect.

It is hereby enacted by the General Assembly of the State of Vermont:

SEC. 1. In all prosecutions for offenses within the jurisdiction of the municipal court to try and determine, and in all civil causes before said court, exceptions to the decisions of said court upon questions of law. may be taken to the supreme court, in the same manner and under the same regulations as provided by law for exceptions from the county court in criminal and civil causes respectively; but no such exceptions shall be allowed when an appeal is taken from such municipal court to the county court.

Sec. 2. Section eight of said act shall be amended so that the fees and costs allowed to parties, witnesses, jurymen and officers for the service of process returnable to such court shall be the same as by law is taxable before a justice of the peace.

Sec. 3. This act shall take effect from its passage.

Approved, November 24, 1874.

No. 51.—AN ACT IN AMENDMENT OF NUMBER FORTY-NINE OF THE ACTS OF 1870, RELATING TO SECTION FORTY-TWO OF CHAPTER TWENTY-FIVE OF THE GENERAL STATUTES, ON THE LIABILITIES OF TOWNS.

It is hereby enacted by the General Assembly of the State of Vermont:

Sec. 1. An act entitled an act in amendment of section forty-two of chapter twenty-five of the general statutes, of repairs of highways and bridges, approved October 20, 1870, is hereby amended so as to read as follows:

No action shall hereafter be had or maintained in any court in this state against any town for injuries received or damage sustained through the insufficiency of any highway or bridge, unless notice shall have first been given in writing, signed by the party so injured or claiming damage, to one or more of the selectmen of the town in which the highway or bridge is situated, by the person injured or claiming damage, within twenty days of the time of the occurrence of such injury or damage, stating the time when and the place where such injury was received, and pointing out the respect or particular in which said highway, road or bridge was insufficient or out of repair; and that he or she so injured or damaged, will claim satisfaction of such town. Such notice shall also contain a description of the injury received or damage sustained by such person so claiming damage, and if bodily injuries be claimed, the part of the body injured shall be given, together with the extent and effect of the injury upon the health of the person so injured; provided, however, that nothing in this section shall be construed to apply to any case where the person injured shall in consequence thereof be bereft of his or her reason.

Approved, November 24, 1874.

No. 52.—AN ACT IN ADDITION TO SECTION SIXTY-FIVE OF CHAPTER TWENTY-FOUR OF THE GENERAL STATUTES, ENTITLED "OF LAYING OUT AND DISCONTINUING HIGHWAYS AND BRIDGES."

SECTION
1. When towns are assessed for expense of repairing highway, court may appoint a commissioner; term of office; duties.
2. To require share of expense from town so assessed; selectmen to draw orders on treas-

SECTION
urer; order valid against town.
3. Commissioner to report each year to the court.
4. Court may remove said commissioner and appoint another.
5. Commissioner to give bonds.
6. To take effect.

It is hereby enacted by the General Assembly of the State of Vermont:

SEC. 1. Whenever any court shall assess any town or towns any proportion of the expense of putting in repair any highway, as is provided for by section sixty-five of chapter twenty-four of the general statutes, entitled "Of laying out and discontinuing highways and bridges," and in all cases where any court has heretofore so assessed any town or towns, the court may in its discretion, on the motion of any town interested as a party to the proceedings, appoint a commissioner, for a time not to exceed five years, who shall have charge of and under whose superintendence and control the putting in repair of said road shall be placed, and by whose direction all moneys expended therefor shall be laid out.

SEC. 2. From time to time, as the commissioner so ap-

pointed shall need, he shall require of the selectmen of
each of the towns which shall have been assessed as aforesaid, and of the town in or through which said road is located, such town's assesment or share of the expense of so
putting in repair said road, in due and ratable proportions;
and upon such requisition, it shall be the duty of the selectmen so required, to draw their order or orders upon the
treasurers of their respective towns for the amount or
amounts so required, which order or orders shall constitute valid and legal claims in favor of the holder or holders thereof against the town or towns upon whose treasurers the same shall have been drawn.

SEC. 3.   Such commissioner shall render to the court by
which he shall have been appointed, an account each year
of his doings and expenditures during said year in the
matters so entrusted to his charge, which account shall at
the expiration of his commission be finally audited and adjusted by such court, and under its order and direction,
upon notice to the several towns interested therein; and
he shall be liable to refund to the several towns, according to their respective interests therein, such moneys or
property as upon such accounting shall be found in his
hands.

SEC. 4.   Said court may at any time in its discretion remove said commissioner and appoint another, who shall be
subject to all the restrictions and libalities herein provided.

SEC. 5.   Such commissioner shall give a bond in such
amount, and with such sureties as the court shall require,
to each of the towns interested as aforesaid, conditioned
for the faithful performance of the duties of his said appointment, and for the re-payment of such moneys or

, property·as upon such accounting shall be found in his
, hands. ´

SEC. 6. This act shall take effect from its passage.

Approved, November 21, 1874.

No. 53.—AN ACT RELATIN G TO HIGHWAYS.

*It is hereby enacted by the General Assembly of the State
of Vermont:*

SEC. 1. The selectmen of any town may, when in their
judgment. the public good requires it, and by a petition
duly presented to them for that purpose they are specially
requested so to do, lay out a highway across any stream
in said town as a fordway, under the same provisions as
are now provided in case of laying out and discontinuing
highways; provided, however, that in case any such
highway shall be laid out as a fordway as above provided,
the town shall not in any event be liable for any injury or
damage that may be sustained by any person by reason of
the insufficiency of said fordway.

SEC. 2. All acts and parts of acts inconsistent with
this act are hereby repealed.

SEC. 3. This act shall take effect from its passage.

Approved, November 24, 1874.

No. 54.—AN ACT IN RELATION TO THE DUTIES OF HIGHWAY SURVEYORS.

It is hereby enacted by the General Assembly of the State of Vermont:

SEC. 1. When the highway surveyor in any town in this state shall have expended all the money in the tax-bill delivered to him by the selectmen, as provided by section nine, chapter twenty-five, of the general statutes, and the amount of such tax shall be found insufficient to complete the ordinary repairs of the highways in his district, it shall be the duty of the highway surveyor to inform the selectmen, or either of them, of the insufficiency of such tax; and upon such notice, it shall be the duty of the selectmen to provide other means for the completion of the ordinary repairs ; and in no case shall the town be chargeable with any expense for such ordinary repairs of highways, except that incurred under the direction of the selectmen,· nor shall the highway surveyor be liable to the town for damages occasioned by the want of any ordinary repairs of highways after he shall have given the notice aforesaid, and the selectmen shall refuse or neglect to furnish means to complets such ordinary repairs.

SEC. 2. All acts and parts of acts inconsistent with this act are hereby repealed.

SEC. 3. This act shall take effect from its passage.

Approved, November 24, 1874.

No. 55.—AN ACT IN AMENDMENT OF SECTION ONE OF AN ACT APPROVED NOVEMBER 20, 1868, ENTITLED "AN ACT RELATING TO WARNING TOWN MEETINGS."

It is hereby enacted by the General Assembly of the State of Vermont:

SEC. 1. Section one of an act approved November 20, 1868, entitled "An act relating to warning town meetings," is hereby amended so as to read as follows :

If the officers of any town or city, whose duty it shall be to warn, or cause to be warned, town or city mee tings shall refuse or neglect to warn, or cause to be warned, a town or city meeting for any purpose, on the petition in writing of thirty or more legal voters, setting forth the purposes of said meeting, for more than ten days after receiving said petition, said officers so refusing or neg· lecting, shall each be liable to a penalty of forty dollars, and a like penalty of forty dollars for every twenty days neglect or refusal to warn or cause to be warned such meetings thereafter.

Approved, October 28, 1874.

No. 56.—AN ACT IN ADDITION TO CHAPTER FIF. TEEN OF THE GENERAL, STATUTES ENTITLED "OF TOWNS, TOWN MEETINGS, AND TOWN OFFICERS."

It is hereby enacted by the General Assembly of the State of Vermont:

Sec 1. No person hereafter elected and qualified as selectman in any town in this state, shall be eligible to the office of first constable and collector of taxes, or town treasurer, for and during the same year he is so elected and qualified as selectman as aforesaid.

Sec. 2. This act shall take effect from its passage.

Approved, November 24, 1874.

No. 57.—AN ACT TO AMEND SECTION FOURTEEN OF CHAPTER FIFTEEN OF THE GENERAL STATUTES, RELATING TO TOWN OFFICERS.

It is hereby enacted by the General Assembly of the State of Vermont:

Section fourteen of chapter fifteen of the general statutes is hereby amended so as to read as follows:

The election of town clerk, selectmen, treasurer, overseer of the poor, constables, superintendent of schools, grand jurors and listers shall be made by ballot when the ballots are required by any three voters present at the meeting. The election of all other town officers shall be in such manner as the meeting may determine.

Approved, November 5, 1874.

No. 58.—AN ACT TO PREVENT ILLEGAL VOTING IN TOWN, VILLAGE OR SCHOOL DISTRICT MEET-INGS.

SECTION
1. Penalty for presiding officers to knowingly receive illegal votes.

SECTION
2. Penalty for knowingly to cast an illegal vote.
3. Recovery of fines.

It is hereby enacted by the General Assembly of the State of Vermont :

SEC. 1. If the presiding officer at any town, village or school district meetings shall knowingly receive and count any vote or votes from any person not a legal voter, or knowingly receive from any legal voter at any one balloting for the same office more than one vote, he shall be punished by fine not exceeding one hundred dollars for each offense.

SEC 2. If any person, knowing that he is not a qualified voter, shall at any of said meetings mentioned in the first section of this act, willfully give in a vote for any officer to be chosen, he shall be punished by a fine not exceeding one hundred dollars for such offense.

SEC. 3. The fines mentioned in this act may be recovered to the use of this state, by information or indictment before the county court in the county where the offense shall be committed.

Approved, November 13, 1874.

No. 59.—AN ACT IN ADDITION TO ACT NUMBER SEVENTY-SIX OF THE ACTS PASSED IN 1870, ENTITLED "AN ACT TO PROTECT BUTTER AND CHEESE MANUFACTURERS."

It is hereby enacted by the General Assembly of the State of Vermont:

SEC. 1. Whoever shall knowingly sell or furnish, o offer to sell, any milk diluted with water, or in any way adulterated, shall forfeit to the person to whom such milk is sold or furnished, the same sum that is forfeited to the manufacturer, as provided in the act to which this is an addition, and to be collected by him in the same manner.

SEC. 2. This act shall take effect from its passage.

Approved, November 17, 1874.

No. 60.—AN ACT IN RELATION TO THE SERVICE OF EXTENTS AGAINST DELINQUENT COL- LECTORS.

It is hereby enacted by the General Assembly of the State Vermont:

SEC. 1. That the extents provided for in sections forty- one and forty-three of chapter eighty-four of the general statutes, may be issued to the sheriff of any county in this state, who is hereby authorized to serve the same and make return thereof as now provided by law for the sheriff of the county in which the delinquent collector may reside.

Approved, October 28, 1874.

No. 61.—AN ACT TO AMEND AN ACT ENTITLED "AN ACT RELATING TO CRIMINAL OFFENSES COMMITTED WITHIN THE LIMITS OF INCORPORATED VILLAGES IN THIS STATE," APPROVED NOVEMBER 22, 1870.

SECTION
1. Fines, penalties and costs to be paid to treasury of village; when unpaid by delinquent, he to be put to hard labor; officer receiving such person to conform to provisions of

SECTION
chapter one hundred and twenty-two, general statutes; justices to draw orders on village treasury for costs.
2. To take effect.

It is hereby enacted by the General Assembly of the State of Vermont:

SEC. 1. That the second section of said act is hereby amended so as to read as follows:

All the fines and penalties which shall be imposed on any person for any such offense, or for the breach of any penal law committed within the limits of any incorporated village in this state, together with the costs of prosecution, if the prosecution be commenced on the complaint or information of any of its police officers, and being within the jurisdiction of a justice oef th peace to try and determine, shall belong and be paid to the treasury of the village in which the offense shall be committed. And if said fine and costs are not paid, the justice of the peace may, in his discretion, order the said person to be put to hard labor, as provided in chapter one hundred and twenty-two of the general statutes, until said fine and costs are paid, or until the avails of such labor received by the officer having charge of the prisoner, as therein provided in said chapter one hundred and twenty-two as aforesaid, shall amount to a sum sufficient to pay said fine and costs. The justice of the peace before whom such prosecution shall be heard and tried, and who shall commit the prisoner, and order such person to be put to hard labor as aforesaid, and the officer receiving such person so assigned to labor as aforesaid, are hereby required to conform fully to the provisions and requirements of chapter one hundred and twenty-two of the general statutes, relating to the assignment of persons to hard labor for minor offenses; and such justices are hereby empowered to draw orders on the treasury of such village to pay the costs of any such prosecution in favor of the persons entitled to the same.

Sec. 2. This act to take effect from its passage.

Approved, November 5, 1874.

No. 62.—AN ACT IN AMENDMENT OF SECTION SEVEN OF CHAPTER ONE HUNDRED AND TWENTY OF THE GENERAL STATUTES, RELATING TO CRIMES AND PUNISHMENTS.

It is hereby enacted by the General Assembly of the State of Vermont:

Sec. 1. Section seven of chapter one hundred and

twenty of the general statutes is hereby amended so as to read as follows:

When any person shall be convicted of any crime punishable with death, and sentenced to suffer such punishment, he shall at the same time be sentenced to hard labor in the state prison for a period of twenty months from the date of his sentence, and to solitary confinement thereafter in the state prison until such punishment of death shall be inflicted.

Approved, November 20, 1874.

No. 63.—AN ACT IN ADDITION TO "AN ACT EMPOWERING INCORPORATED VILLAGES AND TOWNS TO HAVE AND MAINTAIN LOCK-UPS OR JAILS," APPROVED NOVEMBER 19, 1866.

SECTION	SECTION
1. Jailor may be appointed by trustees or bailiffs.	conviction may be committed to lock-ups or village jails, subject to all the restraints of confinement in county jails.
2. Jailors shall be sworn; duties; fees.	
3. Persons held for trial or under	4. To take effect.

It is hereby enacted by the General Assembly of the State of Vermont:

SEC. 1. The trustees or bailiffs of any village incorporated under the laws of this state, which has and maintains a lock-up or jail, shall have power to appoint a ja lor, who shall hold his office during the pleasure of said trustees or bailiffs. The appointment of said jailor shall be in writing, and signed by a majority of said trustees or bailiffs, and shall be recorded in the records of said village. A majority of said trustees or bailiffs may revoke such appointment, and their revocation shall be in writing, and shall be recorded in the records of said village.

SEC. 2. Every jailor so appointed shall be sworn to the faithful discharge of the duties of his office, and shall perform all the duties and be amenable to all the penalties which are imposed by law on county jailors within this state, and shall be entitled to the same fees.

SEC. 3. When any process, issued under the authority of this state, shall be delivered to any officer or other person authorized to serve the same, in any county in this state, by which it shall become the duty of such officer or other person to commit any prisoner to the county jail in said county, and the person required to be committed shall have been convicted by a justice of the peace of any crime or offense against the laws of this state within the jurisdiction of a justice of the peace to try and determine, or shall be committed to await an examination or trial before a justice of the peace, or shall be committed for neglect or refusal to comply with the requirements of section thirty-three of chapter ninety-four of the general statutes, such conviction, commitment, neglect or refusal, being had within the limits of any village incorporated under the laws of this state, such officer or other person may commit the person named in such process to the lockup or jail maintained by such village; and any person so committed shall be subject to all the restraints, and entitled to all the privileges which are provided by law in the case of persons confined in county jail.

SEC. 4. This act shall take effect from its passage.

Approved, November 24, 1874.

No. 64.—AN ACT IN AMENDMENT OF AND IN AD-
DITION TO CHAPTER THIRTY-FOUR OF THE
GENERAL STATUTES, ENTITLED "OF PROCEED-
INGS AGAINST TRUSTEES."

*It is hereby enacted by the General Assembly of the State
of Vermont:*

SEC. 1. If it shall appear that any person is held as
trustee in any suit by reason of any negotiable paper, and
any claimant shall not appear or be cited to appear in such
suit, and a suit shall afterwards be brought against said
trustee by any person holding such negotiable paper by
force of an assignment from the payee thereof, the said
trustee may plead the former judgment against him in
bar; and the court before whom such last mentioned suit
is pending, shall issue a citation, and the holder of such
negotiable paper shall cause the same to be served on the
plaintiff in the first mentioned suit, or his attorney of
record. And the court shall proceed to try and determine
the case as between the holder and the plaintiff in the first
suit, the same as though the holder had been cited to
appear in the first suit; and the judgment against the
trustee shall not be held to be conclusive between the
holder and the plaintiff in the first suit, but the court shall
decide to which the judgment rendered against the trustee
belongs, and if the decision shall be in favor of the holder
of such negotiable paper, the court shall adjudge the

judgment against the trustee to be the property of such holder, and such holder shall have the right to collect the same in the name of the plaintiff in the first suit, at the expense of such holder, if the trustee shall not previously have paid said judgment; but if the trustee shall have previously paid such judgment, or part thereof, then such holder shall recover judgment against the plaintiff in the first suit for the sum so paid, and be entitled to the residue of said judgment as aforesaid if the whole shall not have been paid.

SEC. 2. Costs shall be allowed between the parties in such a manner as the court shall decide to be just and equitable, and either party shall be entitled to have the facts tried by a jury or by a commissioner, as in other cases.

SEC. 3. If the holder of any note or bill of exchange not due, shall, after he has notice that a copy of a trustee writ has been served on the trustee, sell, transfer or assign such note or bill to any person, firm or corporation, without fully informing him or them of such process, with intent to defeat such process, he shall be deemed guilty of a misdemeanor, and on conviction thereof, shall be punished by fine not exceeding five hundred dollars, or by imprisonment in the county jail not exceeding one year, or both of said punishments, in the discretion of the court, together with costs of prosecution.

Approved, November 24, 1874.

No. 65.—AN ACT TO PROTECT CAMP-MEETINGS.

It is hereby enacted by the General Assembly of the State of Vermont:

SEC. 1.   The president, vice-presidents and trustees of any camp-meeting association, chartered by the legislature of this state, or that may hereafter be formed under the existing laws of this state, are authorized to act as a special police at any camp-meeting held by such association, and within two miles of the camp-meeting grounds, during the continuance of said camp-meeting, with the same power as is given to constables by the laws of this state, to seize spirituous liquors, to demand assistance, and to arrest disorderly persons and detain them in custody until proper trial can be had; and such persons so authorized shall, before the exercise of any of the powers specified in this act, be sworn to a faithful performance of the duties of said special police officer, and while on duty shall wear a badge of their office.

SEC. 2.   This act shall take effect from its passage.

Approved, November 24, 1874.

No. 66.—AN ACT IN ADDITION TO CHAPTER TWENTY OF THE GENERAL STATUTES, ENTITLED "OF THE SUPPORT AND REMOVAL OF PAUPERS AND THE RELIEF OF THE INSANE POOR."

SECTION
1. Three dollars per week allowed for the board of insane poor in the Vermont asylum for the insane; trustees may draw seventy-five cents per

SECTION
   week from the state on account of such board; travel fees.
2. Certain laws repealed.
3. To take effect.

It is hereby enacted by the General Assembly of the State of Vermont:

SEC. 1. The trustees of the Vermont asylum for the insane are hereby authorized to charge three dollars per week for supporting the insane poor of this state at said asylum; and said trustees may draw from the treasury of this state upon the order of the auditor of accounts, annually, in the month of August, for the benefit of each town having insane poor persons confined in said asylum, the sum of seventy-five cents per week for each of said insane poor persons, for the time they shall have been confined there during the year next preceding the month of August annually, and ten cents per mile by the nearest practicable route from their respective residences to said asylum, as the expense of transportation.

SEC. 2. Sections thirty-seven, thirty-eight and forty-two of chapter twenty of the general statutes, and an act entitled "An act to amend section thirty-eight of chapter twenty of the general statutes, relating to the relief of

the insane poor," approved October 30, 1869, are hereby repealed.

SEC. 3. This act shall take effect from its passage.

Approved, November 24, 1874.

No. 67.—AN ACT REGULATING THE DISCHARGE OF PATIENTS FROM INSANE ASYLUMS.

SECTION	SECTION
1. If persons desire to remove friends while superintendent does not deem them restored, two physicians, elected by the friends of said person; and	commissioner of insane to examine said person, and if not restored, said person to be retained on their certificate.
	2. To take effect.

It is hereby enacted by the General Assembly of the State of Vermont:

SEC. 1. If the friends or guardian of any person confined in any insane asylum in this state, shall desire to remove such person for the purpose of setting him or her at
liberty, while the superintendent of such asylum shall
deem such person not sufficiently restored to render it safe
for themselves, their friends or for the community, for such
person to be at liberty, then two physicians, not connected
with the said asylum, but selected by the friends or guardians of said person, and the commissioner of insane, shall
together examine such person, and if by them such person
shall be found not sufficiently restored to be allowed their
liberty, then, on the certificates of such examiners, such
person shall be retained in said asylum until some provisions are made by friends or guardians to remove such

person to some other asylum for the insane, or other suitable place of confinement.

SEC. 2. This act shall take effect from its passage.

Approved, November 23, 1874.

No. 68—AN ACT IN AMENDMENT OF AN ACT ENTITLED "AN ACT FOR THE RELIEF OF THE FAMILIES OF INSANE PERSONS," APPROVED NOVEMBER 10, 1870.

SECTION	SECTION
1. Where income of estate and earnings of family are insufficient for support of an insane person, said person shall be maintained at insane asylum at the expense of the town; the balance of said in-	come and earnings, after support of family, shall go to the town affording such income. 2. County court to have jurisdiction. 3. To take effect.

It is hereby enacted by the General Assembly of the State of Vermont :

SEC. 1. Section one of number thirty-three of the public acts of the general assembly of the state of Vermont for the year 1870, entitled "An act for the relief of the families of insane persons," is hereby amended so as to read as follows:

All insane persons having a legal settlement in any town in this state, the annual income of whose estate, together with the earnings of the wife and minor children of such insane person, shall not be sufficient for the support and maintenance of the wife and minor children of such insane person, and the support and maintenance of such insane person, shall be supported and maintained by such town at the insane asylum at Brattleboro. And such town shall be entitled to the use and control of so much of the income of said insane person's estate and property, and the earnings of said wife and minor children of such insane person, as shall be in excess of the expense of supporting and maintaining said wife and minor children.

SEC. 2. The county court in the county where such insane person shall have his legal settlement, upon complaint made by the wife of such insane person, may, on due hearing, either upon the appearance or default of such town, order such town to maintain and support such insane person at the insane asylum; and upon such complaint, said court may inquire into the matters and things pertaining to the income of said estate of said insane person, as well as to the earnings of said wife and minor children, and their support and maintenance, and may make such orders as may be necessary to carry into effect the provisions of this act; and said court may award costs to either party, as justice may seem to require, in the discretion of said court.

SEC. 3. This act shall take effect from its passage.

Approved, November 24, 1874.

No. 69.—AN ACT IN ADDITION TO CHAPTER SEVENTY-TWO OF THE GENERAL STATUTES, ENTITLED "OF GUARDIANS AND WARDS."

SECTION
1. Probate court may appoint guardian of insane married woman when the husband shall have abandoned said wife without making provision for her maintenance.

SECTION
2. Notice of such application to be given.
3. Estate of such woman may be sold.
4. To take effect.

It is hereby enacted by the General Assembly of the State of Vermont:

SEC. 1. The probate court may appoint a guardian of any insane married woman when the husband of said woman shall have left the state and abandoned his insane wife without making sufficient provision for her maintenance, on the application of a relative of said insane married woman, or of the overseer of the poor of the town in which said woman shall reside or be chargeable.

SEC. 2. Whenever there shall be an application to the probate court for the appointment of a guardian as aforesaid, said court shall give notice to such supposed insane married woman, and proceed with the hearing of said application as provided by an act amending section fourteen of chapter seventy-two of the general statutes, approved November 15, 1866.

SEC. 3. The probate court may authorize the guardian of such insane married woman to sell the personal or real estate of said woman and convey the same as provided by an act in amendment of sections thirty-three and thirty-five of chapter seventy-two of the general statutes, approved November 8, 1866.

SEC. 4. This act shall take effect from its passage.

Approved, November 24, 1874.

No. 70.—AN ACT TO AID AND ENCOURAGE DISCHARGED CONVICTS.

It is hereby enacted by the General Assembly of the State of Vermont:

SEC. 1. Every person who has been or shall be hereafter convicted of any offense against the laws of this state, and confined in the state prison in execution of the judgment or sentence upon such conviction, who shall so conduct himself or herself for any month of such sentence that no charge for misconduct shall be sustained against him or her for such month, shall have paid to him or her at the time of his or her discharge from such confinement, by the superintendent of the prison, in case such discharged convict is poor and destitute, the sum of one dollar for every such month; but said sum shall be reduced one dollar whenever in any month a charge for misconduct shall be sustained against him or her; provided, that the sum paid to any such discharged convict shall not exceed one hundred dollars; and the state treasurer, on the order of the said superintendent, shall furnish the moneys required for the carrying out of the provisions of this act.

SEC. 2. This act shall take effect from its passage.

Approved, November 24, 1874.

No. 71.—AN ACT TO AMEND SECTION FORTY-SIX, CHAPTER ONE, GENERAL STATUTES, RELATING TO PLACE FOR CANVASSING VOTES FOR MEMBER OF CONGRESS IN THE SECOND CONGRESSIONAL DISTRICT.

It is hereby enacted by the General Assembly of the State of Vermont:

SEC. 1. Section forty-six, chapter one, of the general statutes shall be amended by striking out the words, "the Congregational meeting house in Royalton," and insert therein, in their place, the words, *White River Junction House in Hartford.*

SEC. 2. This act shall take effect from its passage.

Approved, November 5, 1874.

No. 72.—AN ACT IN AMENDMENT OF SECTION
SEVENTY OF CHAPTER THIRTY-ONE OF THE
GENERAL STATUTES.

*It is hereby enacted by the General Assembly of the
State of Vermont:*

SEC. 1. Section seventy of chapter thirty-one of the
general statutes is hereby amended by adding to same
section the following words:

Provided, however, that in actions when the defendant
shall plead in excuse or justification that he was acting
as public officer, an appeal shall in all cases be allowed
the said defendent.

SEC. 2. This act shall take effect from its passage.

Approved, November 24, 1874.

No. 73.—AN ACT AMENDING SECTION TWENTY-
FOUR OF CHAPTER ONE HUNDRED AND TWEN-
TY-ONE OF THE GENERAL STATUTES.

*It is hereby enacted by the General Assembly of the State
of Vermont:*

SEC. 1. Section twenty-four of chapter one hundred and
twenty-one of the general statutes of this state is hereby
amended by adding thereto the following words, viz:

And the debtor in said execution, first above mentioned

in said section twenty-four, shall be entitled to all and the same relief, and in the same manner, as to the vacating the statement in said execution or endorsed thereon, and as to the privilege and time of being admitted to the poor debtor's oath or the liberties of the jail yard, as is provided for debtors in sections fifty-seven, fifty-eight and fifty-nine of chapter one hundred and twenty-one of the general statutes of this state.

SEC. 2. This act shall take effect from its passage.

Approved, November 12, 1874.

No. 74.—AN ACT TO REPEAL AN ACT IN AMEND-MENT OF SECTION TWENTY-ONE, CHAPTER TWENTY-EIGHT, GENERAL STATUTES, AP-PROVED NOVEMBER 26, 1872.

It is hereby enacted by the General Assembly of the State of Vermont:

SEC. 1. The act to amend an act in amendment of section twenty-one, chapter twenty-eight, general statutes, approved November 26, 1872, is hereby repealed; provided, however, that this act shall not in any way affect any proceedings which have been commenced under the said amendment.

SEC. 2. This act shall take effect from its passage.

Approved, November 24, 1874.

No. 75.—AN ACT IN AMENDMENT OF SECTION
SEVEN OF CHAPTER ONE HUNDRED AND
THIRTEEN OF THE GENERAL STATUTES, EN-
TITLED "OF OFFENSES AGAINST PRIVATE
PROPERTY," AND IN ADDITION TO SAID CHAP-
TER.

SECTION
1. Penalty for breaking and entering with intent to commit
certain crimes.

SECTION
2. Penalty for same in night time
3. To take effect.

*It is hereby enacted by the General Assembly of the
State of Vermont:*

SEC. 1.   That section seven of chapter one hundred and
thirteen of the general statutes shall be so amended as to
read as follows:

Every 'person who shall in the night time break and
enter any dwelling-house, church, court house, town house,
college, academy, school house, or any bank, warehouse,
office, shop, store, grocery, manufactory, mill, or any vessel,
steamboat, or any railroad car or saloon, with the intent to
commit the crime of murder, rape, robbery, larceny, or
any other felony, shall be punished by imprisonment in
the state prison not more than fifteen years, or be fined
not more than one thousand dollars; and shall thereafter
be disabled from giving a verdict in any cause whatever.

SEC. 2.   Every person who shall break and enter in the
night time any of the places mentioned in section one of
this act, which are occupied by any person or persons as
a sleeping apartment, with the intent to commit the crime

of murder, rape, robbery, larceny, or any other felony shall be punished by imprisonment in the state prison for life, or for a term of years not less than four.

SEC. 3. This act shall take effect from its passage.

Approved, November 23, 1874.

No. 76.—AN ACT IN ADDITION TO AN ACT ENTITLED " AN ACT TO AMEND SECTION TWENTY-FIVE OF CHAPTER THIRTY-THREE OF THE GENERAL STATUTES, ENTITLED ' OF PROCESS AND OTHER MATTERS,'" APPROVED NOVEMBER 19, 1868.

It is hereby enacted by the General Assembly of the State of Vermont:

SEC. 1. There shall be added to the list of personal property enumerated in said act, and subject to all the provisions thereof, the following articles: scythe snaths, shovel handles, hoe handles, fork stales, bobbins, and all kinds of lumber, manufactured, or in the process of manufacture.

SEC. 2. This act shall take effect from its passage.

Approved, November 24, 1874.

No. 77.—AN ACT IN ADDITION TO AN ACT EN-
TITLED, "AN ACT TO AMEND SECTION TWENTY-
FIVE OF CHAPTER THIRTY-THREE OF THE
GENERAL STATUTES, ENTITLED 'OF PROCESS
AND OTHER MATTERS,' APPROVED NOVEMBER
19, A. D. 1868."

*It is hereby enacted by the General Assembly of the State
of Vermont :*

SEC. 1. There shall be added to the list of personal
property enumerated in section one of an act entitled
"An act to amend section twenty-five of chapter thirty-
three of the general statutes, entitled, ' Of process and
other matters,' approved November 19, 1868," and subject
to all the provisions of said section, the article of flax,
whether in a raw state or in any stage or process of
curing or manufacturing.

SEC. 2. This act shall take effect from its passage.

Approved, November 20, 1874.

No. 78.—AN ACT REGULATING THE FEES OF AP-
PRAISERS IN CERTAIN CASES.

*It is hereby enacted by the General Assembly of the State
of Vermont:*

SEC. 1. The fees of persons appointed to appraise real

estate set off on execution, or to appraise personal property attached, or to appraise property to be replevied, shall be at the rate of twenty cents for each hour actually spent in such appraisal.

Approved, November 20, 1874..

No. 79.—AN ACT IN AMENDMENT OF SECTION THIRTY-SEVEN, CHAPTER ONE HUNDRED AND TWENTY-SIX, OF THE GENERAL STATUTES, RELATING TO FEES OF PARTIES IN JUSTICE COURTS.

It is hereby enacted by the General Assembly of the State of Vermont:

SEC. 1. Section thirty-seven of chapter one hundred and twenty-six of the general statutes shall be so amended as to read as follows:

There shall be allowed to the party recovering in a justice's court, for attendance, fifty cents; for travel within this state, per mile, six cents; provided, the plaintiff in no case be allowed anything for travel unless he shall personally attend the court. ·

Approved, October 28, 1874.

No. 80.—AN ACT FIXING THE FEES REQUIRED TO
BE PAID TO PROBATE JUDGES FOR THE BENE-
FIT OF THE STATE IN CERTAIN CASES.

*It is hereby enacted by the General Assembly of the State
of Vermont :*

SEC. 1. Instead of the fees now required to be paid to
the judge of probate, of the several probate districts, for
the benefit of the state for granting letters of administra-
tion, or testamentary, upon estates the assets of which
exceed the sum of one hundred and fifty dollars, there
shall be paid the following :

When the assets do not exceed the sum of five thousand
dollars, there shall be paid the sum of two dollars ; and
when the assets exceed the sum of five thousand dollars,
there shall be paid in addition thereto, the sum of two
dollars for each five thousand dollars, and each fraction
thereof in excess of five thousand dollars.

SEC. 2. This act shall take effect on the first day of
December, 1874.

Approved, November 5, 1874.

No. 81.—AN ACT IN AMENDMENT OF SECTION ONE OF AN ACT ENTITLED AN ACT TO AMEND AN ACT ENTITLED AN ACT TO AMEND SECTION TWO OF CHAPTER TWENTY-THREE OF THE GENERAL STATUTES, " ENTITLED OF THE INSTRUCTION OF THE DEAF, DUMB, AND BLIND," APPROVED. NOVEMBER 16, 1869.

It is hereby enacted by the General Assembly of the State of Vermont:

SEC. 1. A sum not exceeding five thousand dollars may be annually drawn from the treasury of this state, by the governor, for the benefit of the deaf and dumb, and a sum not exceeding four thousand dollars may. also be drawn, annually by him, for the benefit of the blind, to be appropriated agreeably to the provisions of said . chapter.

SEC. 2. All acts and parts of acts inconsistent with this act are hereby repealed.

SEC. 3. This act shall take effect from its passage.

Approved, November 20, 1874.

No. 82.—AN ACT TO AMEND SECTIONS SIXTY-
NINE AND SEVENTY-ONE OF CHAPTER EIGHT
OF THE GENERAL STATUTES, RELATING TO
THE DISTRIBUTION OF THE VERMONT REPORTS.

SECTION
1. Reporter to publish and distribute reports; compensation therefor.

SECTION
1. Distribution of by state librarian.

*It is hereby enacted by the General Assembly of the State
of Vermont:*

SEC. 1. Section sixty-nine of chapter eight of the
general statutes is hereby amended so as to read as
follows :

The reporter shall annually, at his own expense, publish
such reports, of which he shall deliver one hundred and
twenty-five copies to the librarian for the use of the state;
and also shall deliver to the librarian of the state library
one copy of the same for each organized town in the state,
and shall be entitled to receive from the state an amount
equal to the actual costs of the publication, binding and
transportation of all such copies so furnished.

SEC. 2. Section seventy-one of chapter eight of the
general statutes shall be amended so as to read as follows :

It shall be the duty of the state librarian to deliver, on
request, out of the one hundred and twenty-five copies so
delivered to the state, a copy to each county clerk for the
use of the courts in their counties ; one copy to each of
the registers of probate for the use of the respective probate courts in their districts ; one copy to each of the

judges and ex-judges of the supreme court; one copy
to the judges of the United States district court for the
district of Vermont; and one copy each to the librarians
of the University of Vermont, Middlebury College, and
Norwich University, and the remainder of said reports
shall be subject to the control of the trustees of the state
library for the library.

Approved, November 5, 1874.

No. 83.—AN ACT PROVIDING FOR THE CARE OF
THE COLLECTIONS IN THE STATE CABINET,
AND FOR ADDITIONS TO THE SAME.

Section	Section
1. Two hundred dollars appropriated; how to be expended.	2. How to be drawn from state treasurer.
	3. To take effect.

*It is hereby enacted by the General Assembly of the State
of Vermont:*

Sec. 1. A sum not exceeding two hundred dollars per
annum for the next two years is appropriated for the purpose of defraying the necessary expenses of the state
cabinet; said sum to be expended by the curator in the
proper care of specimens now in the cabinet, and in the
collections of such specimens as he may deem of public
value, and in properly caring for and labeling the same.

Sec. 2. The auditor of accounts is hereby directed to draw his order on the state treasurer, at such times and and for such sums, not exceeding the sum mentioned in section one of this act, in favor of the curator of the state cabinet, as shall appear to said auditor, that said curator is entitled to receive under section one of this act.

Sec. 3. This act shall take effect from its passage.

Approved, November 20, 1874.

No. 84.—AN ACT TO PROCURE THE PRINTING AND DISTRIBUTION OF THE REPORT OF THE SECRETARY OF THE VERMONT DAIRYMEN'S ASSOCIATION.

It is hereby enacted by the General Assembly of the State of Vermont:

Sec. 1. The secretary of state is hereby authorized and directed, annually to procure the printing of thirteen hundred copies of the report of the secretary of the Vermont Dairymen's Association: nine hundred copies of said report for the use of the association; one hundred copies for the state library; and three hundred copies to be distributed by the secretary of state annually, among the members of the general assembly.

Sec. 2. The expense of printing such report shall be paid from the treasury of the state in like manner as the expense of printing public documents is now defrayed.

Sec. 3. This act shall take effect from its passage.

Approved, November 17, 1874.

No. 85.—AN ACT TO CONFIRM THE TITLE TO CERTAIN STRUCTURES IN LAKE CHAMPLAIN.

It is hereby enacted by the General Assembly of the State of Vermont:

Sec. 1. Whenever any railroad company in this state shall have constructed their railroad beyond low water mark into Lake Champlain, or shall have built out into said lake any wharf, dock, pier or other structure in connection with such railroad, for its accommodation or use, which shall not impede ordinary navigation in passing up and down said lake, such building and structures are hereby declared to be lawful, and the legal title thereto is hereby confirmed to such railroad companies respectively, which built the same, or others lawfully claiming through them.

Sec. 2. This act shall take effect from its passage.

Approved, November 24, 1874.

No. 86.—AN ACT RELATING TO REPORTERS FOR THE SENATE.

It is hereby enacted by the General Assembly of the State of Vermont:

SEC. 1. It shall be the duty of the president of the senate, immediately upon the organization of the senate, to appoint one assistant reporter thereof, whose duty it shall be to assist the reporter to furnish at the close of each day's session, daily reports of the proceedings of the senate, for publication in the daily newspapers of the state, and whose compensation shall be three dollars per day.

SEC. 2. Section two of the act approved November 22, 1870, entitled "An act to amend an act entitled 'An act for the appointment of reporters,' approved November 8, 1867," is hereby repealed.

SEC. 3. This act shall take effect from its passage.

Approved, October 14, 1874.

No. 87.—AN ACT ENLARGING THE POWERS OF THE INSPECTOR OF FINANCE, AND DEFINING HIS DUTIES.

Section	Section
1. Inspector of finance to visit and inspect savings banks; duties and powers of, in relation thereto.	any savings bank to be appointed inspector.
2. To make report to auditor of accounts annually.	5. Same powers conferred as upon bank commissioner.
3. Compensation.	6. Acts inconsistent herewith repealed.
4. No stockholder or officer of	7. To take effect.

It is hereby enacted by the General Assembly of the State of Vermont:

SEC. 1. The inspector of finance, in addition to the duties imposed upon him by section sixty-six, chapter eight, of the general statutes, shall at least, once a year visit and inspect the condition and affairs of every savings bank and trust company in this state, and oftener, if he believes the interest and safety of the depositors in and creditors of any such corporation shall require such inspection and examination; and if, upon such examination, such inspector shall find that the officers of any such corporation have violated the provisions of their acts of incorporation or any acts relating thereto, he may in his discretion cause proceeding to be instituted in the court of chancery, for the restraining and enjoining of such institution and the officers thereof, from the collection, disposition and distribution of the effects and property of any such corporation, agreeably to the provisions of chapter eighty-six of the general statutes, entitled " Of private corporations."

Sec. 2. The inspector aforesaid shall, on or before the first Monday of August in each year, make a report to the anditor of accounts of the condition of every savings bank and trust company in this state, which report shall embrace all the particulars named in section twenty-eight of chap - ter eighty-six of the general statutes.   •

Sec. 3. Said inspector of finance shall receive, by way of compensation for his services, five dollars per day for all the time expended in said inspection and examination, to be paid by the treasurer of the state, upon the warrant of the auditor of accounts ; and said treasurer shall divide the sum so paid as aforesaid to said inspector, among the several corporations so examined and inspected as aforesaid, in proportion to the capital and deposits of the same.

Sec. 4. No stockholder or officer in any savings bank or trust company shall be appointed inspector of finance.

Sec. 5. The inspector of finance is hereby fully authorized, in the discharge of his duties as aforesaid, to exercise in such inspection and examination as aforesaid, all and singular, the powers heretofore conferred upon the bank commissioner by virtue of chapter eighty-six of private corporations.

Sec. 6. All acts and parts of acts inconsistent with this act are hereby repealed.

Sec. 7. This act shall take effect from its passage.

Approved, November 24, 1874.

No. 88.—AN ACT MAKING PROVISION FOR THE SUPPORT OF GOVERNMENT.

It is hereby enacted by the General Assembly of the State of Vermont:

SEC. 1. A tax of thirty cents on the dollar is assessed on the list of the polls and ratable estate of the inhabitants of this state for the year one thousand eight hundred and seventy-four, to be paid into the treasury by the first day of June next, in money or orders drawn on the treasury by authority of law.

SEC. 2. A tax of thirty-five cents on the dollar is assessed on the list of the polls and ratable estate of the inhabitants of this state, which shall be made for the year one thousand eight hundred and seventy-five, to be paid into the treasury of this state by the first day of June, A. D. 1876, in money or orders drawn on the treasury by authority of law.

SEC. 3. The sum of eighty thousand dollars is appropriated for the purpose of paying the debentures of the lieutenant governor, the senate, and house of representatives, and the contingent expenses of the general assembly.

SEC. 4. The sum of six hundred and fifty thousand dollars is appropriated for paying such demands against the state as may be allowed by the auditor of accounts, and such orders on the treasury as may be drawn by county clerks, as provided by law.

SEC. 5. The sum of sixteen thousand dollars is appropriated for the purpose of paying such orders as may be drawn to pay the contingent and incidental expenses of the executive and treasury departments.

SEC. 6. The sum of forty thousand dollars is appropriated for the purpose of paying the interest on the bonds and other debts of the state.

SEC. 7. The sum of one hundred and eighty-nine thousand dollars is appropriated for the purpose of paying the bonds of this state.

SEC. 8. A sum not exceeding forty-five thousand dollars is appropriated to pay the expenses of the Vermont reform school, to be allowed by the auditor of accounts, who shall draw his orders on the treasurer in favor of the superintendent, on his presenting proper vouchers for the amount of the expenses incurred, and on the approval of one or more of the trustees of said institution.

SEC. 9. For all taxes assessed by virtue of this act and paid to the collectors of the same before the first day of

February, next after the issuing by the treasurer of his warrant authorizing the collection of the same, there shall be allowed by the collectors to the individuals or corporations making such payment, four per cent on the amount paid; and the sums so allowed, the treasurer shall credit to the collector on settlement of his tax account; provided, the collector pays the money so collected into the treasury before the fifth day of said February; and provided further, that no allowance shall be made on a sum exceeding the amount due from the collector to the state.

Sec. 10. Instead of the credit mentioned in section sixty-four of chapter eighty-four of the general statutes, the treasurer shall credit the several collectors one fortieth part of the whole sum contained in the warrant by him issued for the collection of the taxes hereby authorized to each collector, who shall be accountable to their respective towns for so much of such fortieth part so credited as is not allowed by way of abatements to such collector; and this section shall not apply to any tax but those assessed by this act.

Sec. 11. This act shall take effect from its passage.

Approved, November 24, 1874.

RESOLUTIONS.

Resolved by the Senate and House of Representatives:

That, having an intelligent regard for the best interests of Vermont, as well as the whole country, it is the duty of our senators and representatives in congress to use their influence against the consummation of any treaty relating to reciprocity in trade with the Dominion of Canada; and to insist that the subject of trade and commercial inter-course with Canada, as well as with all other foreign coun-tries, is not a proper matter of treaty stipulation, but be-longs to congress, and should be wisely regulated by judi-cious legislation.

Resolved, That in common with the Canadian people, we earnestly desire and hope for the early completion of the ship canal connecting the waters of the St. Lawrence and Hudson rivers with Lake Champlain, as forming an impor-tant line of communication between the great cities on the Atlantic seaboard and the grain and lumber regions of Can-ada and the Northwest, and in this work we invite the co-operation respectively of the governments of the Domin-ion of Canada and the United States.

Resolved, That the governor of this state be and is hereby requested to transmit a copy of these joint resolutions
to each of our senators and representatives in congress;
also, a copy each to the president of the United States and
the governor-general of the Dominion of Canada.

H. HENRY POWERS,
Speaker of the House of Representatives.

LYMAN G. HINCKLEY,
President of the Senate.

No. 90.—A JOINT RESOLUTION IN RELATION TO THE SO-CALLED ST. ALBANS RAID CLAIMS.

WHEREAS, on the 19th day of October, 1864, there was
a rebel raid from Canada on the town of St. Albans in
this state, and by means thereof a number of individuals
and corporations were plundered and thereby suffered
heavy losses, for which they have never been indemni-
fied; therefore,

Be it resolved by the Senate and House of Representatives:

That our senators and representatives in Congress be
and hereby are requested to use their best endeavors
towards securing proper indemnity from the United States
government for such losses, by an appropriation from congress or otherwise.

Resolved, That the secretary of state be required to
transmit a copy of this preamble and resolutions to each
of our senators and representatives in congress.

LYMAN G. HINCKLEY,
President of the Senate.

II. HENRY POWERS,
Speaker of the House of Representatives.

No. 91.—REPORT OF SPECIAL COMMITTEE TO WHOM WAS REFERRED THE CLAIM OF IROQUOIS IN-DIANS, AND JOINT RESOLUTION RELATING TO THE SAME.

To the House of Representatives:

The special committee to whom was referred the petition of the delegates of the Iroquois Indians have fully considered the same, and respectfully report:

That the claim made, covers all the land on the west side of the Green Mountains lying northerly of a straight line from Ticonderoga to the Great Falls of Otter Creek, (now called Sutherland Falls,) from thence to be continued to the top of the Green Mountains; thence along the top of said mountains to Canada line, containing some 2,240,000 acres of land, for which is demanded the sum of $89,600.

This claim is not a new one, the first claim having been presented to Governor Tichenor in 1798, and it was by him referred to the legislature, and a committee was appointed to examine into the claim, and the same was referred back to Governor Tichenor, and in 1799 he reported that the claim of the Indians to the lands in question had been extinguished.

Again in 1812 a like petition was presented.

A similar memorial was presented in 1826 to Governor Butler, and by him referred to the legislature, and a committee was appointed, who reported that the petitioners had no claim on this state.

The subject was up again in 1854 and 1855, and at no time has a favorable report on the petition been made.

Your committee further find that the land claimed by the petitioners was ceded by France to Great Britain in 1763, and that the tribes of Indians, whom your petitioners claim to represent, about that time moved into the limits of the Dominion of Canada, and have since resided there; and there was no evidence before the committee that they have ever occupied or been in possession of the territory claimed from 1763 to the present time, though the petitioners claim, that a party of their tribe came on to said territory on a hunting excursion in 1799, or thereabouts.

If the petitioners' claim was not extinguished by the treaty between France and Great Britain in 1763, your committee are of the opinion that all legal and equitable title to the property claimed was transferred to the United States by the treaty with Great Britain in 1783.

Whereupon your committee recommend the adoption of the following joint resolution:

Resolved by the Senate and House of Representatives:

That the governor be requested to notify the petitioners that the state of Vermont has fully examined their claim, and are of the opinion that if such claim ever existed it was extinguished by the treaty between France and Great Britain in 1763, and by the treaty between Great Britain and the United States in 1783; and that the petitioners, at this time, have no legal or equitable claim or interest in or to any of the lands described in their petition.

B. B. SMALLEY, *for Committee.*

H. HENRY POWERS,
Speaker of the House of Representatives.

LYMAN G. HINCKLEY,
President of the Senate.

No. 92.—A JOINT RESOLUTION IN RELATION TO THE ORIGINAL ROLLS OF CAPT. GILES HARRINGTON'S MILITIA COMPANY.

WHEREAS, the original rolls of Capt. Giles Harrington's militia company, called into service for the suppression of the northern frontier disturbance at Alburgh, Vermont, in April, 1839, bear evidence of having been altered without authority, by attempting to change figures "6" and "5" into figures "8" and "3" in several places on said rolls, and it also being manifestly the intention of the maker of said rolls that the original, unaltered rolls should be the true and correct rolls of said company; now, therefore,

Resolved by the Senate and House of Representatives:

That with a view of furnishing a correct and authentic record of the service of said company, the original rolls of said company, before such alterations were made, be and hereby are declared and adopted as the true and genuine rolls of said company, and the secretary of state is hereby directed to record such original rolls in his office, without reference to such unauthorized alterations, as the proper evidence of the service of said company.

LYMAN G. HINCKLEY,
President of the Senate.

H. HENRY POWERS,
Speaker of the House of Representatives.

9

No. 93.—JOINT RESOLUTION AUTHORIZING THE TRANSFER OF CERTAIN MILITARY RECORDS.

Resolved by the Senate and House of Representatives:

That the secretary of state is hereby authorized and directed to transfer all military records in his office to the department of the adjutant and inspector general.

LYMAN G. HINCKLEY,

President of the Senate.

H. HENRY POWERS,

Speaker of the House of Representatives.

No. 94.—JOINT RESOLUTION RELATING TO THE PORTRAITS OF THE GOVERNORS OF THE STATE.

WHEREAS, a desire has long been expressed by many persons interested in the history and reputation of the state and her public men, and by persons having a personal interest in many of our governors, that portraits of all of the governors aforesaid be collected and preserved in our capitol; and whereas, several such portraits have been already presented to the state; now, therefore,

Be it resolved by the Senate and House of Representatives:

That the secretary of state be and he is hereby directed to obtain the portraits of such of the governors as are not already in possession of the state, without expense to the state, and cause the same to be properly placed in the capitol.

LYMAN G. HINCKLEY,

President of the Senate.

H. HENRY POWERS,

Speaker of the House of Representatives.

No. 95.—JOINT RESOLUTION RELATING TO THE BOOKS AND PAPERS OF THE STATE IN THE POSSESSION OF THE BOARD OF EDUCATION.

Resolved by the Senate and House of Representatives:

That the secretary of state be, and he hereby is directed to procure all books, records, blank forms and papers belonging to the state, in the hands or possession of the board of education, or any member thereof, or in the hands or possession of the secretary of said board, and deposit the same in his office for the use of the state superintendent of education.

LYMAN G. HINCKLEY,

President of the Senate.

H. HENRY POWERS,

Speaker of the House of Representatives.

No 96.—JOINT RESOLUTION OF THANKS TO THE CEN-
TRAL VERMONT RAILROAD COMPANY.

Resolved by the Senate and House of Representatives:

That the members of the general assembly acknowledge
the kindness and courtesy extended to them by the Central Vermont Railroad Company in furnishing a special
train to enable them to visit the state reform school at
Waterbury, on Wednesday, October 28, 1874; and that the
thanks of the two houses are tendered to Superintendent
Hobart and to the other officers and managers of the company; and that the secretary of state is hereby directed
to transmit a copy of this joint resolution to the president
of the company.

H. HENRY POWERS,
Speaker of the House of Representatives.

REDFIELD PROCTOR,
President pro tem. of the Senate.

No. 97.—JOINT RESOLUTION OF THANKS TO D. A. CLIF-
FORD FOR PORTRAIT OF GOVERNOR PECK.

Resolved by the Senate and House of Representatives:

That the presentation to the state of Vermont of the
finely finished photographic portrait of Governor Asahel
Peck, by D. A. Clifford, artist photographer, of St. Johnsbury, Vt., merits our grateful acknowledgments, and we

hereby tender to him the thanks of the general assembly for said portrait.

Resolved, That the sergeant-at-arms be and he hereby is instructed to cause said portrait to be properly placed in the executive chamber in the state capitol.

H. HENRY POWERS,
Speaker of the House of Representatives.

LYMAN G. HINCKLEY,
President of the Senate.

No. 98.—JOINT RESOLUTION TO CHANGE THE LOCATION OF THE AVENUE THROUGH THE STATE CAPITOL GROUNDS.

Resolved by the Senate and House of Representatives:

The sergeant-at-arms, with the advice and consent of the governor, is hereby authorized to change the location of Eastern avenue to the easterly line of the state house grounds; provided, that the expense of said change shall be borne by the town of Montpelier.

H. HENRY POWERS,
Speaker of the House of Representatives.

LYMAN G. HINCKLEY,
President of the Senate.

No. 99.—JOINT RESOLUTION PROVIDING FOR THE PRINTING OF THE ADDRESS OF GEORGE T. CHILDS, DELIVERED BEFORE THE REUNION SOCIETY OF VERMONT OFFICERS, NOVEMBER 5, 1874.

Resolved by the Senate and House of Representatives:

That the clerk of the house and secretary of the senate be directed to procure for the use of the general assembly, the printing of one thousand copies of the address of George T. Childs, delivered before the Reunion Society of Vermont officers, November 5, 1874; and also one thousand copies of the address of P. O'Meara Edson, at the Reunion of the First Vermont Cavalry, November 4, 1874.

LYMAN G. HINCKLEY,
President of the Senate.

H. HENRY POWERS,
Speaker of the House of Representatives.

No. 100.—JOINT RESOLUTION TO PAY THE DEBENTURE OF CERTAIN WITNESSES.

Resolved by the Senate and House of Representatives:

That the auditor of accounts is hereby authorized and directed to draw his order on the treasurer for the purpose of paying the witnesses summoned to attend before the joint committee to investigate into the expenditure of the funds of the University of Vermont and State Agricultural College, the usual mileage and per diem compensation.

LYMAN G. HINCKLEY,
President of the Senate.

H. HENRY POWERS,
Speaker of the House of Representatives.

No. 101.—JOINT RESOLUTION DIRECTING THE TREAS-URER TO PAY THE SUMS SPEICFIED.

Resolved by the Senate and House of Representatives:

That the treasurer of the state be and he is hereby directed to pay to the secretary and assistant secretary of the senate and to the clerk of the house of representatives the full salary provided by law for each of said officers, upon the rising of the present session of the legislature.

H. HENRY POWERS,
Speaker of the House of Representatives.

LYMAN G. HINCKLEY,
President of the Senate.

No. 102.—JOINT RESOLUTION EQUALIZING THE PAY OF REPORTERS.

Resolved by the Senate and House of Representatives:

That the pay of assistant reporter of the senate, for the present session, shall be the same as that of the other official reporters of the general assembly; and that the auditor of accounts is hereby authorized to draw his order on the treasurer for the same.

LYMAN G. HINCKLEY,
President of the Senate.

H. HENRY POWERS,
Speaker of the House of Representatives.

No. 103.—JOINT RESOLUTION RELATING TO THE PAY OF ENGINEERS AND OTHER EMPLOYES.

Resolved by the Senate and House of Representatives:

That the pay of the engineers, sweepers and night watchmen, for the present session, be at the rate of three dollars per day.

LYMAN G. HINCKLEY,
President of the Senate.

H. HENRY POWERS,
Speaker of the House of Representatives.

CORPORATIONS.

No. 104.—AN ACT RELATING TO BENNINGTON GRADED SCHOOL DISTRICT.

It is hereby enacted by the General Assembly of the State of Vermont :

SEC. 1. It shall be lawful for Bennington Graded School District, by vote at any meeting thereof duly warned and holden for the purpose, to accept all such devises, bequests, legacies, gifts, or donations, as may be made to it for the purpose of establishing and maintaining professorships, procuring and keeping apparatus, ordaining and administering rewards, or for any other purpose relating to the maintenance of public schools, or buildings, or grounds connected therewith, upon such terms and subject to such conditions or limitations as may be prescribed or imposed by the testators or donors.

SEC. 2. This act shall take effect from its passage.

Approved, November 5, 1874.

No. 105.—AN ACT IN ADDITION; TO AN ACT TO ESTABLISH BENNINGTON GRADED SCHOOL DISTRICT.

It is hereby enacted by the General Assembly of the State of Vermont:

SEC. 1. It shall be lawful for Bennington Graded School District to pay to its principal and subordinate teachers, at any time, any part of their wages, except that one month's wages shall be retained until the due return, according to law, of the register, properly filled and completed, and other full performance of his contract by the teacher.

SEC. 2. This act shall be deemed a public act, and shall take effect from its passage.

Approved, November 24, 1874.

No. 106.—AN ACT TO CHANGE THE NAME OF THE DOUGLAS GRADED SCHOOL DISTRICT IN THE TOWN OF CHELSEA.

It is hereby enacted by the General Assembly of the State of Vermont:

SEC. 1. The "Douglas Graded School District," in the town of Chelsea, shall hereafter be named and called the *Douglas Academy and Graded School District.*

SEC. 2. This act shall take effect from its passage.

Approved, November 24, 1874.

No. 107.—AN ACT TO AUTHORIZE THE TRUSTEES OF CHESTER ACADEMY TO TRANSFER THE ACADEMY BUILDING AND OTHER PROPERTY.

SECTION	SECTION
1. Trustees authorized to transfer building and property to two districts when they shall vote to unite in establishment of graded school district.	2. Deed, how executed. 3. Duties of trustees of academy to cease, on transfer. 4. To take effect.

It is hereby enacted by the General Assembly of the State of Vermont:

SEC. 1. The trustees of Chester Academy, an institution located at Chester, Windsor county, established by the legislature in 1814, are hereby authorized to transfer, by deed, the academy building and all the property appertaining thereto, and to deliver any and all funds in their hands, belonging to said institution, to any two or more of the school districts in said Chester, which shall be contiguous, whenever such districts shall, by vote, respectively agree to unite in the establishment of a graded school within and for the district so formed, which deed shall become operative and binding upon the establishment of said graded school.

SEC. 2. The deed referred to in the foregoing section may, on the part and in behalf of the said trustees, be executed by any one of their number who may be authorized so to do by a vote of the majority of the said board of trustees.

SEC. 3. Upon the transfer of said academy building and property, and the establishment of said graded school, the powers and duties of the board of trustees of Chester Academy shall cease.

SEC. 4. This act shall take effect from its passage.

Approved, November 18, 1874

No. 108.—AN ACT TO ESTABLISH THE COOKESVILLE GRADED SCHOOL DISTRICT.

SECTION
1. Boundaries; name; powers; privileges; liabilities; proviso.
2. Other school districts may be annexed on certain conditions.
3. Officers.

SECTION
4. By-laws.
5. Distribution of public money; how made.
6. Subject to future legislation; to take effect.

It is hereby enacted by the General Assembly of the State of Vermont:

SEC. 1. All that territory now in school district number three in the town of Corinth, and all the inhabitants within school district number three, are incorporated and constituted a body politic and corporate, by the name of Cookesville Graded School, and the present school houses and school property of said graded school district, and all the debts and liabilities of said district number three, shall be assumed and paid by said graded school district; and said graded school district shall have all the powers and privileges, and shall be subject to all the duties and liabilities, that are incident to school districts established under the general statutes of the state; provided, that no part of the territory hereby incorporated shall be hereafter taken from said graded school district, unless by future amendment of this act, and that territory shall be added to said graded school district in manner provided by this act.

SEC. 2. If any other school district or districts in the town of Corinth shall, at any time, by their vote at any annual meeting, or at a special meeting of said district or districts, duly warned for the purpose, signify their desire to unite with and become a part of said graded school district, and if the said graded school district at any annual meeting, or at a special meeting of said district duly warned for that purpose, shall vote to agree to such union, then the said district or districts shall, to all intents and purposes, become and form a part of said Cookesville Graded School District; and such union of said districts may be upon such terms, in regard to debts, liabilities and assets of each, as may be mutually agreed upon; and by vote of the town of Corinth, and consent by vote of said graded school district, at the annual meeting of said town and said district, or at a special meeting of said town and of said district, duly warned for that purpose, territory may be added to said graded school district from any school district in said town.

SEC. 3. The officers of said graded school district shall be the same as are or may be provided by law for other school districts in the state; shall be elected at the same time and hold their offices for the same terms, and have the same power and perform the same duties as the same officers in other districts ; and the present officers to hold their offices for the time for which they have been chosen.

SEC. 4. Such graded school district may make such by-laws, rules and regulations as.it may deem expedient, not inconsistent with the laws of this state, and may provide for the establishment and maintenance of such number of schools, and of such grades, and for teaching therein such branches, as it may deem expedient, and may receive scholars not belonging in said district on such terms as the district or its prudential committee may determine.

SEC. 5. In the distribution of the public moneys, that portion which may be divided among the several districts, irrespective of the number of scholars or their attendance at school, shall be so divided as to give said graded school district the share of the original district or districts of which it is or may hereafter be composed.

SEC. 6. This act shall be deemed a public act; it shall be under the control of future legislatures to alter, amend or repeal as the public good may require; and shall take effect on the adoption of all the provisions of the same by a vote of a majority of the legal voters of said district number three, at a meeting duly warned for that purpose at any time before December 1, 1876.

Approved, November 24, 1874.

No. 109.—AN ACT AMENDING SECTION EIGHT OF AN ACT TO ESTABLISH THE DOUGLAS GRADED SCHOOL DISTRICT IN THE TOWN OF CHELSEA.

It is hereby enacted by the General Assembly of the State of Vermont:

SEC. 1. Section eight of an act entitled " An act to establish the Douglas Graded School District in the town of Chelsea," approved November 26, 1872, is hereby amended so as to read as follows:

Sec. 8. This act shall be deemed a public act, and shall take effect on the adoption of all the provisions of the same by a vote of the majority of the legal votes of said district number two, present at a meeting duly warned for that purpose, at any time before December 1, 1876.

SEC. 2. This act shall take effect from its passage.

Approved, November 20, 1874.

No. 110.—AN ACT TO LEGALIZE THE ISSUING OF NOTES OF SCHOOL DISTRICT NUMBER ONE IN THE TOWN OF NEWBURY.

It is hereby enacted by the General Assembly of the State of Vermont:

SEC. 1. The vote of the legal voters of school district number one, in the town of Newbury, voted the twenty-first day of August, A. D. 1873, authorizing the building committee to issue notes of five hundred dollars each, to pay for a school house, and all notes and bonds issued by said committee for the purposes of paying for said school house, the same being authorized by the voters of said school district at a meeting legally warned and holden for that purpose, are hereby declared legal and valid, and the legal indebtedness of said school district.

SEC. 2. This act shall take effect from its passage.

Approved, November 20, 1874.

No. 111.—AN ACT TO INCORPORATE ESSEX CLAS-SICAL INSTITUTE, IN ESSEX, VERMONT.

It is hereby enacted by the General Assembly of the State of Vermont :

SEC. 1. The association organized in Essex, May 11th, A. D. 1869, under the name of the Essex Academy Association, is hereby incorporated under the name of Essex Classical Institute.

SEC. 2. A. B. Halbert, S. G. Butler, I. R. Reynolds, Amasa Osgood, Edwin Andrews, A. M. Butler, F. W. Joyner James Nichols, L. M. Bates, C. W. Warner, H. N. Tracy, E. F. Whitcomb, William Brew, L. C. Butler, P. C.

Abbey, J. W. Johnson, Noah Taylor, Charles Nichols, B. A. Stevens, George Gates, and their associates and successors, are hereby constituted a body politic and corporate, with all the powers, rights, privileges and duties belonging to similar institutions, by and under the name specified in section one of this act.

Sec. 3. The said corporation may have a common seal, and the same alter at pleasure, may sue and be sued by their corporate name, may make all by-laws, rules and regulations needful for the government of said corporation and for securing its object, provided, they shall not be repugnant to the constitution and laws of this state, and may take and hold property, both real and personal either by purchase, gift or bequest, including the building and land now occupied by the aforesaid Essex Academy Association, and also the bonds, notes, mortgages and all other personal property now belonging to and in the possession of the aforesaid Essex Academy Association.

Sec. 4. The trustees shall have power to use only the income derived from gifts, legacies or bequests that may come into their possession.

Sec. 5. The said corporation shall have power to perpetuate its existence by the election of new members to fill vacancies caused by the death, resignation or removal of a trustee from the town, at any meeting regularly warned and held for that purpose, according to the rules and by-laws which the said corporation may adopt.

Sec. 6. The said corporation is hereby further empowered to establish such courses of study, either English,

10

scientific or classical, as are commonly pursued in the best academies, seminaries and female colleges of the country; to prescribe the terms of admission to each course, the studies to be pursued through it, and the number of years it shall continue.

SEC. 7.   This act shall be under the control of the legislature to alter, amend or repeal as the public good and the cause of education may require.

SEC. 8.   This act shall take effect from the time when the trustees, as enumerated in section two of this act, shall, at a meeting warned and held for that purpose, proceed to organize under the provisions thereof; and A. B. Halbert is hereby authorized to call the first meeting of the trustees, or, in his absence or failure, any one of the trustees named in this act, by giving a written notice to each of the trustees at least six days before the day of the meeting.

Approved, November 23, 1874.

No. 112.—AN ACT TO ESTABLISH THE FAIRHAVEN GRADED SCHOOL DISTRICT.

It is hereby enacted by the General Assembly of the State of Vermont:

Sec. 1.   Such portions of the territory of the town of Fairhaven as now constitute Center school district, number one, is hereby constituted a school district in Fairhaven, by the name of the Fairhaven Graded School District, and the existing school house and school property embraced within the territory constituting said school district, of whatever character, shall become the general property of said graded school district.   All debts and liabilities of said district number one shall be assumed and paid by the said graded school district, and said graded school district shall have all the powers and privileges, and shall be subject to all the duties and liabilities, that are incident to school districts established under chapter twenty-two of the general statutes, and the laws in relation thereto and in amendment thereof.

Sec. 2.   Instead of the prudential committee required by law to be elected, said graded school district, at its first annual meeting, shall elect three trustees, as follows: one for the term of one year; one for the term of two years, and one for the term of three years; and at all subsequent annual meetings, vacancies caused by the expiration of the term of office of trustees shall be filled by the election of trustees for the term of three years each; and all vacancies caused by resignation, death, removal from the district, or other cause, shall be filled at an annual or special meeting warned for the purpose, for the unexpired term of such trustees only.   Such trustees shall have all the powers and perform all the duties of a prudential committee, and shall choose one of their number to be president, and shall appoint a secretary of said board of trustees, who shall hold office for the term of one year and until their successors are chosen and appointed.

SEC. 3. The time of holding the annual elections and meetings shall be the same as now is or hereafter shall be fixed by law for all school districts in the state, and the term of office of the trustees elected for the first year, as hereinbefore specified, shall expire on that day or when their successors are appointed. All other officers of said district shall be elected in the manner prescribed by law.

SEC. 4. The first regular meeting under this act shall be holden on the last Tuesday of March, A. D. 1875; provided, the said school district number one, at a special meeting to be duly warned and holden for this purpose in the month of February next, shall vote to adopt the provisions of this act.

SEC. 5. Said graded school district may make such by-laws, rules and regulations as it may deem expedient, not inconsistent with the laws of this state, and may provide for the establishment and maintenance of such number of schools, and of such grade or grades, and for teaching such branches of knowledge, as it may deem expedient.

SEC. 6. This act shall be deemed a public act, and shall take effect upon its adoption as herein provided.

Approved, November 18, 1874.

No. 113.—AN ACT TO INCORPORATE THE LAMPSON GRADED SCHOOL DISTRICT IN NEW HAVEN.

It is hereby enacted by the General Assembly of the State of Vermont:

SEC. 1. School district number six, in the town of New Haven, is hereby constituted a school district in said town by the name of the Lampson Graded School District.

SEC. 2. Said district may make all such necessary rules and regulations in regard to its buildings, finances, attendance of scholars, and the course of instruction in its school or schools, as shall not be inconsistent with the laws of this state.

SEC. 3. Instead of the prudential committee now required by law to be elected, said graded school district, at its first annual meeting hereafter, shall elect three or more trustees; and said trustees shall have all the powers and perform all the duties of a prudential committee, and shall choose one of their number to be president, and shall appoint a secretary of said board of trustees, who shall hold office for the term of one year, and until their successors are chosen and appointed. All other officers of said district shall be elected in the manner now prescribed by law.

The time of holding the annual meetings shall be the same as now is or may hereafter be fixed by law for all school districts in the state.

SEC. 4.   The board of trustees of said district may admit scholars from without said district upon such terms as they may prescribe.

SEC. 5.   The said Lampson Graded School District, in addition to the powers conferred by this act, shall have all the powers and rights that are or may be conferred upon common school districts in this state, and shall be subject to all the provisions of law concerning school districts and district schools, not inconsistent with the provisions of this act.

SEC. 6.   This act shall be under the control of any future legislature to alter, amend or repeal as the public good may require.

SEC. 7.   This act shall take effect from its passage.

Approved, November 24, 1874.

No. 114.—AN ACT TO AMEND AN ACT TO ESTABLISH MILTON GRADED SCHOOL DISTRICT.

It is hereby enacted by the General Assembly of the State of Vermont:

SEC. 1.   That the boundaries of Milton Graded School

District be enlarged by embracing within its territory the whole of lot number eight in the ,fourth division, now owned by William Bean and Richard' Martin, and lying east of the highway upon which the said Bean and Martin's residence is situated in Milton.

SEC. 2. This act shall take effect from its passage.

Approved, November 5, 1874.

No. 115.—AN ACT TO ENLARGE THE BOUNDARIES OF MILTON GRADED SCHOOL DISTRICT.

It is hereby enacted by the General Assembly of the State of Vermont:

SEC. 1. The boundaries of Milton Graded School District are hereby enlarged so as to include within its boundaries all of the real estate now owned by John Nay in Milton.

SEC. 2. This act shall take effect from its passage.

Approved, November 18, 1874.

No. 116.—AN ACT TO ESTABLISH THE NEWPORT
ACADEMY AND GRADED SCHOOL.

It is hereby enacted by the General Assembly of the State of Vermont :

SEC. 1. Such portions of the town of Newport as lie within the present limits of school district number six, and the inhabitants thereof, are hereby incorporated and constituted a school district of the town of Newport, by the name of the Newport Academy and Graded School District ; and the school house and all other property of school district number six, of whatever character, shall become the general property of said Newport Academy and Graded School District; and all debts and liabilities of said district shall be assumed and paid by said Newport Academy and Graded School District; and said Newport Academy and Graded School District shall have all the powers and privileges, and shall be subject to all the duties and liabilities, that are incident to school districts established under chapter twenty-two of the general statutes, and the laws in addition thereto or in amendment thereof.

SEC. 2. If any other school district or districts in the

town of Newport shall at any time, by their vote at a meeting duly warned for that purpose, signify their desire to become united with the said Newport Academy and Graded School District, and if the said Newport Academy and Graded School District, at a meeting duly warned for that purpose, shall vote to agree to such union, then the said additional district or districts shall become and form a part of said Newport Academy and Graded School District; and such union of said districts may be made upon such terms in regard to the school property of each as may be mutually agreed upon by said districts. And by vote of the town of Newport, and consent by vote of said academy and graded school district, at any annual or special meeting of said town and said district, duly warned for that purpose, territory from adjoining districts may be added to the said graded school district; or territory may be taken from said graded school district by vote of the town as aforesaid, and by the consent of two thirds of the voters in said graded school district present at any meeting legally warned for that purpose.

SEC. 3. All property, of whatever character, belonging to the Newport Academy, an institution incorporated by the legislature by act approved November 9, 1860, shall become the property of the Newport Academy and Graded School District. The selectmen of the town of Newport shall annually pay over the rents and profits arising from the grammar school lands in said town to the trustees of said Newport Academy and Graded School, together with all sums arising from that source now in their hands and unappropriated.

SEC. 4. Instead of the prudential committee required

by law to be elected, said academy and graded school district, at its first annual meeting, shall elect three trustees as follows: one for the term of one year, one for the term of two years, and one for the term of three years; and at all subsequent annual meetings, vacancies caused by. the expiration of the term of office of trustees shall be filled by the election of trustees for the term of three years each; and all vacancies caused by death, resignation, removal from the district, or other cause, shall be filled at an annual or special meeting warned for the purpose, for the unexpired term of such trustees only. The trustees shall have all the powers and perform all the duties of a prudential committee; and shall choose one of their number to be president, and may appoint a secretary of said board, each of whom shall hold office for the term of one year and until their successors are chosen and appointed. The other officers of said graded school district shall be the same as now or may hereafter be provided for all school districts in the state; shall be elected in the same manner and be subject to the same duties and liabilties as now or hereafter prescribed by law.

SEC. 5. The time of holding the annual meeting in said graded school district shall be the same as now is or hereafter shall be fixed by law for all school districts in the state; and in accordance therewith the first meeting for the election of trustees, as hereinbefore provided, shall be held on the last Tuesday of March, A. D. 1875.

SEC. 6. Said Newport Academy and Graded School District may make such by-laws, rules and regulations as it may deem expedient, not inconsistent with the laws of

this state, and may provide for the establishment and maintenance of such number of schools, of such length, and of
such grade or grades, and for teaching such branches
therein, as it may deem expedient; and may in its option
give instruction in the studies usually taught in higher
academic schools and which are requisite to prepare
scholars for entering college. Said academy and graded
school shall not be required to teach gratuitously drawing,
music or the languages, other than English, but may at its
option. All residents of the district, between the ages of
five and twenty years, may attend said academy and graded
school free of tuition for all branches except those above
mentioned, tuition to be charged upon the branches excepted at the option of said district.

SEC. 7. The trustees may make such by-laws, rules
and regulations for the gradation, instruction and management of said academy and graded school, and for the care
of the property of said district, as they may deem expedient,
not inconsistent with the laws of the state; they shall
establish a course or courses of study in each of the schools,
and shall, in conjunction with the teachers of the schools
and the town superintendent of schools, arrange and hold
a public examination of all the schools at the close of each
term thereof and assign each scholar to the particular
grade or department which each shall be found qualified
to enter; shall assign each pupil to the proper grade upon
admission to the school, and may change pupils from one
grade to another during term time, whenever the interest
of the pupils or the good of the school may seem to require
it. The trustees shall, unless otherwise directed by a vote
of the district at any annual meeting thereof, allow scholars
from other districts in the town of Newport, or from other

towns, to attend said academy and graded school with equal advantages of resident scholars, at rates of tuition corresponding as nearly as may be to the usual rates for the same instruction in schools of like character in the state.

Sec. 8. The said academy and graded school district is hereby empowered to receive any endowment, fund or legacy in fee or in trust that may be donated as an endowment toward the support or for the use of said academy and graded school on such terms and conditions as may be prescribed by the donor or legator, not inconsistent with the laws of this state; and the trustees of such academy and graded school shall be the custodians of such fund and of the income of the same, subject to instructions of the district in regard to the use of said fund or income, unless otherwise provided by the terms of the endowment, donation or legacy.

Sec. 9. In the distribution of the public moneys, that portion which may be divided among the several school districts, irrespective of the number of scholars or the attendance at school, shall be so divided as to give said Newport Academy and Graded School District the share of the original district of which it is composed.

Sec. 10. This act shall be under the control of future legislatures to alter or amend as the public good may require, and shall take effect on the last Tuesday in March, A. D. 1875; provided, that a majority of the legal voters in said school district number six present at the next annual meeting, to be held on the last Tuesday of March, A. D. 1875, shall vote to accept the provisions of this act;

and the clerk of said district number six is hereby directed to insert in the warning of the next annual meeting an article requesting the voters in said district to vote upon the acceptance of the provisions of this act, and to elect the officers herein provided for.

Approved, November 24, 1874.

No. 117.—AN ACT TO AMEND AN ACT ENTITLED " AN ACT TO ESTABLISH NORTHFIELD GRADED SCHOOL DISTRICT IN NORTHFIELD," APPROVED NOVEMBER 22, 1872.

It is hereby enacted by the General Assembly of the State of Vermont:

SEC. 1.   Section five of an act entitled "An act to establish Northfield Graded School District in Northfield," approved November 22, 1872, is hereby amended so as to read as follows:

The annual meetings of said school district shall be held on the second Tuesday of June in each year.

SEC. 2.   The directors of said school district are hereby authorized and empowered to provide for a spring term of said graded school in the year A. D. 1875, in said district, at the expense of said district.

SEC. 3.   This act shall take effect from its passage.

Approved, November 24, 1874.

No. 118.—AN ACT CHANGING THE CORPORATE NAME OF RIPLEY FEMALE COLLEGE. ·

It is hereby enacted by the General Assembly of the State of Vermont:

SEC. 1. An act changing the corpoiate name of Troy Conference Academy, approved November 13, 1866, is hereby repealed.

SEC. 2. No rights or privileges now existing under said acts of assembly shall in any way be affected by the provisions of this act; and the corporate name of said academy shall hereafter be Troy Conference Academy.

SEC. 3. This act shall take effect from its passage.

Approved, November 24, 1874.

No. 119.—AN ACT TO AUTHORIZE THE TRUSTEES OF THE RUTLAND COUNTY GRAMMAR SCHOOL TO TRANSFER THEIR SCHOOL BUILDING AND OTHER PROPERTY.

SECTION
1. Trustees of Rutland County Grammar School may transfer by deed said property to any graded school district, or other parties.

SECTION
2. Deed, how executed; avails of sale after payment of indebtedness to be devoted to educational purposes.

It is hereby enacted by the General Assembly of the State of Vermont :

SEC. 1.　The trustees of the Rutland County Grammar School, an institution located at Castleton, in the county of Rutland, established by the legislature of this state, are hereby authorized to transfer, by deed, the said grammar school property, both real and personal, except the rents and reversions of lands granted to grammar schools, and any moneys in their hands belonging to said institution, to any graded school district or other parties, whenever in the judgment of the board of trustees it may be necessary or expedient so to do ; provided, that the avails of such transfer, if any, after the payment of the just indebtedness of said corporation, shall be devoted to educational purposes.

SEC. 2.　The deed referred to in section one may, on the part and in behalf of the said board of trustees, be executed by any one of the members of said board of trustees, who may be authorized so to do by a vote of a majority of the said board of trustees at any meeting duly called for that purpose, and notice of which shall have been served upon each member of said board of trustees, either verbally or by letter through the mails.

SEC. 3.　This act shall take effect from its passage.

Approved, November 24, 1874.

No. 120.—AN ACT IN AMENDMENT OF "AN ACT TO INCORPORATE THE VERMONT CONFERENCE SEMINARY AND FEMALE COLLEGE," APPROVED NOVEMBER 6, 1865.

SECTION	SECTION
1. Name changed.	3. Trustees, by whom elected; vacancies, how filled.
2. Number of trustees; tenure of office and classification therein.	4. To take effect.

It is hereby enacted by the General Assembly of the State of Vermont:

SEC. 1.　The corporate name of the corporation created by the "Act to incorporate the Vermont Conference Seminary and Female College," approved November 6, 1865, shall be the Methodist Conference Seminary and Female College; and the first and second sections of said act are hereby so far amended as is necessary to accomplish said change of corporate name.

SEC. 2.　Section three of the act to which this is an amendment is hereby amended so as to read as follows:

The trustees of said Vermont Methodist Seminary and Female College shall not exceed forty, and shall hold office for a term of four years, as hereinafter provided; and the present board of trustees shall divide themselves into four classes, each class to consist of not more than ten trustees,—one class to hold office for one year, one class for two years, one class for three years, and one class for four years. At the expiration of the term of service of each class of said trustees, their successors shall be elected for a term of four years.

SEC. 3. The trustees of said corporation may elect annually five trustees, on the nomination of the Vermont Annual Conference of the Methodist Episcopal Church. The Vermont Annual Conference of said church may elect annually two trustees. The Laymen's Electoral Conference of the Vermont Annual Conference of said church may, at each quadrennial session thereof, elect eight trustees,—two of said eight to become trustees from the date of their election, two to take office in one year from the date of their election, two in two years from the date of their election, and two in three years from the date of their election. The associated alumni of the seminaries at Newbury, Springfield and Montpelier may elect at each annual meeting of said alumni one trustee. Vacancies occurring in said board of trustees by death, resignation, or otherwise, may be filled for the unexpired term in which such vacancy occurs by the board of trustees.

SEC. 4. This act shall not take effect until it has been accepted by the trustees of said Vermont Methodist Seminary and Female College, at an annual meeting of said trustees.

Approved, November 24, 1874.

No. 121.—AN ACT TO ESTABLISH THE WEST CONCORD GRADED SCHOOL DISTRICT, IN CONCORD.

SECTION
1. Boundaries; voters of districts must agree to enlargement; property to be transferred and contracts assumed.
2. Officers to elect prudential committee at annual meeting; tenure of office.
3. By-laws, powers, rights and privileges; scholars from other districts may be allowed to attend; and from other towns.

SECTION
4. Provisions for adding other territory.
5. Annual meeting.
6. Distribution of public moneys. .
7. Nothing herein to prevent collection of present tax.
8. To be deemed a public act; subject to future legislation; to take effect.

It is hereby enacted by the General Assembly of the State of Vermont :

SEC. 1.   School district number four in Concord is hereby enlarged so as to include within its boundaries such portions of the territory of the town of Concord as on the first day of May, A. D. 1874, constituted school districts numbers four and eleven; provided, that a majority of the legal voters of said school districts numbers four and eleven, at any meeting legally warned for that purpose, shall vote in favor of the same, and such portions of territory are hereby incorporated and constituted a school district of the town of Concord, hereafter to be known by the name of West Concord Graded School District, and the school houses and other property of said school districts numbers four and eleven, of whatever character, shall become the general property of said graded school district, and all debts and liabilities of said two districts shall be assumed and paid, and all contracts, agreements, leases and stipulations made by either of said districts,

with any person, firm or corporation, shall be assumed
and carried out by said West Concord Graded School District the same as though the said graded school district
was the original contracting party; and said persons, firms
or corporations, having so contracted, agreed, leased or
stipulated with either of said districts, are hereby held
and bound to duly fulfill and carry out all such contracts,
agreements, leases or stipulations, the same as though
originally entered into with said West Concord Graded
School District. Said graded school district shall have all
the powers and privileges, and be subject to all the duties
and liabilities, that are incident to school districts established under chapter twenty-two of the general statutes,
and the laws in addition thereto and in amendment thereof; provided, that no part of the territory hereby incorporated shall be hereafter taken from said graded school
district unless by future amendment of this act, and that
territory shall be added to said graded school district in
the manner provided by this act.

SEC. 2. The present officers of school district number
four shall be the officers of West Concord Graded School
District, and shall in all things perform the duties of said
officers until the time of holding the annual election of
school district officers as now provided by law, at which
annual meeting, in lieu of the number of prudential committee prescribed by statute, said 'West Concord Graded
School District shall elect three prudential committee
who shall hold their office in the following manner: the
first for one year, the second for two years, the third for
three years, and annually thereafter one prudential committee shall be elected for the term of three years,—the

remaining officers the same as now or shall be hereafter proscribed by law for school districts in this state.

SEC. 3.   Said West Concord Graded School District may make such by-laws, rules and regulations as it may deem expedient, not inconsistent with the laws of this state, and may provide for the establishment and mainte- nance of such number of schools, and of such grade or grades, and for teaching therein such branches of knowl- edge, as it may deem expedient, and said district may at its option give instruction in the studies usually taught in higher academic schools, and which are requisite to pre- pare scholars to enter college.   Said graded school is not required to gratuitously teach drawing, painting, modern languages and music, but may at its option.   All resi- dents of the district between the ages of five and twenty years may attend said graded school free of tuition, for all branches except drawing, painting, modern languages and music, tuition to be charged upon the branches ex- cepted, at the option of said district.   The prudential committee shall allow scholars from other districts in Con- cord to attend said school with equal advantages of schol- ars in the district, when said scholars are qualified to en- ter either department of said school, at rates of tuition corresponding as nearly as may be to the usual rates for the same instruction in schools of like character in this state.   The prudential committee are also authorized to receive students from other towns, in their discretion, and upon such terms as they may see fit to impose.

SEC. 4.   Other territory may be added to said graded school district by vote of the town in which said territory may be situated, and consent by vote of said graded school district at the annual meeting of said town and said district, or at a special meeting of said town and said district duly warned for that purpose.

SEC. 5. The annual meeting of said graded school district shall be held at the same time as is now or hereafter shall be fixed by law for all school districts in this state.

SEC. 6. In the distribution of the public moneys, that portion which may be divided among the several school districts, irrespective of the number of scholars or their attendance at school, shall be so divided as to give said graded school district the shares of the several original districts of which it is or shall be composed.

SEC. 7. Nothing in this act shall be construed to prevent or impede the collection of the tax now in the hands of the collector of district number four.

SEC. 8. This act shall be deemed a public act and shall take effect from its passage, and this act shall at all times be under the control of the legislature to amend or repeal as the public good may require.

Approved, November 12, 1874.

No. 122.—AN ACT TO INCORPORATE THE EMERSON AQUEDUCT COMPANY.

It is hereby enacted by the General Assembly of the State of Vermont :

SEC. 1.   Thomas Emerson and Esther Emerson, of Northfield, in the county of Washington and state of Vermont, and Charles W. Emerson, of Fitchburgh, county of Worcester and commonwealth of Massachusetts, their associates and successors, are hereby constituted a corporation for the purpose of constructing and maintaining an aqueduct or aqueducts to supply the inhabitants of the village of Northfield, and the inhabitants of the outlying and adjacent territory, with water for domestic and culinary purposes,— said corporation to be known by the name of the Emerson Aqueduct Company; and by that name may sue and be sued, may purchase and hold real and personal estate, and convey the same, so far as shall be necessary for carrying on the business mentioned in this act, and shall be vested with all the rights, powers and privileges incident to a corporation for the purposes aforesaid.

SEC. 2. The capital stock of said company shall be one hundred shares of twenty-five dollars each, which stock may be increased by said corporation to three hundred shares, as shall be necessary, and said corporation may provide for the sale and mode of transfer thereof, as said corporation may from time to time deem expedient, and may levy and collect assessments on said shares, according to law, and fix the rates of rents and the same alter at pleasure, and shall have the power to sue for and collect said water rates or rents when necessary.

SEC. 3. Said corporation may at its annual meeting, and at all other meetings legally notified for that purpose, make, alter and repeal such by-laws, rules and regulations as may be thought necessary, and which are not repugnant to the laws of this state.

SEC. 4. The first meeting of this corporation shall be held at Northfield, and shall be called by the first person named in this act by giving six days notice in writing to all the stockholders, or by publishing the same in some newspaper printed in Washington county two successive weeks prior to the day of said meeting, and at said meeting the company may organize and elect all necessary officers.

SEC. 5. Said corporation created by this act may purchase any aqueduct now in use, or in process of construction, and take a conveyance of title by deed or otherwise, and divide the same into shares, agreeably to the by-laws of said corporation.

SEC. 6. The officers of said company shall be a president, three or five directors, a clerk and treasurer, and such other officers as it may deem expedient; and such officers shall hold their offices for such times, shall perform such duties, shall give such bonds for faithful performance of said duties, shall be entitled to such compensation, and generally shall be governed and controlled in such manner and to such extent, as said company by its by-laws shall provide.

SEC. 7. The said corporation may take the waters of such fountains and springs as they have purchased or may purchase of the owners for that purpose, or purchase any aqueduct now constructed, and may dig up and open any street, common or highway, for the purpose of construct- ing and laying down or repairing such aqueduct or aque- ducts and reservoirs connected with the same; provided, they shall first obtain the [consent of a majority of the board of trustees of the village of Northfield for that purpose; and the same may be done in such a manner as not to prevent their convenient use for travel, and to be completed in a reasonable time and in such a manner as not to disfigure or injure said street, common or highway; and in all cases where said corporation shall lay or repair any of their pipes in any enclosed field they shall pay all damages done to crops thereon, and leave the surface of said lands, as near as may be, in as good condition as be- fore laying or repairing said pipes.

SEC. 8. The said corporation may enter upon and use any land and enclosure through which it may be neces- sary for said aqueduct to pass, on the most practicable route from whence its waters may be taken for the pur- pose of placing such reservoirs and pipes as may be nec- essary for constructing, completing and repairing said aqueduct, and may agree with the owner or owners thereof for the use of the same; but in case of disagreement, or if any owner thereof be a minor, insane, or out of the state, or otherwise incapacitated to sell and convey, said corporation, or the owners or persons interested in lands so entered upon, may apply to the judges of the county court for the county of Washington, by petition, who shall appoint forthwith three disinterested persons to view the premises and assess the damages sustained by the owners or occupants of or interested parties in said lands, by the construction of said aqueduct, and said committee shall appraise such damage on oath, and report the same to the county court aforesaid at its first session thereafter; and if said report shall be accepted by said court, the court shall render judgment thereon, and may issue an execution therefor, with costs.

SEC. 9. Any person who shall maliciously or willfully disturb or injure said aqueduct or aqueducts, springs or reservoirs, or any enclosure or appurtenant of the same shall be liable to be prosecuted by information, complaint or indictment, and on conviction thereof shall be fined not less than five nor more than twenty dollars and costs of prosecution, for each offense proved against him, and shall also be liable to said corporation in an action on the case for all damages.

SEC. 10. This corporation shall not contract debts to an amount exceeding three fourths of the capital stock actually paid in, and if the indebtedness of said company shall at any time exceed the amount aforesaid, the directors and stockholders shall be personally liable for such excess to the creditors of such corporation.

SEC. 11. This act shall be subject to the control of future legislatures to alter, amend or repeal, and also to all general laws now or hereafter enacted relative to private corporations.

SEC. 12. This act shall take effect from its passage.

Approved, November 24, 1874.

No. 123.—AN ACT TO INCORPORATE THE GUILD-HALL AQUEDUCT COMPANY.

It is hereby enacted by the General Assembly of the State of Vermont:

SEC. 1. Such persons as shall hereafter become stockholders are hereby constituted a body corporate by the name of the Guildhall Aqueduct Company, with powers incident to corporations, and may hold real and personal estate, not exceeding ten thousand dollars in value, for the purpose of constructing and maintaining an aqueduct for the purpose of supplying the inhabitants of the village of Guildhall with water for domestic and other purposes.

SEC. 2.   Said corporation may at any annual or other meeting legally notified make, alter and repeal such by-laws, rules and regulations as may be thought necessary, not repugnant to the laws of this state.

SEC. 3.   The capital stock of said company shall consist of one hundred shares, at one hundred dollars each, which stock may be increased by said corporation to an amount sufficient to carry into effect the object of this act, and said corporation may provide for the sale and mode of transfer thereof as said corporation may from time to time deem expedient, and may levy and collect assessments on such shares according to law, and fix the rates and rents on the same at pleasure, and shall have the power to sue for and collect said water-rents when necessary.

SEC. 4.   Said corporation may dig or open any street, common or highway, for the purpose of constructing, laying down or repairing such aqueduct, as may be found desirable; provided, the same may be done in such a manner as not to injure or disfigure said street, common or highway; and in all cases when said corporation shall lay or repair said aqueduct in any enclosed field, they shall pay all damages done to crops thereon, and leave the surface of said lands, as near as may be, in as good condition as before laying or repairing said aqueduct.

SEC. 5.   The said corporation may enter upon and use any enclosure or land through which it may be necessary for said aqueduct to pass, on the most practicable route from where its water may be taken, for the purpose of placing such reservoirs and pipes as may be necessary for constructing, completing and repairing said aqueduct, and may agree with the owner or owners thereof for the use of the same; but in case of disagreement, or if any owner thereof be a minor, insane, or out of the state, or otherwise incapacitated to sell and convey, said corporation, or the owner or owners, or persons interested in lands so entered upon, may apply to the judges of the county court for the county of Essex, by petition, who shall appoint forthwith three disinterested persons to view the premises and assess the damages sustained by the owners or occupants of said land, by the construction of said aqueduct, and said committee shall appraise said damages on oath, and report the same to the county court for the county aforesaid, at its first session thereafter, and if their report shall be accepted by said court, the court shall render judgment thereon, and may issue an execution therefor with costs.

Sec. 6. Any person who shall maliciously disturb or injure said aqueduct, or any works or enclosures connected with the same, shall be liable to be prosecuted by information, complaint, or indictment, and on conviction thereof shall be fined not less than five dollars nor more than twenty dollars, and costs of prosecution, and shall also be liable to said corporation for all damages.

Sec. 7. This act shall be subject to the provisions of chapter eighty-six of the general statutes, entitled of private corporations, and may be altered, amended or repealed as the public good may require.

SEC. 8. This act shall take effect from its passage.

Approved, November 23, 1874.

No. 124.—AN ACT TO INCORPORATE THE ST. JOHNSBURY ACADEMY.

It is hereby enacted by the General Assembly of the State of Vermont:

SEC. 1. Thaddeus Fairbanks, William W. Thayer, Horace Fairbanks, Henry Fairbanks, Franklin Fairbanks, Edward T. Fairbanks, and Homer T. Fuller, their associates and successors, are hereby constituted a body politic and corporate by the name of the St. Johnsbury Academy, to be located in the village of St. Johnsbury, in the county of Caledonia, with all the rights, privileges and powers belonging to similar corporations, for the purpose of instructing pupils in the English, modern and ancient languages, and in the various sciences, and for the improvement of such pupils in general culture and in morals; and by that name may sue and be sued, may have a common seal, and may alter the same at pleasure.

SEC. 2. The said corporation may make such by-laws, rules and regulations as it may deem necessary for the establishment, control and government of said institution, not repugnant to the constitution and laws of this state, or of the United States; may appoint and agree with professors and instructors, may establish a course or courses of study, and confer diplomas upon those pupils who shall have completed such course or courses of study; and for said purposes may purchase books, cabinet and apparatus, and provide such other educational furniture and facilities as are deemed requisite; may take and hold by gift, grant, bequest, devise or purchase, property real, personal or mixed, to any amount, the net annual income of which shall not exceed thirty thousand dollars, and may manage, control, use and dispose of the same for the benefit of said academy. Said corporation may take any or all of the kinds of property hereinbefore named, and hold the same intact for a permanent fund or an endowment, with the right to use only the net income arising therefrom, either for the general purposes of said academy or for such of said purposes as the donor shall specify; but if the donor to such permanent fund shall fail to specify the particular use or uses to which he desires to have such income appropriated, it shall be used, in the discretion of the trustees, for the general purposes of the academy.

SEC. 3. The said corporation shall have power to perpetuate its existence by the election of new corporators to fill vacancies caused by death, resignation or removal from this state, and to increase the number of said corporators to a number not exceeding at any one time thirty.

SEC. 4. The management and control of the affairs of said corporation shall be vested in a board of trustees, consisting of not less than three nor more than nine members of said corporation, who shall be elected at such times and places, and shall hold their offices for such length of time, as said corporation shall by by-law establish, who shall elect a president from their number and also a secretary and treasurer of said institution, and who shall biennially, or as often as the legislature of this state shall meet, make a report of the condition and work of said institution to the secretary of state. The persons named in section one of this act shall be the trustees of said corporation until others are duly elected. A majority of the board of trustees, when assembled at any regularly notified meeting, shall have power to transact the business of such meeting.

SEC. 5. Any two of the corporators named in section one of this act may call the first meeting of the corporation at such time and place in the village of St. Johnsbury as they may think proper, for the purpose of organizing said corporation, prescribing the duties of the officers thereof and transacting the necessary business thereof, by giving the other corporators notice in writing of the time and place of said meeting at least six days before the time appointed for such meeting.

Sec. 6. The trustees of the St. Johnsbury Academy, an associate corporation organized under the laws of this state and located in St. Johnsbury, may convey to the corporation hereby created, when organized, all the property, of whatsoever kind, of said associate corporation, on such conditions, limitations and restrictions as it may deem best, and the corporation hereby created may receive and accept such conveyance, and on its acceptance of such conveyance it shall be liable for all the debts and obligations of every kind of said associate corporation.

Sec. 7. This act shall be under the control of future legislatures to alter, amend or repeal.

Sec. 8. This act shall take effect from its passage.

Approved, November 23, 1874.

No. 125.—AN ACT IN AMENDMENT OF AN ACT ENTITLED AN ACT TO INCORPORATE THE ST. JOHNSBURY AQUEDUCT COMPANY, APPROVED NOVEMBER 21, 1859.

It is hereby enacted by the General Assembly of the State of Vermont:

SEC. 1. The said St. Johnsbury Aqueduct Company may take and hold real and personal estate not exceeding one hundred thousand dollars in value.

SEC. 2. The said corporation may take the waters of any pond or stream for the purposes named in said act, but not to the extent of depriving any owner or person having an interest in. the same of such portion of said water as is necessary for agricultural and domestic purposes, and may take lands for the construction of necessary reservoirs. And all damages for injury to water rights and for lands taken for reservoirs shall be determined, if the parties are unable to agree upon the amount of the same, in the manner prescribed in said act.

SEC. 3. Any person who shall maliciously disturb or injure said aqueducts, springs or reservoirs, or any works or enclosures connected with the same, shall be liable to be prosecuted by information, complaint, or indictment, and on conviction thereof shall be fined not less than five dollars nor more than twenty dollars and costs of prosecution, and shall also be liable to said corporation for all damages.

SEC. 4. This act shall take effect from its passage.

Approved, November 23, 1874.

No. 126.—AN ACT TO INCORPORATE THE WALLINGFORD AQUEDUCT COMPANY.

It is hereby enacted by the General Assembly of the State of Vermont :

SEC. 1. Such persons as shall hereafter become stockholders are hereby constituted a body corporate by the name of the Wallingford Aqueduct Company, with powers incident to corporations, and may hold real and personal estate, not exceeding five thousand dollars in value, for the purpose of constructing and maintaining an aqueduct for the purpose of supplying the inhabitants of the village of Wallingford with water for domestic and other purposes.

SEC. 2. Any three stockholders may call the first meeting of the corporation, to be held in the village of Wallingford at such time and place as they shall appoint, at any time within one year from the passage of this act, by posting a written notice thereof at two public places in said Wallingford village, at least six days prior to said meeting, for the purpose of choosing such officers as may be deemed necessary; and the said corporation at such meeting, and at all meetings legally notified, may make such by-laws and regulations as may be deemed necessary, not repugnant to the laws of this state ; and said corporation may divide their stock into as many shares as they shall deem expedient, and may levy and collect assessments on the same according to law.

SEC. 3.   The said corporation may take the waters of such fountain, brooks and springs as they may purchase of the owners for that purpose, and may dig up or open any street, common or highway, having first obtained the, consent of a majority of the board of selectmen of said town, for the purpose of constructing and laying down or repairing such aqueduct, or reservoirs connected therewith; provided, the same be done in such a manner as not to prevent their convenient use for travel, and to be completed in a seasonable time and in such a manner as not to disfigure or injure the said street, common or highway.   And in all cases when said corporation shall lay or repair any of their pipes or logs in any enclosed field, they shall pay all damages done to crops thereon, and leave the surface of said lands, as near as may be, in as good condition as before laying or repairing such reservoirs or pipes.

SEC. 4.   The said corporation may enter upon and use any lands and enclosures through which it may be neces sary for said aqueduct to pass, on the most practicable route from whence its waters may be taken, for the purpose of placing such reservoirs and pipes or logs as may be necessary for constructing, completing and repairing said aqueduct, and may agree with the owner or owners thereof for the use of the same; but in case of disagreement, or if the owner be a minor, insane, or out of the state, or otherwise incapacitated to sell and convey, said corporation, or the owners or persons interested in lands so entered upon, may apply, by petition in writing, setting forth the cause of complaint, to the judges of the county court for the county of Rutland, praying that a committee may be appointed to appraise the damages sustained by such owners or occupants of the lands so entered upon; and the clerk of said court, on the filing of said petition, shall issue a citation to all persons interested in such lands, giving at least twelve days notice of the time and place of hearing before said judges, to appear and show cause, if any, why the prayer of said petition should not be granted; and said judges, on such hearing, may appoint three disinterested persons to appraise the damages sustained by such owners or occupants of such lands, and said committee, before proceeding to appraise such damages, shall give reasonable notice to all persons interested in such lands, claiming damages, and to said corporation, of the time and place of hearing on such damages; and said committee on such hearing shall assess such damages to the owners or occupants of such lands as shall be just and equitable, and make report of the same to the county court for the county of Rutland at its first session thereafter; and if the report of said committee shall be accepted upon hearing, said court may render judgment thereon for such damages and costs as said court shall deem just and equitable, and issue execution for the same.

Sec. 5. This act shall be subject to the provisions of chapter eighty-six of the general statutes, entitled "Of private corporations," and may be amended, altered or repealed as the public good may require. . . . .

Sec. 6. This corporation shall not at any time contract

debts to an amount exceeding two thirds of its capital stock actually paid in ; and if the debts of said corporation shall at any time exceed such an amount, the directors and stockholders shall be personally liable to the creditors of such corporation for such excess.

SEC. 7. This act shall take effect from its passage.

Approved, November 20, 1874.

No. 127.—AN ACT TO INCORPORATE THE ¡WEST PAWLET CEMETERY ASSOCIATION.

It is hereby enacted by the General Assembly of the State of Vermont:

SEC. 1. S. S. Brown, Hiel Hollister and Allen Whedon, their associates and successors, are hereby constituted a corporation by the name of the West Pawlet Cemetery Association, under the provisions of chapter ninety of the general statutes, and amendments thereto; and in addition to the privileges thereby conferred, said corporation may sue for and collect the taxes levied upon the lots in said cemetery, not exceeding two dollars upon each lot in any year.

SEC. 2. This act shall take effect from its passage.

Approved, November 24, 1874.

No. 128.—AN ACT TO INCORPORATE E. AND T. FAIRBANKS AND COMPANY.

It is hereby enacted by the General Assembly of the State of Vermont:

SEC. 1. Thaddeus Fairbanks, Horace Fairbanks and Franklin Fairbanks, of St. Johnsbury, in the county of Caledonia, and all others who are or shall hereafter become associated with them, with their successors and assigns, are hereby made and established a body politic and corporate by the name of E. and T. Fairbanks and Company, for the purpose of manufacturing scales and all kinds of weighing instruments, and all kinds of machines and machinery, and all kinds of implements, made in whole or in part from iron, brass or other metals and wood, or other materials, for grinding grain and manufacturing fabrics in the most advantageous manner, and for buying, selling and trafficking in the same, and mercantile purposes in connection with the aforesaid business in St. Johnsbury. By that name they and their successors and assigns shall be, and. they are hereby authorized to purchase, take, hold, occupy, possess and enjoy to them, their successors and assigns, any letters patent, and any goods, chattels and effects, of whatever kind they may be, the better to enable them to carry on such business in a profitable manner. Also to purchase, take, hold, occupy and enjoy such lands, tenements, or hereditaments as shall be necessary for the accomplishment of the purposes of the corporation; and the same, or any part thereof, to sell and dispose of at pleasure, or to take a lease or leases of any such lands and real estate for a term or terms of years. Also to sue and be sued, to plead and be impleaded, defend and be defended, answer and be answered to, in all courts of record or elsewhere. Said corporation may have and use a common seal, which it may alter at pleasure. Said corporation may as a partner unite with other partners in establishing and maintaining in other of the United States, and in foreign countries, agencies or houses for the carrying on, management and transaction of the business of said corporation in such states and countries in an economical and profitable manner.

SEC. 2. The capital stock of said corporation shall be two million dollars, which may be increased from time to time to an amount not exceeding in the whole five million dollars. One share of said capital stock shall not be more than one thousand dollars, and shall be deemed and considered personal estate, and be transferable only on the books of said corporation, in such form as the directors of said corporation shall prescribe ; and said corporation shall at all times have a lien on all the stock or property of the members of said corporation, invested therein, for all debts due from them to said corporation, and the said corporation may be organized whenever and as soon as one million dollars of said stock shall be taken up and subscribed for.

SEC. 3. Said corporation shall be located at St. Johns-bury, in the county of Caledonia, and there have its principal office for the transaction of its business, and there hold its corporate meetings.

SEC. 4. The stock, property and affairs of said corporation shall be managed by a board of not less than three nor more than seven directors, one of whom shall be chosen president by them, and all of whom shall be stockholders, and shall be elected annually, at such times and places within this state as the by-laws of said corporation shall prescribe, and shall hold their offices for one year and until others are elected. A majority of said directors when met shall in all cases constitute a board for transacting business, and a majority of the stockholders present at any legally notified meeting shall be capable of transacting the business of such meeting, each share entitling the owner thereof to one vote, which vote shall be given by the stockholder in person, or by lawful proxy, but no stockholder shall be entitled to cast more than one third of the votes which might be lawfully cast by the stockholders of said corporation. The first meeting of the corporation hereby formed may be called by any two of the corporators named in the first section of this act, at such time, and on giving such notice, as is prescribed by the general statutes in relation to private corporations.

SEC. 5. The president and directors, or a majority of

them for the time being, shall have power to fill any vacancy in their board, which may happen by death, resignation or otherwise, for the then current year, and to employ a secretary, treasurer, and such other officers, mechanics and laborers, as they may think necessary for the transaction of the business and concerns of said corporation, and may require said secretary, treasurer and other officers to give security, by bond or otherwise, for the faithful discharge of their trust and duty, as said directors may think proper; and also to make and establish, subject to the ratification of the stockholders at their next regular meeting, such by-laws, rules and regulations as they shall deem expedient and proper for the better management of the affairs of said corporation, and the same alter and repeal; provided always, said by-laws, rules and regulations be not inconsistent with the laws of this state or of the United States. And said directors may and shall as often as the interests of the stockholders shall require, and the affairs of said corporation shall permit, make and declare a dividend or dividends of the profits on each share, which shall be paid by the treasurer of said corporation.

SEC. 6. If the annual election of directors shall not be made on the day appointed by the by-laws of said corporation, the corporation shall not be deemed dissolved for such cause, but said election may be holden on any subsequent day which shall be appointed by said directors.

SEC. 7. The present members of the firm of E. and T. Fairbanks and Company, a copartnership existing and doing business under that name and style at St. Johnsbury, in the county of Caledonia, may become subscribers to the capital stock of this corporation to an amount equal to their respective interests in said copartnership; and their subscriptions may be paid by a conveyance or release to said corporation of their respective interests in said property of said copartnership, upon such terms as may be agreed upon by and between the said copartners and said corporation, and such payment shall be deemed good and valid as if paid in cash, and stock certificates may be issued for the full amount of the stock by them so subscribed and paid for as aforesaid. And the corporation formed by this act shall assume and pay all the liabilities and debts of said copartnership. Whenever, and as soon as one million dollars shall have been subscribed and paid, as provided in this section, said corporation may go into operation and commence business.

Sec. 8. The books of said corporation, containing their accounts, shall at all reasonable times be open forthe inspection of any of the stockholders of said corporation, and an annual statement of the accounts of said corporation shall be made by the order of and under the direction of the directors. And the directors may obtain at any time new subscriptions to the capital stock until the same shall amount to the sum of five million dollars; always provided, that before the directors shall obtain subscriptions as aforesaid, they shall be authorized so to do by a vote of the stockholders, at a meeting especially called for that purpose, increasing the capital stock, and directing the directors to open subscriptions for the same, and the then stockholders shall have the right to subscribe for such increase *pro rata*.

Sec. 9. For the debts which may at any time be due

from said corporation, the stockholders thereof shall not be responsible in their private capacity, but only the stock property and estate of the corporation; but nothing in this act shall be construed to authorize or empower said corporation to use its funds or property for any banking purposes or transactions, or any business inconsistent with the provisions of section one of this act.

SEC. 10.   The directors may call in the subscriptions to the capital stock by installments, in such proportions and at such times and places as they may deem proper, giving such notice as the by-laws and regulations of said corporation shall prescribe; and if any stockholder shall neglect or refuse to pay such installment or installments within sixty days after the same shall become due and payable, and after said stockholder shall have been notified thereof, said corporation may through its directors declare the stock of such negligent and delinquent stockholder forfeit to said corporation, and may proceed to sell the same at public auction, after having given at least twelve days notice in some newspaper printed at St. Johnsbury, in Caledonia county, of such forfeiture and sale, and of the time and place of sale, and after paying from the avails of such sale the installment or installments so in arrears and unpaid, and all reasonable expenses and costs of such sale, shall refund the balance, if any, to such delinquent stockholder.   Nothing in this section shall be construed to take away the right of said corporation to collect such install-ment or installments of such delinquent stockholder, in-stead of declaring his or her stock forfeit to said corpora-tion, and selling the same in the manner aforesaid.

SEC. 11.   The said corporation shall, within the period

of one year next after the same shall become organized, lodge a certificate with the secretary of state, containing the amount of capital stock actually paid in and belonging to said corporation, which certificate shall be signed by the president and secretary of said corporation, and verified by their oaths; and also a like certificate of all subsequent installments paid in, and new shares thereafter created shall be verified and lodged in the same manner. And the amount of the capital stock thus·verified shall not be withdrawn so as to reduce the same below the amount stated in the certificate, and if any part of the capital stock paid in and certified shall be withdrawn, by dividends or otherwise, without the consent of the general assembly, the directors consenting thereto shall be jointly and severally liable as traders in company, in case of the insolvency of said corporation at any period afterwards, for all debts owing by said corporation at the time of or subsequently to the reduction or diminution of the capital as aforesaid. And if said corporation shall be delinquent in filing with the secretary of state the certificate or certificates prescribed in this section, within the time herein prescribed, the directors of said corporation shall be jointly and severally liable as traders in company for all debts contracted by said corporation while such delinquency of said corporation shall continue. And if the indebtedness of such corporation shall at any time exceed its capital stock, the directors of said corporation shall be jointly and severally liable for such excess to the creditors of said corporation.

Sec. 12. This act shall be under the control of the

legislature to alter, amend or repeal as the public good shall require.

SEC. 13. This act shall take effect from its passage.

Approved, November 24, 1874.

No. 129.—AN ACT GRANTING A FERRY TO ALLEN L. HALE.

It is hereby enacted by the General Assembly of the State of Vermont:

SEC. 1. The exclusive right and privilege of keeping a ferry is hereby granted to Allen L. Hale and his heirs, for the term of fifteen years' from the first day of January, A. D. 1875, from the shore of Lake Champlain at Benson Landing, so-called, in the town of Benson, to the town of Putnam, on the opposite shore of said lake, in the state of New York,—said right and privilege to extend one mile each way north and south from said landing.

Sec. 2. It shall be the duty of said Allen L. Hale and his heirs, at all proper and suitable times for ferrying at said ferry, to be provided with suitable boats and ferry-men for carrying passengers, teams, beasts, and other property across, said ferry, under the penalty of forfeiting all right to this grant.

Sec. 3. The rates of ferriage to be allowed to the said Allen L. Hale or his heirs, for ferrying across said ferry, shall be adjusted and determined by the selectmen of the town of Benson, upon the application of said Allen L. Hale or his heirs.

Sec. 4. This act shall be subject to the action of any future legislature of this state to alter, amend or repeal as the public good may require.

Approved, November 17, 1874.

No. 130.—AN ACT GRANTING A FERRY TO VOLNEY RICE.

It is hereby enacted by the General Assembly of the State of Vermont:

SEC. 1.　The exclusive right of keeping a ferry, from the landing place at Cold Spring in West Haven, and for one half mile north and south from such landing place, is hereby granted to Volney Rice, of said West Haven, his heirs and assigns, for the term of twenty years from and after the first day of January, A. D. 1875.

SEC. 2.　The terms and rates of toll upon said ferry shall be established by the county court for the county of Rutland, agreeably to the provisions of section eight of chapter twenty-six of the general statutes.

SEC. 3.　It shall be the duty of the said Volney Rice, or his heirs or assigns, as the case may be, to provide at the said ferry and keep in repair ferry boats which, in the judgment of the selectmen of said town of West Haven, are suitable and proper for the said ferry.

SEC. 4.　This act shall be subject to the general laws of this state to alter, amend or repeal as the public good may require.

SEC. 5.　This act shall take effect from its passage.

Approved, November 18, 1874.

No. 131.—AN ACT GRANTING A FERRY TO CHARLES F. WITHERBEE.

It is hereby enacted by the General Assembly of the State of Vermont:

SEC. 1. The exclusive right and privilege of keeping a ferry is hereby granted to Charles F. Witherbee and his heirs and assigns, for the term of twenty years from the first day of January, A. D. 1875, from the shore of Lake Champlain, at the Mount Ferry Place, so-called, in the town of Orwell, to a place on the opposite shore of said lake, at or near Port Marshal, in the state of New York,—said right and privilege to extend one half mile each way north and south from the present landing at the said Mount Ferry Place.

SEC. 2. It shall be the duty of the said Charles F. Witherbee and his heirs and assigns, at all proper and suitable times for ferrying at said ferry, to be provided with suitable boats and ferrymen for carrying passengers, teams, beasts, and other property across said ferry, under the penalty of forfeiting all right to this grant.

SEC. 3. The rates of ferriage to be allowed to the said Charles F. Witherbee, or his heirs and assigns, for ferrying across said ferry, shall be adjusted and determined by the selectmen of the town of Orwell aforesaid, and may be re-adjusted and determined by the selectmen of said

·Orwell, upon the application of said Charles F. Witherbee, or his heirs and assigns.

SEC. 4. This act shall be subject to the action of any future legislature of this state to alter, amend or repeal as the public good may require.

Approved, November 17, 1874.

No. 132.—AN ACT TO AMEND AN ACT ENTITLED "AN ACT FOR THE INCORPORATION OF THE TRUSTEES OF THE PAROCHIAL FUND OF THE PROTESTANT EPISCOPAL CHURCH IN THE DIOCESE OF VERMONT."

It is hereby enacted by the General Assembly of the State of Vermont:

SEC. 1. That section eight of an act entitled "An act for the incorporation of the trustees of the parochial fund of the Protestant Episcopal Church in the diocese of Vermont," approved November 10, 1869, be amended so as to read as follows:

Sec. 8. The said trustees are further authorized to re-

13

ceive, by donations or devise, moneys and land devoted by the giver to the purposes of clerical support, parsonage aid in particular parishes, and parochial and theological schools and missions within the said diocese; also lands or money for the site or erection of churches of the Protestant Episcopal Church in said diocese, and they shall hold and apply the same in strict accordance with the condition attached to any such donation or devise, if not incompatible with the laws of this state. And in cases where the bishop of the diocese has been heretofore, or shall be hereafter, made a testamentary trustee for any of the purposes contemplated by this act, he shall have the right to surrender the said trust to the trustees of this fund at will; and in case of his not doing so before his death, the said testamentary trust shall inure on his death to the trustees of this fund, subject to all the conditions prescribed by the donor; but the annual income, accruing from the property said trustees are allowed to hold by virtue of this section and of section four, shall not exceed thirty thousand dollars in the aggregate.

SEC. 2. This act shall take effect from its passage.

Approved, November 24, 1874.

No. 133.—AN ACT IN AMENDMENT OF THE CHAR-TER OF THE HOME FOR DESTITUTE CHILDREN.

It is hereby enacted by the General Assembly of the State of Vermont:

SEC. 1. Section eight of an act entitled " An act to incorporate the Home for Destitute Children at Burlington," approved November 1, 1865, is hereby amended so as to read as follows:

The said corporators shall have power, with the approval of the judge of probate for the district of Chittenden, to receive any such child as shall be relinquished to it by its parent or guardian, or by the overseer of the poor of the town or city of which such child is an inhabitant, in cases where such overseer would have the right, under section six of chapter seventy-three of the general statutes, to bind such child as an apprentice or servant, and such relinquishment shall be in writing and signed by such parent, or guardian, or overseer of the poor, and shall be recorded in the records of the probate court for said district; and said corporation shall have the sole and exclusive care, guardianship and education of such child, and shall have and be entrusted with all the legal powers of a guardian over it; provided, that said corporation shall not be the guardian of the property of any such child. And said corporation may also, with the approval of such judge of probate, hire or bind out any such child so received as aforesaid, for such time as said corporation shall think fit, not longer than the age of legal majority of such child, to some proper person, to be instructed in some suitable trade, pursuit or profession, according to the rules and regulations which may from time to time be adopted by said corporation.

SEC. 2. Whoever shall entice or remove any child, who shall have been duly relinquished to such Home for Destitute Children, as aforesaid, from the care and custody thereof, or of any person to whom such Home for Destitute Children shall have hired or bound out such child as aforesaid, shall, on conviction thereof, be punished by imprisonment in the county jail for not more than one year, or by a fine of not exceeding three hundred dollars, or both of said punishments, in the discretion of the court.

SEC. 3. Section two of said charter is hereby amended so as to read as follows:

Said corporation shall have power to prescribe from time to time terms and conditions on which persons may be admitted as members of said corporation. In the distribution of the benefits and charities of said corporation, whenever there shall be more applications than can be granted, the destitute children of soldiers and sailors of the United States shall be entitled to preference.

SEC. 4. This act shall take effect from its passage.

Approved, November 24, 1874.

No. 134.—AN ACT TO INCORPORATE THE WALTER N. GREENE INDEPENDENT HOSE COMPANY.

It is hereby enacted by the General Assembly of the State of Vermont:

SEC. 1. W. N. Greene, J. A. Harvey, H. K. Weaver and others, and their associates and successors, are hereby constituted a corporation and body politic by the name of the W. N. Greene Independent Hose Company, of the city of Burlington; and by that name may sue and be sued, plead and be impleaded, may purchase and hold real and personal estate for their own use, and such real and personal estate shall not at any time be disposed of except as a grant to the city, and shall have all the privileges incident to corporations; and said corporation shall be located in the city of Burlington.

SEC. 2. The buildings and apparatus of the said corporation being paid for by the private subscription of the lumbermen, mill-owners and others, in that part of the city situated in the western part of ward five, it is deemed prudent that the apparatus be not enjoined at any time, unless fire in any other ward of the city be immediately hazardous, to leave said ward.

SEC. 3. The corporation shall at all times adhere to the ordinances of the fire department of the city of Burlington, when on duty.

SEC. 4. All business of the corporation shall be managed by the members, of whom ten shall form a quorum. Officers of the corporation shall be elected at an annual meeting, to be held on the second Tuesday of October, and shall hold their offices until their successors shall be appointed.

SEC. 5. The corporation may adopt or make such by-laws and regulations as they may deem necessary and proper, not inconsistent with this act or in conflict with the laws of the city.

SEC. 6. This act shall not be construed to confer on said corporation any rights or powers to make any contracts, or to accept or execute any trust whatever, which it would not be lawful for any individual under the general rules of law which are or shall be in force, to make, accept or execute.

SEC. 7. This act shall be under the control of the legislature to alter, modify or repeal.

SEC. 8. This act shall take effect on its passage.

Approved, November 21, 1874.

No. 135.—AN ACT TO AMEND AN ACT TO INCOR-
PORATE THE CONNECTICUT RIVER MUTUAL
FIRE INSURANCE COMPANY, APPROVED NO-
VEMBER, 23, 1858.

*It is hereby enacted by the General Assembly of the State
of Vermont:*

SEC. 1.   Section eighteen of an act to incorporate the
Connecticut River Mutual Fire Insurance Company, ap-.
proved November 23, 1858, is hereby amended so as to
read as follows :

Sec. 18.   The board of directors of said company shall
consist of a number not exceeding fifteen nor less 'than
nine, any five of whom shall constitute a quorum for the
transaction of business; and all vacancies happening in
said board may be filled by the remaining members until
the next annual meeting.   Special meetings of the company may be called by order of the directors, or in such
other manner as the by-laws may have prescribed.

SEC. 2.   Section fifteen of said act is hereby repealed.

SEC. 3.   This act shall take effect from its passage.

Approved, November 12, 1874.

No. 136.—AN ACT TO INCORPORATE THE PEOPLE'S MUTUAL FIRE INSURANCE COMPANY.

SECTION
1. Corporators; name; purpose; powers, rights and privileges.
2. Members.
3. First directors; tenure of office; subsequent directors, how elected.
4. Duties of directors; other officers; powers of directors.
5. Liability of members, with proviso.
6. Alienation of property voids the policy, with proviso.
7. Mutual liability of members.
8. Loss or damage of property, how determined and adjusted; right of appeal, with proviso.
9. Assessments upon members, how made and collected.
10. Insufficiency of assets; losses may be paid *pro rata;* release of membership, how effected.
11. Limitation of insurance.
12. Limitation of time for settlement of losses and payment thereof.
13. Alteration of buildings without notice being given, voids insurance.

SECTION
14. Notes given for insurance in certain cases may be retained after loss of property, during term of insurance.
15. Directors to give bonds.
16. Existing insurances in other companies void insurance by this company, unless by consent.
17. Subject to future legislation.
18. Board of directors, number of; special meetings, how called.
19. Judges of courts, not prejudiced by reason of membership.
20. Jurors, not prejudiced by reason of membership.
21. Sheriff, or other officers, not prejudiced by reason of membership.
22. No policies to be issued until fifty thousand dollars insurance applied for.
23. Location.
24. To take effect.

It is hereby enacted by the General Assembly of the State of Vermont:

SEC. 1.   Francis Leclair, Harvey V. Horton, Orville Sinclair, Bernard J. Heineberg, Peter Leclair, William C. Whiteman and Albert O. Hood, and all other persons who may hereafter become members of said company in the manner herein prescribed, be and hereby are incorporated and made a body politic by the name of the People's Mutual Fire Insurance Company, for the purpose of insuring any description of property, real or personal, against loss or damage by fire, whether the same shall happen by accident, lightning, or by any other means, excepting that of design in the insured, or by the invasion of an enemy, or insurrection of the citizens of this or any of the United States, and also to insure against loss or damage by lightning; and by that name may sue and be sued, appear, prosecute and defend, in any court of record, or other place whatever; may have and use a common seal, may purchase and hold such real and personal estate as may be necessary to effect the objects of their association, and the same may sell and convey at pleasure; may make, establish and put in execution such by-laws, ordinances and resolutions, not being contrary to the laws of this state, as may seem necessary or convenient for their regulation and government, and for the management of their affairs; and do and execute all such acts and things as may be necessary to carry into full effect the purposes intended by this grant.

SEC. 2. All and every person and persons, who shall at any time become interested in said company by insuring therein, and also their respective heirs, executors and administrators and assigns, continuing to be insured therein, as hereinafter provided, shall be deemed and taken to be members thereof, for and during the terms specified in their respective policies, and no longer; and shall at all times be concluded and bound by the provisions of this act.

SEC. 3. Francis Leclair, Harvey V. Horton, Orville Sinclair, Bernard J. Heineberg, Peter Leclair, William C. Whiteman and Albert O. Hood shall be the first directors of said corporation, and shall continue in office for one year after the passage of this act, and until others shall be chosen in their stead; which board of directors shall thereafter be elected in each year, at an annual meeting to be held at the city of Burlington, in the state of Vermont, at such time as the corporation in their by-laws shall direct, of which election public notice shall be given in at least one of the newspapers printed at said Burlington, thirty days immediately preceding such election; and such election shall be made by ballot or otherwise, as said company shall direct, and the persons, being members of said company, receiving a plurality of all the the votes shall be duly elected.

SEC. 4. The board of directors shall superintend the concerns of said company, and shall have the management of the funds and property thereof, and of all matters and things thereunto relating, and not otherwise provided for by said company; they may from time to time appoint a secretary, treasurer, and such other officers, agents and assistants as to them may seem necessary, and prescribe their duties, fix their compensation, take such security from time to time as they may deem necessary for the faithful performance of their respective duties, and remove them at pleasure; they shall determine the rates of insurance, the sum to be insured on any building or other property, and the sum to be deposited for the insurance thereof; they shall order and direct the making and issuing of all policies of insurance, the providing of books, stationery, and all other things needful for the office of said company, and for carrying on the affairs thereof, and may draw upon the treasurer for the payment of all losses that may have happened, and for expenses incurred in transacting the business of said company; they shall elect one of their own number president, and may hold their meetings monthly, or oftener if necessary, for transacting the business of the company; and they shall keep a record of their proceedings, and any director disagreeing with a majority of the board at any meeting, may enter his dissent, with his reasons therefor, on record.

Sec. 5. Every person who shall become a member of said company, by effecting insurance therein, shall, before he receives his policy, pay such sum of money and deposit his promissory note for such further sum of money as shall be determined by the directors; and said deposit note shall be payable, in part or the whole, at any time when the directors shall deem the same requisite for the payment of losses or other expenses. And at the expiration of the term of insurance, the said note, or such part of the same as shall remain unpaid, after deducting all losses and expenses during said term, shall be relinquished and given up to the maker thereof; provided, nevertheless, that it may and shall be lawful for said company to receive from the insured a certain sum in full for insurance, which said sum shall be in lieu and place of a premium note; and the insured shall not be liable to said company during the continuance of his, her or their policy, for any assessment or further payment; provided, that the property insured aforesaid shall in no case exceed ten per cent of the whole amount insured.

Sec. 6. Whenever any building or other property shall be alienated by sale or otherwise, the policy shall thereupon be void, and be surrendered to said company; and the insured shall be entitled to receive his, her or their

deposit notes, upon the payment of his, her or their proportion of all the losses and expenses that have accrued
prior to such surrender; provided, however, that the
grantee or alienee, having the policy assigned, may have
the same ratified and confirmed to him, her or them, for
his, her or their use and benefit, upon application to the
directors, and with their consent, within thirty days next
after their alienation, on giving proper security to the
satisfaction of said directors for such portion of the deposit or premium note as shall remain unpaid; and by
such confirmation and ratification, the party causing the
same shall be entitled to all the rights and privileges, and
subject to all the liabilities, to which the original party
insured was entitled and subjected under this act.

Sec. 7. Every member of said company shall be and
hereby is bound and obliged to pay his proportion of all
losses and expenses happening or accruing in and to said
company; and all buildings insured by and with said company, together with the right, title and interest of the
assured to the lands on which they stand, shall be pledged
to such company; and the said company shall have a lien
thereon against the assured during the continuance of
his, her or their policies; and said lien shall extend to the
assignees of said insured, and shall be considered the
same in law as though the insured executed a mortgage
to said company to secure the payment of his proportion
of all losses and expenses happening or accruing in and
to said company.

Sec. 8. In case of any loss or damage by fire or lightning happening to any member, upon property insured in
and with said company, the said member shall give notice

thereof in writing to the directors, or some one of them, or to the secretary of said company, within thirty days from the time such damage or loss may have happened; and the directors, upon a view of the same, or in such other way as they may deem proper, shall ascertain and determine the amount of said loss or damage; and if the party suffering is not satisfied with the determination of the directors, the question may be submitted to referees, or the said party may bring an action against said company for loss or damage, returnable to the county court to be holden in the county of Chittenden, or in the county in which said party may reside, or in which said loss or damage by fire or lightning may have happened, which action shall be commenced within one year next after such determination, and not afterwards. And if upon trial of said action, a greater sum shall be recovered than the amount determined upon by said directors, the party suffering shall have judgment therefor against said company, with interest thereon from the time such loss or damage happened, and costs of suit; but if no more shall be recovered then the amount aforesaid, the party shall become nonsuit, and the said company shall recover their costs; provided, however, that the judgment last mentioned shall in no wise affect the claim of said suffering party to the amount of loss or damage as determined by the directors aforesaid.

SEC. 9. The directors shall, after receiving notice of any loss or damage by fire sustained by any member, and ascertaining the same, or after the rendition of any judgment, as aforesaid, against said company for such loss or damage, settle and determine the sum to be paid by the several members, which shall always be in proportion to the original amount of his deposit note, and publish the same in such manner as they shall see fit, or as the by-laws shall have prescribed, which sum shall be paid to the treasurer within thirty days after the publication of said notice; and if any member shall, for the space of thirty days after the publication of said notice, neglect or refuse to pay the sum assessed upon him, her or them, or his, her or their proportion of any loss as aforesaid, in such case the directors may sue for and recover the whole amount of his, her or their deposit note or notes, with cost of suit, and the money thus collected shall remain in the treasury of said company, subject to the payment of such losses as may have accrued, or may thereafter accrue; and the balance, if any remain, shall be returned to the party from whom it was collected, on demand, after the expiration of the term for which insurance was made.

Sec. 10. If it shall ever happen that the whole amount of deposit notes shall be insufficient to pay the losses occasioned by fire or lightning, in such case the sufferers insured by said company shall receive, towards making good their respective losses, a proportionate dividend of the whole amount of said notes, according to the sums by them insured. Any member upon the payment of the whole of his assessments on his deposit notes, and surrendering his policy before any subsequent loss or expense has accrued, may be discharged from said company; but no person shall be allowed to surrender his policy after he shall have sustained a total loss of the property insured in such policy, except in cases where the by-laws of the company may authorize such surrender.

Sec. 11. The said company may make insurance for

any term not exceeding ten years; and any policy of insurance issued by said company, signed by the president and countersigned by the secretary, shall be deemed valid and binding on said company in all cases when the assured has a title in fee-simple, unencumbered, to the building or buildings insured, and to the land covered by the same; but if the insured have less estate therein, or if the premises be encumbered, the policy shall be void, unless the true title of the assured, and the encumbrances on the premises, be expressed therein and in the application therefor.

Sec. 12. The directors shall settle all losses within three months after they have been notified thereof; and when said losses shall have been ascertained and adjusted on or before the first day of August in any year, they shall be paid by said company on the first day of December then next following; and all losses, which shall be ascertained and adjusted between the first day of August and the first day of December in any year, shall be paid by said company on the first day of November next following the first day of December. And the assured shall be entitled to an order for the amount of such loss, drawn by the secretary and accepted by the treasurer of said company, on interest after three months from notice of loss; but in estimating damage and adjusting losses, no allowance shall be made for any gilding, historical or landscape painting, sketch or carved work.

Sec. 13. If any alteration should be made in any house or building by the proprietor thereof, after insurance has been made thereon with said company, whereby it may be exposed to greater risk or hazard from fire than it was at the time it was insured, the insurance made upon such house or building shall be void unless an additional premium and deposit, after such alteration, be settled with and paid to the directors; but no alteration or repairs in buildings, not increasing such risk or hazard, shall in any wise affect insurance previously made thereon.

SEC. 14. In case any building or buildings, situated upon lease lands, and insured by said company, be destroyed by fire, the directors may retain the amount of the premium note given for insurance thereof until the time for which insurance was made shall have expired; and at the expiration thereof the assured shall have the right to demand and receive such part of said retained sum or sums as has not been expended in losses and assessments.

SEC. 15. Each and every one of the directors of said company shall, before he enters upon the duties of his office, give bonds to the treasurer of this state in the sum of three thousand dollars, with good and sufficient surety or sureties, to the satisfaction of said treasurer, conditioned for the faithful discharge of the duties of his office, agreeably to the regulations, requirements and restrictions of this act; and on the complaint of any person who has been injured by the misconduct of any director, the said treasurer shall cause such bond to be put in suit on receiving surety to indemnify the state against costs, and shall certify to the court who is the prosecutor in such case; and the said court, on motion of the defendants in such cause, may order the prosecutor to find sureties to indemnify the defendants for their costs, should he fail to prosecute or recover thereon; and if the defendants shall plead the performance of the conditions of said bond, the prosecutor may reply as many breaches respecting his interest as he shall think fit; and the jury, on the trial of such issues as shall be put to them, shall assess damages for such breaches as the prosecutor shall prove, and the court shall enter up judgment for the whole penalty of the bond, and issue execution in favor of the prosecutor for such sum as the jury shall have found for damages and costs; and the judgment shall remain for the benefit of such person or persons as may, by a *scire facias* thereon, show that they have been injured by any breaches of the condition of said bond. And if the prosecutor shall fail to recover in such suit, the court shall award costs to the defendants, and thereof issue execution against such prosecutor.

SEC. 16. If insurance on any house or building shall be and subsist in said company, and in any other office, or from and by any other person or persons, at the same time, the insurance made in and by said company shall be deemed and become void, unless such double insurance subsist with the consent of the directors.

SEC. 17. This act shall be under the direction and control of the legislature to alter, amend or repeal as the public good and interests of the company may require, and shall at all times be subject to any general laws relating to fire insurance companies.

SEC. 18. The board of directors of said company, after the first year, shall consist of a number not exceeding eighteen nor less than five, any three of whom shall constitute a quorum for the transaction of business; and all

14

vacancies happening in such board may be filled by the remaining members until the next annual meeting. Special meetings of the company may be called by order of the directors, or in such other manner as the by-laws may have prescribed.

SEC. 19. The judges of the supreme and county courts, within their respective jurisdictions, are hereby authorized and required to hear, try and determine all actions and causes that come before them in which said company is a party, notwithstanding they may be members of said company by having property insured therein, unless the adverse party in such actions or suits object thereto.

SEC. 20. Jurors in all courts in this state shall be required to sit in the trial of all actions and suits in which the said company is a party, notwithstanding they be members thereof by having property insured therein, unless specially objected thereto for this cause by one of the parties to such action or suit.

SEC. 21. Any sheriff or other officer, within his jurisdiction, may serve or execute any writ or other process to him directed, in which said company is a party, notwithstanding such officer shall be a member of said company by being insured therein, any law or usage to the contrary notwithstanding.

SEC. 22. No policies shall be issued until application for insurance shall have been made to the amount of fifty thousand dollars.

SEC. 23. This corporation shall be located in the city of Burlington.

SEC. 24. This act shall take effect from its passage.

Approved, November 24, 1874.

No. 137.—AN ACT TO INCORPORATE THE UNION MUTUAL FIRE INSURANCE COMPANY.

It is hereby enacted by the General Assembly of the State of Vermont:

Sec. 1. Henry C. McDuffie, Marcus D. Gilman, E. B. Campbell, Luther R. Graves, M. J. Francisco, James M. Slade, Jr., James A. Shedd, E. Henry Powell, E. P. Colton, Samuel Wells, N. P. Bowman, J. C. Parker, E. P. Mudgett and James W. Brock, and all other persons who may hereafter become members of said company, in the manner herein prescribed, are hereby constituted a corporation by the name of the Union Mutual Fire Insurance Company, for the purpose of insuring any description of property, real or personal, against loss or damage by fire, whether the same shall happen by accident, lightning, or by any other means, except that of design in the insured, or by the invasion of an enemy, or insurrection of the citizens of this or of any of the United States; and by that name may sue and be sued, appear, prosecute and defend, in any court of record or other place whatever; may have and use a common seal; may purchase and hold such real and personal estate as may be necessary to effect the objects of their association, and the same may sell and convey at pleasure; may make, establish and put in operation such by-laws, ordinances and resolutions, not repugnant to the laws of this state, as may seem necessary or convenient for their regulation and government, and for the management of their affairs, and do and execute all such acts and things as may be necessary to carry into effect the purposes intended by this grant.

Sec. 2. All persons who shall at any time become interested in said company, by insuring therein, and also their respective heirs, executors, administrators and assigns, continuing to be insured therein, as hereinafter provided, shall be deemed and taken to be members thereof, for and during the term specified in their respective policies, and no longer; and shall at all times be concluded and bound by the provisions of this act.

SEC. 3. Henry C. McDuffie, Marcus D. Gilman, E. B. Campbell, Luther R. Graves, M. J. Francisco, James M. Slade, Jr., James A. Shedd, E. Henry Powell, E. P. Colton, Samuel Wells, N. P. Bowman, J. C. Parker, E. P. Mudgett and James W. Brock shall be the first directors of said corporation, and shall continue in office, as shall their successors, for one year, and until others be chosen in their stead; which board of directors shall thereafter be elected in each year, at an annual meeting to be held at Montpelier, in the state of Vermont, at such time as the corporation in their by-laws shall direct; of which election public notice shall be given in at least one of the newspapers printed at Montpelier, thirty days immediately preceding such election; and such election shall be made by ballot or otherwise, as said company may direct, and the persons, being members of said company, receiving a plurality of all the votes shall be duly elected.

SEC. 4. The board of directors shall superintend the concerns of said company, and shall have the management · of the funds and property thereof, and all matters and things thereunto relating, and not otherwise provided for by said company; they may from time to time appoint a secretary, treasurer, and such other officers, agents and assistants as to them may seem necessary, and prescribe their duties, fix their compensation, take such security from time to time as they may deem necessary for the faithful performance of their respective duties, and remove them at pleasure; they shall determine the rates of insurance, the sum to be insured on any building or buildings, or property therein, and the sum to be deposited in advance for the insurance thereof; they shall order and direct the making and issuing of all policies of insurance, the providing of books, stationery, and all other things needful for the office of said company, and for carrying on the affairs thereof, and may draw on the treasurer for all losses that may have happened, and for all the expenses incurred in transacting the business of said company; they shall elect one of their own number president, and may hold their meetings monthly, or oftener, if necessary for transacting the business of the company; and they shall keep a record of their proceedings, and any director disagreeing with a majority of the board at any meeting, may enter his dissent, with his reasons therefor, on record.

Sec. 5. Every person who may become a member of said company, by effecting insurance, shall, before he receives his policy, deposit his promissory note for such a sum of money as shall be determined by the directors, and shall pay a sum not exceeding one third of the amount of said note to the treasurer of said company in money; and the said deposit note shall be payable in part, or in whole, at any time when the directors shall deem the same requisite for the payment of losses by fire, and such incidental expenses as shall be necessary for transacting the business of said company; and at the expiration of the term of insurance, or at the time of cancelling said policy, the said note or notes, or such part thereof as shall remain unpaid, after deducting all losses and expenses accruing and due on the same, shall be relinquished and given up to the maker thereof; and said company may loan such portion of the moneys on hand as may not im- mediately be wanted for the purposes of said company, to be secured by mortgage on unincumbered real estate of double the value of the amount loaned.

SEC. 6. Whenever any building or personal property, insured in this company, or the land upon which any such building may be located, shall be alienated by sale, mort- gage, or other encumbrance or lien, the policy of insur- ance thereon shall be void; provided, however, that the alienee or grantee, having the policy assigned in writing, may have the same ratified and confirmed, upon such terms and conditions as the directors of said company shall prescribe, on giving proper security, to the satisfac- tion of said directors, for such proportion of the deposit or premium note as shall remain unpaid; and by such certi- fication and confirmation, the party causing the same shall be entitled to all the rights and privileges, and subject to all the liabilities, to which the original party was entitled and subject under this act.

· SEC. 7. Every member of said company shall be and hereby is bound and obliged to pay his proportion of all losses and expenses happening or accruing in and to said company; and all buildings insured by and with said com- pany, together with the right, title and interest of the assured to the lands on which they stand, shall be pledged to said company; and the said company shall have a lien thereon against the assured during the continuance of his, her or their policies; and the pledge and lien mentioned in this section, shall extend to the assignees of said insured, and shall be considered the same in law as though the in- sured gave a direct mortgage to said company to secure the payment of his proportion of all losses and expenses happening or accruing in and to the said company.

SEC. 8.   In case of any loss or damage by fire happening to any member, upon property insured in and with said company, the said member shall give due notice thereof in writing to the directors, or some one of them or to the secretary of said company, within thirty days from the time such damage or loss may have happened; and the directors, upon a view of the same, or in such other way as they may deem proper, shall ascertain and determine the amount of said loss or damage; and if the party suffering is not satisfied with the determination of the directors, the question may be submitted to referees, or the said party may bring an action against said company for loss or damages, at the next court to be held in and for the county of Washington, or in the county in which said party may reside, or in which said loss or damage by fire may have happened, and not afterwards, unless said court shall be held within sixty days after such determination, but if held within that time, then at the next court held in said county thereafter.   And if upon trial of such action, a greater sum shall be recovered than the amount determined upon by the directors, the party shall have judgment thereof against said company, with interest thereon from the time such loss or damage happened, with costs of suit; but if no more shall be recovered than the amount aforesaid, the party shall become nonsuit, and the company shall recover their costs; provided, however, that the judgment last mentioned shall in no wise affect the claim of said suffering party to the amount of loss or damage as determined by the directors aforesaid; and provided, also, that execution shall not issue on any judgment against said company until the expiration of three months from the rendition thereof.

SEC. 9. The directors shall, after receiving notice of any loss or damage by fire sustained by any member, and ascertaining the same, or after the rendition of any judgment, as aforesaid, against said company for such loss or damage, settle and determine the sum to be paid by the several members, which shall always be in proportion to the original amount of his deposit note, and publish the same in such manner as they shall see fit, or as the by-laws shall have prescribed, which sum shall be paid to the treasurer within thirty days after the publication of said notice; and if any member shall, for the space of thirty days after the publication of said notice, neglect or refuse to pay the sum assessed upon him, her or them, as his, her or their proportion of any loss as aforesaid, in such case the directors may sue for and recover the whole amount of his, her or their deposit note or notes, with costs of suit, and the money thus collected shall remain in the treasury of said company, subject to the payment of such losses as may have accrued, or may thereafter accrue; and the balance, if any remain, shall be returned to the party from whom it was collected, on demand, after thirty days from the expiration of the term for which insurance was made.

SEC. 10. If it shall ever happen that the whole amount of deposit notes shall be insufficient to pay the losses occasioned by fire, in such case the sufferers insured by said company shall receive, towards making good their respective losses, a proportionate dividend of the whole amount of said notes, according to the sums by them insured. Any member upon the payment of the whole of his assessments on his deposit notes, and surrendering his policy before any subsequent loss or expense has accrued, may be discharged from said company; but no person shall be allowed to surrender his policy after he shall have sustained a total loss of the property insured in such policy, except in cases where the by-laws of the company may authorize such surrender.

SEC. 11. The said company may make insurance for any term not exceeding ten years; and any policy of insurance issued by said company, signed by the president and countersigned by the secretary, shall be deemed valid and binding on said company in all cases where the assured has a title in fee-simple, unencumbered, to the building or buildings insured, and to the land covered by the same; but if the insured have less a estate therein, or if the premises be encumbered, the policy shall be void, unless the true title of the assured, and the encumbrances of the premises, be expressed therein and in the application therefor.

SEC. 12. The directors shall settle all losses within three months after they shall have been notified thereof; and when said losses shall have been ascertained and adjusted on or before the first day of August in any year, they sha be paid by said company on the first day of December then next following; and all losses, which shall be ascertained and adjusted between the first day of August and the first day of December in any year, shall be paid by said company on the first day of November next following the first day of December. And the assured shall be entitled to an order for the amount of such loss, drawn by the secretary and accepted by the treasurer of said company, on interest after three months from notice of loss; but in estimating damage and adjusting losses, no allowance shall be made for any gilding, historical or landscape painting, stucco or carved work.

Sec. 13.   It may and shall be lawful for said company, upon any person or persons applying for insurance in said company, to receive from them a certain sum of money in full for such insurance, which said sum shall be in lieu and place of a premium note, and such person or persons shall not be liable to said company during the continuance of his, her or their policy for any assessment or further payment; provided, however, that the property insured as aforesaid shall in no case exceed ten per cent of the amount insured in said class.

Sec. 14.   If any alteration should be made in any house or building by the proprietor thereof, after insurance has been made thereon with said company, whereby it may be exposed to greater risk or hazard from fire than it was at the time it was insured, the insurance made upon such house or building shall be void unless an additional premium and deposit, after such alteration, be settled with and paid to the directors; but no alteration or repairs in buildings, not increasing such risk or hazard, shall in any wise affect insurance previously made thereon.

Sec. 15.   In case any building or buildings, situated upon lease lands, and insured by said company, be destroyed by fire, the directors may retain the amount of the premium note given for insurance thereof until the time for which insurance was made shall have expired; and at the expiration thereof the assured shall have the right to demand and receive such part of said retained sum or sums as has not been expended in losses and assessments.

SEC. 16. Each and every one of the directors of said company shall, before he enters upon the duties of his office, give bonds to the treasurer of this state in the sum of five thousand dollars, with good and sufficient surety or sureties, to the satisfaction of said treasurer, conditioned for the faithful discharge of the duties of his office, agreeably to the regulations, requirements and restrictions of this act; and on the complaint of any person who has been injured by the misconduct of any director, the said treasurer shall cause said bond to be put in suit on receiving surety to indemnify the state against costs, and shall certify to the court who is prosecutor in such case; and the said court may, on motion of the defendants in such cause, order the prosecutor to find sureties to indemnify the defendants for their costs, should he fail to prosecute or recover thereon; and if the defendants shall plead the performance of the conditions of said bond, the prosecutor may reply as many breaches respecting his interest as he shall think fit; and the jury, on the trial of such issues as shall be put to them, shall assess damages for such breaches as the prosecutor shall prove, and the court shall enter up judgment for the whole penalty of the bond, and issue execution in favor of the prosecutor for such sum as the jury shall have found for damages, and the costs; and the judgment shall remain for the benefit of such person or persons as may, by a *scire facias* thereon, show that they have been injured by any breaches of the condition of said bond; and if the prosecutor should fail to recover in such suit, the court shall award costs to the defendants, and thereof issue execution against such prosecutor.

SEC. 17. If insurance on any house or building shall be and subsist in said company, and in any other office, or from and by any other person or persons, at the same time, the insurance made in and by said company shall be deemed and become void, unless such double insurance subsist with the consent of the directors.

SEC. 18. This act shall be unlimited in its duration, and shall be under the direction and control of the legislature to alter, amend, or repeal as the public good and interest of the company may require.

SEC. 19. The board of directors of said company, after the first year, shall consist of a number not exceeding twenty, nor less than nine, any five of whom shall constitute a quorum for the transaction of business; and all vacancies happening in said board may be filled by the remaining members, until the next annual meeting, and a majority of the whole number shall constitute a quorum for the transaction of said business. Special meetings of the company may be called by order of the directors, or in such other manner as the by-laws thereof may have prescribed.

SEC. 20. The judges of the supreme and county courts, within their respective jurisdictions, are hereby authorized and required to hear, try and determine all actions and causes that come before them in which the company is a party, notwithstanding they be members of said company by having property insured therein, unless the adverse party in such actions or suits object thereto.

SEC. 21. No person shall be adjudged incompetent to testify as a witness in any action or cause, in which said insurance company is a party, by reason of his being a member of said company.

SEC. 22.   Jurors in all courts in this state shall be required to sit in trial of all actions and suits in which the said insurance company is a party, notwithstanding they may be members thereof by having property insured therein unless specially objected thereto for this cause by one of the parties to such action or suit.

SEC. 23.   Any sheriff or other officer, within his jurisdiction, may serve or execute any writ or other process to him directed, in which said insurance company is a party, notwithstanding such officer shall be a member of said company by being insured therein, any law or usage to the contrary notwithstanding.

SEC. 24.   No policies shall be issued until application for insurance shall have been made to the amount of fifty thousand dollars.

SEC. 25.   This corporation shall be located at Montpelier in the county of Washington.

SEC. 26.   This act shall take effect from its passage.

Approved, November 24, 1874.

No. 138.—AN ACT ENABLING THE WINDSOR COUNTY MUTUAL FIRE INSURANCE COMPANY TO INSURE AGAINST LOSS BY LIGHTNING.

It is hereby enacted by the General Assembly of the State of Vermont:

SEC. 1. The Windsor County Mutual Fire Insurance Company is authorized and empowered to insure against loss or damage by lightning.

SEC. 2. This act shall take effect from its passage.

Approved October 28, 1874.

No. 139.—AN ACT TO CHANGE THE NAME OF THE NYE MANUFACTURING COMPANY TO THE BERLIN MANUFACTURING COMPANY.

It is hereby enacted by the General Assembly of the State of Vermont:

SEC. 1. The name of the Nye Manufacturing Company, a corporation chartered by an act approved November 25, A. D. 1872, is hereby changed to the Berlin Manufacturing Company.

SEC. 2. This act shall take effect from its passage.

Approved, November 5, 1874.

No. 140.—AN ACT TO INCORPORATE THE ASCUT. NEY MILLS.

It is hereby enacted by the General Assembly of the State of Vermont:

SEC. 1. Russell L. Jones, Eastburn E. Lamson, Charles J. Jones, Henry D. Stone, Edward E. Floyd, and their associates and successors, are hereby constituted a body politic and corporate by the name of the Ascutney Mills, for the purpose of manufacturing cotton and other textile fabrics, wood and metal wares, and machinery and lumber, and of acquiring, using, selling, and leasing to others to use, real estate, water power, tenements and machinery, and for such other purposes, and such other business, as may be incidental thereto; and by that name may sue and be sued, have a common seal, and have and enjoy all the rights incident to corporations.

SEC. 2. Said corporation shall comply in all respects with the provisions and requirements of an act entitled " An act to authorize the formation of private corporations by voluntary association," approved November 20, 1870, and all amendments thereto, and subject to all the liabilities of corporations, under said acts, except that said corporation shall have the right to increase its capital stock to six hundred thousand dollars, and said corporation shall have all the rights and privileges conferred by said acts.

SEC. 3. This act shall be subject to the control of the legislature to alter, amend or repeal as the public good may require.

SEC. 4. This act shall take effect from its passage.

Approved, November 24, 1874.

No. 141.—AN ACT TO CHANGE THE NAME OF THE ST. ALBANS PRINTING, BINDING AND PAPER MANUFACTURING COMPANY.

It is hereby enacted by the General Assembly of the State of Vermont:

SEC. 1. The name of the St. Albans Printing, Binding and Paper Manufacturing Company is hereby changed to the St. Albans Advertiser Company; and by the latter name said company shall hereafter be known and styled; and all debts, demands, contracts, obligations and liabilities now outstanding in favor of or against said company may be enforced by or against said company by the name of the St. Albans Advertiser Company.

SEC. 2. This act shall take effect from its passage.

Approved, November 24, 1874.

15

No. 142.—AN ACT TO INCORPORATE THE DEERFIELD RIVER RAILROAD COMPANY.

It is hereby enacted by the General Assembly of the State of Vermont :

SEC. 1. Such persons as shall hereafter become stockholders are constituted a body corporate by the name of the Deerfield River Railroad Company, for the purpose and with the right of building a railroad from some point on the southern boundary of the state of Vermont, in the town of Halifax or Whitingham, and running northerly through such of the following towns as may be finally determined upon by said company in locating their said railroad namely: Wilmington, Marlboro, Somerset, Dover, Newfane, Townshend, Stratton, Wardsboro, Jamaica and Londonderry, in the county of Windham, Searsburgh and Winhall in the county of Bennington, Andover, Weston, Ludlow, Plymouth and Bridgewater, in the county of Windsor, Mt. Holly and Shrewsbury, in the county of Rutland, to connect with the proposed Montpelier and Rutland Railroad, at some point in the town of Sherburne in said county of Rutland, with the right of building said railroad, with single or double track, and with the right to transport and carry persons and property, by the power of steam or otherwise; and by that name may sue and be sued, may have a seal, and shall have all the rights incident to corporations.

SEC. 2. The capital stock of said company shall be four hundred thousand dollars, which may be increased from time to time to such an amount as may be necessary to complete said road and furnish all necessary buildings, road furniture and other apparatus useful or convenient for the use of said road, and said capital stock shall be divided into shares of one hundred dollars each.

SEC. 3. Charles A. Scott, E. J. Whitcomb, M. Tarbell, Fred Parmenter, C. W. Sprague, J. Q. A. Cragin, David Arnold, J. L. Martin, H. H. Felton, J. G. Eddy, O. O. Fitts, Rufus Lyman, Lucius Smith, Hollis Town, Simon Doane, D. P. Leonard, Ashley Stone, John Patch, N. L. Stetson, L. A. Warren and Jed Stark shall be commissioners to receive subscriptions to the capital stock of said company, who shall open the books thereof at such time and place as they or a majority of them shall elect, giving ten days notice thereof by publication in one or more newspapers in each of the several counties in which said road is to be built.

SEC. 4. Said commissioners may cause such preliminary surveys and examinations to be made as they deem expedient, and the expense thereof shall be paid by said company when organized.

SEC. 5. The commissioners shall, as soon as three

hundred shares of the capital stock of said company shall have been subscribed, cause notice to be given to the stockholders of said company for a meeting of said stockholders, for the election of not less than five or more than nine directors of said company, which notice shall be given by publication in one or more newspapers in each of the several counties in which said road is to be built, at least two weeks prior to the time of holding such election; at which time and place designated in said notice, the stockholders shall elect said directors who shall hold their office for one year and until others are elected. If any vacancy shall occur in said board of directors during said year, the clerk of said company may call a special meeting of the stockholders to fill said vacancy.

SEC. 6. Said directors may cause such examinations and surveys of the line of said road to be made, and after such examination and survey may locate said road, not exceeding six rods in width, and shall, by a certificate under their hands and the corporate seal, designate the line or route on which they have located their said road, and shall cause the same to be recorded in the town clerk's office in the towns through which said road passes. Said directors may at any time make such alterations in the route or location of said road as they may deem necessary or expedient, always causing the same to be recorded in the town clerk's office in the towns where such alterations are made.

SEC. 7. Said railroad company may, in the construction and running of their said railroad, have the right to cross the track or roadway of any railroad now built, or any railroad which may hereafter be built; and the damages and terms of such crossing, if not agreed upon and amicably settled by the parties, shall be determined by the commissioners appointed to settle land damages, and the same proceedings shall be had in all respects as in case of settling land damages under the statutes.

Sec. 8. Said railroad company may contract with the managers of any other railroad company to do and perform all transportations of persons and property upon and over their road; and may lease their road, and do such other things as may be necessary to build and run their said railroad.

Sec. 9. If said company shall not within ten years commence the survey and construction of said road, and expend at least the sum of fifty thousand dollars, and shall not within fifteen years, complete and put in operation said road, so far as practicable, said corporation shall take no benefit of this act, and the same shall be null and void except so far as said road may be completed.

Sec. 10. The directors may establish for said railroad such guage or width of track as they deem advisable for the interest of the company.

Sec. 11. This act shall be deemed and taken to be a public act, and shall be construed favorably and beneficially for all purposes for which the same is intended, and shall be subject to all the general laws which shall have been or may hereafter be enacted; provided, said company shall not be required to commence or complete their said road except as is provided in section nine.

Sec. 12. Said company may at any annual meeting or special meeting called for that purpose, adopt such rules and regulations, not inconsistent with the provisions of this act or the laws of this state, as they may deem expedient and necessary.

SEC. 13. This act shall be under the control of the legislature to amend or repeal as the public good may require.

SEC. 14. This act shall take effect from its passage.

Approved, November 24, 1874.

No. 143.—AN ACT TO INCORPORATE THE GRAND JUNCTION RAILROAD COMPANY.

SECTION
1. Corporators; name; purpose; powers, rights and privileges.
2. Capital stock.
3. Commissioners to receive subscriptions, to give notice.
4. May cause surveys to be made.
5. First meeting; directors, how elected.
6. Directors may cause surveys; to be made; to record same in town clerk's office.
7. May cross tracks of other roads; damage, how determined.
8. Limitation of construction.

SECTION
9. To be deemed a public act and subject to general laws.
11. Towns may aid in the construction of the road.
12. Aid, how. given.
13. Vote and assent to be recorded in office of town clerk and secretary of state.
14. Towns may issue bonds.
15 Selectmen or commissioners to carry votes into effect.
16, Corporation may lease their road.
17. Subject to future legislation; to take effect.

It is hereby enacted by the General Assembly of the State of Vermont:

SEC. 1. Mark Blake, Daniel Colby, Calvin Morrill, of St. Johnsbury, F. A. Follansby, E. S. Bailey, George F.

Wells, Luther Russell, Jr., Enoch Ware, of Victory, Samuel Ford, Edwin Turner, Solon S. Gould, of Concord, Orville Lawrence, of Waterford, George H. Weeks and J. M. Weeks, of Lyndon, and such persons as shall hereafter become stockholders, are hereby constituted a body corporate by the name of the Grand Junction Railroad Company, for the purpose of building a railroad, with a single or double track, from some point in the town of Concord to some point on the Grand Trunk Railroad in the town of Brighton or Ferdinand, through the towns of Victory, Granby, Ferdinand and Brighton, in Essex county, with the right of crossing the railroad of any other company, with the right to connect with any or all of the railroads now built and centering at Concord or any of the other towns mentioned, with the right to carry and transport persons and property by the power of steam or otherwise; and in that name may sue and be sued, may have a common seal; and shall have all the rights incident to corporations.

SEC. 2. The capital stock of said company shall be five hundred thousand dollars, which may be increased to such an amount as may be required to complete said road, and furnish all necessary buildings, equipments and appurtenances needful or convenient for the use of said road, and said capital stock shall be divided into shares of fifty dollars each.

SEC. 3. Solon S. Gould of Concord, Calvin Morrill and Horace Fairbanks, of St. Johnsbury shall be commissioners to receive subscriptions to the capital stock of said corporation, who shall open books therefor at such times and places as they may elect, giving ten days notice thereof by publication of the same in some one or more papers published in Essex or Caledonia counties.

SEC. 4. Said commissioners may cause such surveys and explorations to be made as they may deem expedient; and the expense thereof shall be paid by the said corporation when organized.

SEC. 5. Said commissioners shall, as soon as two hundred shares of the capital stock of said company shall have been subscribed, proceed to give notice to the stockholders of said company, for a meeting of the said stockholders for the election of nine directors of said company, which notice shall be given by publication in one or more newspapers published in Essex or Caledonia counties, Vermont, at least two weeks preceding the time fixed for said election, at which time and place said stockholders' shall elect said directors. A new election of directors shall be made annually at such time and place as the said board of directors may direct, and said directors shall hold office for one year, and until others are elected.

SEC. 6. Said directors may cause such surveys and examinations of the line of such road as they deem necessary, and afterward may locate the said road not exceeding six rods in width, and shall, by certificates under their hands and seals, designate the line or route on which they have located said road, and shall cause the same to be recorded in the several town clerks' offices in the towns in which said road is located. Said directors may at any time make such alterations in the route or location of said road as they may deem necessary or expedient, always causing such alterations to be recorded in the town clerk's office in the towns where such alterations shall be made.

SEC. 7. Said railroad company may, in the construction and running of their said railroad, have the right to cross the track or roadway of any railroad now built, or of any railroad which may hereafter be built, and the damages and terms of such crossing, if not agreed upon and amicably settled by the parties, shall be determined by the commissioners appointed to settle land damages, and the same proceedings shall be had in all respects as in cases for settling land damages under the statute.

SEC. 8. If the said corporation shall not within five years from the approval of this act, commence the construction of said railroad, and shall not within ten years complete and put in operation some portion of said railroad, then said corporation shall be dissolved and this act become void.

SEC. 9. This shall be deemed a pubic act, and shall be construed favorably and beneficially for all persons for which the same is intended, and shall be subject to all general laws which have been or may hereafter be enacted, as far as the same may be applicable to all railroads; provided, said corporation shall not be required to commence or complete their road except as provided in section eight of this act.

SEC. 11. Any town in Essex county may aid in the construction of the said road, by subscribing to the stock in said road, or by issuing bonds to said road, or in such manner as said town shall direct; provided, that no town shall assume any liability for said road, exceeding eight times the grand list of said town at the time said aid is granted.

SEC. 12. Such aid shall be given in the following manner, to wit:

The selectmen of said town, on the application of ten
or more legal voters of said town, shall, within ten days
after the receipt of said application, warn a meeting of
the legal voters of such town, to be held at the usual
place of holding town meetings in such town, which
notice shall specify the time and place of the meeting,
which shall not be more than twenty days nor less than
twelve days from the time of posting such notice, and
the warning shall be sufficient, if it state the business to be done at said meeting is to aid in the construction of said road; and if a majority of the votes
given at said meeting shall be to aid said road, then the
town shall fix the amount of the aid to be given, and the
terms thereof, and may appoint three commissioners, who
shall be resident tax-payers of the town; and if no commissioners be appointed, the selectmen shall act as commissioners until commissioners shall be appointed by said
town. Said commissioners or selectmen shall be duly
sworn, and shall, as soon as may be, procure suitable books
in which said vote shall be set forth, in which the tax-payers of the town may sign their names assenting to said
vote, and the grand list of each person signing said assent shall be annexed to his name, and when a majority of
the tax-payers of said town, both in number and amount
of grand list, shall have signed the same, the same shall be
binding on the town; provided, the signatures are procured
within six months after the first signature to the paper is
made; and all persons or corporations liable to pay taxes,
and all persons who shall be owners of real estate of said
town, taxed at the time the assent is given, shall have the
right to assent to said vote.

SEC. 13. The said vote and assent, when so signed as aforesaid, shall be duly certified by the commissioners or selectmen, and recorded by the town clerk in the town clerk's office at length in the land records of said town, and a duly certified copy of the vote of the town, and a certificate of the commissioners or selectmen to the same, that the act has been complied with by a majority of the tax-payers, both in number and amount, who have duly signed the same, with the certificate of the town clerk that the same has been duly recorded in his office, shall be recorded in the office of the secretary of state; and certified copies from either office shall be full proof in any court that the law has been complied with.

SEC. 14. Said towns may issue bonds, with coupons payable semi-annually, at any rate of interest not exceeding seven and three tenths per cent, for the purpose of aiding said road.

SEC. 15. The selectmen or commissioners aforesaid, as soon as the assent is given and recorded as aforesaid, shall proceed to carry into effect the vote of said town, according to the terms and conditions thereof, and shall have power to vote and act for said town on all proper occasions to carry into effect the aforesaid vote, and their votes and acts shall be binding on said town.

SEC. 16. Said corporation may lease their road and do such other things as are necessary to build and run said road.

SEC. 17. This act shall be under the control of the legislature to alter, amend or repeal as the public good may require, and shall take effect from its passage.

Approved, November 24, 1874.

No. 144.—AN ACT TO INCORPORATE THE HARD-WICK AND MARSHFIELD RAILROAD COMPANY

It is hereby enacted by the General Assembly of the State of Vermont:

SEC. 1. Such persons as shall hereafter become stockholders are constituted a body corporate by the name of the Hardwick and Marshfield Railroad Company, for the purpose and with the right of building a railroad from some point on the line of the Lamoille Valley Railroad in the town of Hardwick, thence through the towns of Hardwick, Woodbury, Cabot and Marshfield, to intersect with the Montpelier and Wells River railroad at Marshfield, with the right of building said railroad with single or double track, to be operated by steam or otherwise, for the purpose for which railroads are generally used; by that name may sue and be sued, may have a seal, and shall have all the rights incident to corporations.

SEC. 2. The capital stock of said company shall be four hundred thousand dollars, which may be increased from time to time to such an amount as may be necessary to build and complete, and furnish said road with all necessary buildings, furniture and appurtenances necessary for said road, and the capital stock shall be divided into shares of fifty dollars each.

SEC. 3. M. P. Wallace, J. P. Lamson of Cabot, A. F. Putnam of Marshfield, S. C. Eaton of Hardwick, John C. Dow of Albany, James G. French of Montpelier, Isaac N. Hall of Groton, shall be commissioners to receive subscriptions to the capital stock of said company, who shall open the books therefor at such times and places as a majority of them shall elect, giving ten days notice thereof by publication in one newspaper in Caledonia and Washington counties.

SEC. 4. Said commissioners may cause such surveys and explorations to be made as they may deem expedient, and the expenses thereof shall be paid by said company when organized.

SEC. 5. The commissioners, as soon as two hundred shares of said stock shall be subscribed for, shall cause notice to be given to the stockholders of said company for a meeting for the election of five directors, which notice shall be given by mailing a notice to each, signed by the acting chairman of said board of commissioners, stating therein the time and place of such meeting, and said directors shall hold their office until others are elected.

SEC. 6. Said company may locate said road on the route aforesaid, at such width as they may deem necessary, and shall by their certificate under their hands, designate the line of said road, and shall cause the same to be recorded in the town clerk's office of each of said towns, and may at any time make such alterations in the route as they may deem expedient, causing such alterations to be recorded as aforesaid.

SEC. 7. If said company shall not within six years

commence the survey of said railroad, and shall not within ten years commence the construction of said road and expend at least thirty thousand dollars thereon, and shall not in fifteen years complete and put in operation said railroad, then this act shall be null and void, except so far as said railroad is completed and put in operation.

SEC. 8. This act shall be deemed to be a public act, and shall be construed favorably and beneficially for all purposes for which the same is enacted, and shall be subject to any general law of the state respecting railroad corporations which is now in force or may hereafter be enacted, and all the general laws of the state relating to railroad corporations shall be deemed and taken to be a part of this act, and shall be under the control of the legislature to alter, amend or repeal as the public good shall require; provided, that said company shall not be required to commence the construction except as it is mentioned in section seven.

SEC. 9. This act shall take effect from its passage.

Approved, November 24, 1874.

No. 145.—AN ACT TO AMEND AN ACT ENTITLED "AN ACT TO INCORPORATE THE MIDLAND RAILROAD COMPANY."

Be it enacted by the General Assembly of the State of Vermont :

SEC. 1. Section one of an act entitled "An act to incorporate the Midland Railroad Company," approved November 12, 1872, is hereby amended so as to include the town of Jay, in the county of Orleans, in the proposed route of said railroad.

SEC. 2. This act shall take effect from its passage.

Approved, November 5, 1874.

No 146.—AN ACT TO AMEND THE CHARTER OF THE MONTPELIER AND BLACK RIVER RAILROAD COMPANY.

SECTION
1. Charter amended; corporators; purpose and right; route of railroad: powers, rights and privileges;

SECTION
2. Section two of act of incorporation repealed.
3. To take effect.

It is hereby enacted by the General Assembly of the State of Vermont:

SEC. 1. Section one of the act to incorporate the Montpelier and Black River Railroad Company, approved November 12, 1872, is hereby amended to read as follows:

Such persons as shall hereafter become stockholders are constituted a body corporate by the name of the Montpelier and Black River Railroad Company, for the purpose and with the right of building a railroad from some point in tho town of Montpelier, and running northerly through such of the following towns as may be finally determined upon by said company in locating said railroad, namely, Montpelier, East Montpelier, Middlesex, Worcester, Elmore, Woodbury, Morristown, Hydepark, Eden, Lowell, Westfield, Troy, Newport, Coventry, Irasburgh, Albany, Craftsbury, Wolcott and Jay, to connect with any railroad now or that may hereafter be built, at some point in tho towns of Troy or Newport, or both of said towns, with the right to build such railroad with a single or double track, with the right to transport and carry persons and property on said road by the power of steam or otherwise; and by that name may sue and be sued, may have a seal, and shall have all the rights incident to corporations.

SEC. 2.   Section one of said act is hereby repealed.

SEC. 3.   This act shall take effect from its passage.

Approved, November 5, 1874.

No. 147.—AN ACT IN RELATION TO THE LOCATION OF THE MONTPELIER AND WHITE RIVER RAILROAD.

It is hereby enacted by the General Assembly of the State of Vermont:

SEC. 1.   The Montpelier and White River Railroad Company are hereby authorized to locate and build their railroad between the Coffee House, so-called, and the Vermont Central Railroad depot, in Montpelier, within the surveyed limits of the Montpelier and Wells River Railroad, but not to interfere with the track or the moving of the trains on said Montpelier and Wells River Railroad. And if the parties in possession of said railroad cannot agree upon said location and the damages and compensation therefor, the same may be determined by commissioners appointed in the same manner as commissioners for the appraisal of damages for land taken for railroad purposes, notice to be given to the Montpelier and Wells River Railroad Company of the time of appointment of said commissioners.

SEC. 2. This act shall take effect from its passage.

Approved, November 24, 1874.

No. 148.—AN ACT IN AMENDMENT OF AN ACT TO INCORPORATE THE RUTLAND AND WOODSTOCK RAILROAD COMPANY, APPROVED NOVEMBER 3, 1865.

It is hereby enacted by the General Assembly of the State of Vermont:

SEC. 1. Section two of said act is hereby amended by
16

striking out the word "ten" in the second line of said section, and inserting instead thereof the word *fifteen*.

SEC. 2. This act shall take effect from its passage.

Approved, November 20, 1874.

No. 149.—AN ACT TO AMEND AN ACT ENTITLED "AN ACT TO INCORPORATE THE WEST RIVER RAILROAD COMPANY," APPROVED NOVEMBER 6, 1867.

It is hereby enacted by the General Assembly of the State of Vermont:

SEC. 1. Section one of said act is hereby amended so as to read as follows :

Such persons as shall become stockholders therein, are hereby constituted a body corporate by the name of the West River Railroad, for the purpose and with the right of building and operating a railroad for the transportation of persons and property from some point in the town of Brattleboro, near the village thereof, along the valley of West river, through the towns of Brattleboro, Dummerston, Newfane, Brookline, Townshend and Jamaica, to some point near the village of Jamaica, in the county of Windham.

SEC. 2. This act shall take effect from its passage.

Approved, November 24, 1874.

No. 150.—AN ACT TO EXTEND THE TIME FOR THE LOCATION OF THE WOODSTOCK RAILROAD.

It is hereby enacted by the General Assembly of the State of Vermont:

SEC. 1. Section one of an act to amend an act entitled "An act to incorporate the Woodstock Railroad Company," approved November 8, 1867, is hereby amended so as to extend to the said Woodstock Railroad Company all the rights and privileges therein contained until the first day of January, A. D. 1876, the same as though the provisions of this act were a part of the act herein amended.

SEC. 2. This act shall take effect from its passage.

Approved, October 28, 1874.

No. 151.—AN ACT TO EMPOWER THE RAILROAD COMPANIES THEREIN NAMED TO CONSOLIDATE WITH EACH OTHER AND WITH CONNECTING RAILROADS.

It is hereby enacted by the General Assembly of the State of Vermont:

SEC. 1. The Essex County Railroad Company, the Montpelier and St. Johnsbury Railroad Company, the Lamoille Valley Railroad Company, the Lamoille Valley Junction Railroad Company, the Lamoille Junction Railroad Company, the Lamoille Valley Extension Railroad Company, and the Burlington and Lamoille Railroad Company, shall each have the right, by a vote of a majority of the stockholders of each of said companies voting at any meeting called for that purpose, to consolidate the maintenance, management and working of each of said roads with any one or more of the other of said roads, and with any other road or roads now built or hereafter to be built between the city of Portland, in the state of Maine, and the cities of Montreal and Ottawa, in the Dominion of Canada, and Ogdensburgh, in the state of New York, connecting with each other and such other road or roads on such terms, and subject to such restrictions, as shall be mutually agreed upon by the companies so consolidating; and the several railroad companies so consolidating may each have the right, by vote of its stockholders as aforesaid, mutually to agree upon and adopt a name for such consolidated line; or said companies, or any one or more of them, may join with the company or companies so consolidating in the issue of joint or consolidated bonds secured by a joint or consolidated mortgage of the roads and property of the companies forming such consolidated line of railroad. And such consolidated line of railroad, or any one or more of said companies, shall have the right to lease or purchase, on such terms as may be mutually agreed upon, the Montreal, Chambly and Sorel Railway, of Canada, or any other railroad or railroads now built or hereafter to be built between the termini before named.

SEC. 2. Whenever there shall be a consolidation under the provisions of section one of this act and a name assumed by said consolidated company, it shall be the duty of the clerk of such consolidated company to file in the office of the secretary of state a certified copy of the articles of consolidation, together with the name of such consolidated company, within thirty days from the time of such consolidation.

SEC. 3. This act shall take effect from its passage; shall be taken to be a public act, and shall be subject to alteration, amendment or repeal as the public good may require.

Approved, November 20, 1874.

No. 152.—AN ACT TO INCORPORATE THE BELLOWS SAVINGS INSTITUTION AND TRUST COMPANY.

It is hereby enacted by the General Assembly of the State of Vermont:

SEC. 1. Such persons as shall hereafter become stock-holders, and their successors, are hereby constituted a corporation and body politic by the name of the Bellows Savings Institution and Trust Company; and by that name may sue and be sued, have a common seal and the same alter at pleasure, may purchase and hold real and personal estate for their own use, and such real and personal estate as may be received in the collection of debts, and may sell and convey the same, and shall have and enjoy all the privileges incident to corporations; and said corporation shall be located at St. Albans, in the county of Franklin.

SEC. 2. The capital stock of said corporation shall be one hundred thousand dollars, with power to increase the same to an amount not exceeding three hundred thousand dollars, which shall be divided into shares of one hundred dollars each.

SEC. 3. In addition to the general powers and privileges of a corporation, said Bellows Savings Institution and Trust Company shall have power:

First. To receive moneys on deposit or in trust, at such rate of interest or on such terms as may be agreed upon, the rate of interest to be allowed for deposits not to exceed the legal rate.

Second. To accept and execute all such trusts of every description, not inconsistent with the laws of this state, as may be committed to them by any person or persons whomsoever, or by any corporation, or by order of any probate court, or other court of record of this state.

Third.   To take and accept by grant, assignment, transfer, deviso or bequest, and hold any real or personal estate, on trust created in accordance with the laws of this state, and execute such trusts on such terms as may be declared, established or agreed upon.

Fourth.   To receive upon deposit for safe keeping, stocks, bonds and other securities; also plate, jewelry and other valuable property, and to act as agent for the purpose of issuing, registering or countersigning the cer-tificates of stock, or other evidences of debt, of any corpo-. ration, association, municipality, state, or public authority, and for collection of interest or dividends on the same, on such terms as may be agreed upon.

Fifth.   To accept from and execute trusts for married women in respect to their separate property, whether real or personal, and act as agent for them in the management of such property.

Sixth.   To accept deposits where public officers or mu-nicipal or private corporations are authorized or required by law to deposit moneys in banks; and such deposits may be made by such officers or corporations with the said Bellows Savings Institution and Trust Company.

Sec. 4.   No bond or other collateral security shall be required from the said corporation when appointed guar-dian, receiver or depositary, but all investments of such character shall be at the sole risk of the said corporation; and for all losses of such moneys, or of any moneys or securities received by said corporation on deposit or in trust, the capital stock, property and effects of the said corporation shall be absolutely liable (the act of God or the public enemies excepted); and in case of the dissolution of the said corporation, by act of law or otherwise, the debts due from said corporation or guardian, received as depositary of moneys in court, and for deposits in favor of minors, insane persons, or married women in their own right, shall have a preference.

SEC. 5. All the business of said corporation shall be managed by five trustees, a majority of whom shall be a quorum for the transaction of business, who shall be stockholders in said corporation, each to the amount of at least one thousand dollars, and a majority of whom shall be inhabitants of this state and who shall be elected annually, at such time as the by-laws of such corporation shall provide, and shall hold their offices for one year from the time of their election and until their successors are chosen and qualified. Notice of such election shall be given by publication in a newspaper printed at St. Albans, for three weeks next previous to such election, and all such elections shall be made by ballot, (each stockholder shall be entitled to one vote for each share of the capital stock standing in his name on the books of the corporation,) by the stockholders of said corporation who shall be present in person or by proxy, and the five persons who shall receive the greatest number of votes at such election shall be trustees; and in case any vacancy shall happen by death, resignation or otherwise, the vacancy shall be filled from among the stockholders by a majority of the remaining trustees. After their election, the trustees shall elect from among their number a president and vice president if necessary, and such other officers as they shall deem necessary. The said trustees shall be liable to the creditors and stockholders of said corporation for any loss which may be sustained in consequence of any incompetency, unfaithfulness or remissness in the discharge of their official duties imposed by this act, and any number of such trustees may be sued in the same action by any claimant under these provisions.

SEC. 6. Albert Sowles, N. B. Atwood, J. S. Weeks, A. G. Safford and C. G. Lawrence, or a majority of them, shall be commissioners, whose duty it shall be to receive subscriptions to the capital stock of said corporation, who shall open books for that purpose at such time or times as they shall deem proper, giving at least four weeks notice in some public newspaper printed in St. Albans, of the time and place when such books will be open for the purpose of receiving such subscriptions to said stock, and such commissioners or a majority of them may continue their sittings for that purpose from day to day, or from time to time, as they may deem proper, until the amount of said capital stock is subscribed for; and as soon as the whole amount of such stock shall be subscribed for, or as soon thereafter as said commissioners shall think proper, not exceeding six months, said commissioners, or a majority of them, shall call a meeting of the stockholders of said corporation, at such place in St. Albans as they shall think proper, by publishing a notice thereof, signed by said commissioners, or the survivors of them, in one or more newspapers printed in St. Albans, three weeks successively previous to such meeting, for the purpose of electing five trustees of said corporation; and said commissioners, or a majority of them, shall deliver to said trustees of said corporation when elected, and within ten days after they shall enter upon the duties of their office, a list of all the names of persons entitled to shares in said corporation, and the number of shares to which each is entitled, and the sum by each deposited with them, also the moneys received by them or deposited on said shares; which list said trustees shall cause to be recorded in the books of said corporation, and thereupon issue certificates to such subscribers for their stock.

SEC. 7. The shares of such corporation shall be transferred only in such manner and under such regulations as shall be prescribed by the by-laws thereof; provided, no transfer shall be valid until recorded by the cashier or treasurer, or in his absence, by one of the trustees, in a book for that purpose, nor until the person making the same shall have previously discharged all debts due from him to said corporation.

SEC. 8. The trustees of such corporation may make such by-laws and regulations as they may deem necessary and proper, not inconsistent with this act or the laws of this state.

SEC. 9. The said corporation shall be allowed as compensation for the care of trust property, the investment and collection of the same, and for other services rendered in the execution of such trust, such sum as shall be agreed upon; and in the absence of any agreement, such compensation as is fixed by the by-laws or regulations of said corporation in force at the time such trust is created.

SEC. 10. The trustees and other officers of said corporation may, at their discretion, pay to any minor or married woman such sums as may have been deposited by and be due to him or her, the same as if such minor were of age and such married woman unmarried; and the check, receipt or acquittance of such minor or married woman shall be a full discharge for the amount for which it is given.

SEC. 11. The trustees shall have a discretionary power to invest the moneys received by them on deposit or in trust, in stock or bonds of the United States, of the states of New England or New York, or any of the towns, cities or counties in either of said states, or in such real or personal security as they shall deem proper; provided, that when a special agreement or direction is given or made by or with those making deposits, or leaving trust property with said corporation, as to the mode of investment thereof the same shall be strictly followed.

SEC. 12. No trustee, officer or employe of said corporation shall be, at any one time, directly or indirectly indebted thereto for more than five per cent of its capital paid in; and for any violation of this section, any director or officer assenting thereto shall be liable to the corporation for the whole amount of such unauthorized indebtedness.

SEC. 13. This act shall not be construed to confer on said corporation any rights or powers to make any contract or to accept or execute any trust whatever which it would not be lawful for any individual under the general rules of law which are or shall be in force, to make, accept or execute.

SEC. 14. If at any time the capital stock paid into said corporation shall be impaired by losses or otherwise, the trustees shall forthwith repair the same by assessments upon the stockholders, or suspend all dividends until the net earnings of said company shall be sufficient to make up such loss ; and no dividends shall be made or declare upon the capital stock of said corporation until the same are actually earned and realized over and above all losses and expenses.

SEC. 15. Any president, trustee or other officer of said corporation who shall misapply or divert the moneys, funds or other trust property confided to and accepted by said corporation, from the purposes and objects prescribed by this act, or who shall participate in such misappropriation or diversion, shall, on conviction thereof, be punished by imprisonment not exceeding two years, or fined not exceeding one thousand dollars, or either of said punishments in the discretion of the court.

SEC. 16. The commissioners herein named shall be sworn to a faithful discharge of their duties, and shall require the subscribers at the time of subscribing for said stock of said company to deposit with said commissioners ten dollars on each share by them subscribed for. The commissioners may allot the subscriptions to said stock in such manner as may be most conducive to the interests of said company, in the event that there is any excess of subscriptions above the amount for which they may receive subscription.

SEC. 17. The corporation shall not commence business, further than to organize, until at least twenty-five per cent of the whole capital stock shall have been paid into said corporation. After the shares shall have been distributed and allotted, each stockholder shall pay the whole amount remaining due on shares held by him, at such time or times as the trustees shall appoint, on which ten days notice at least shall be given to each subscriber by mail, and by publishing the same in some newspaper printed in the town of St. Albans; and the shares of each subscriber omitting to make such payment shall be forfeited, together with all previous payments made thereon; provided, that there shall be at least fifteen thousand dollars of the capital stock paid in yearly until the whole one hundred thousand dollars shall have been paid in.

SEC. 18. This corporation shall be subject to the provisions of sections twenty-five, twenty-six, twenty-seven twenty-eight, twenty-nine, thirty, thirty-one, thirty-two, thirty-three, thirty-four and thirty-five of chapter eighty-six of the general statutes, relating to private corporations or other moneyed corporations.

Approved, November 24, 1874.

No. 153.—AN ACT TO INCORPORATE THE FACTORY POINT SAVINGS BANK.

It is hereby enacted by the General Assembly of the State of Vermont:

SEC. 1. Robert Ames, Jared Burrit, James Lamson, A. G. Clark, Richard W. Dean, D. S. Wilson, R. Howard, A. G. Clark, M. S. Colburn, Loveland Munson, S. W. Bowen, I. N. Sykes, Wm. H. Bebee, Andrews Bowen, John G. Walker, Zadoc Canfield, Jerome Hill, and such other persons as shall be duly elected members of the corporation hereby constituted, according to such by-laws as may hereafter be established, are hereby constituted a body politic and corporate by the name of the Factory Point Savings Bank, for the purpose of enabling industrious persons of all classes to invest such part of their earnings as they can conveniently spare, in a safe and profitable manner; and by that name may sue and be sued may have a common seal, and the same alter at pleasure; and all deeds, conveyances, grants, covenants and agreements made by their treasurer, or other person by them authorized, shall be good and valid in law.

SEC. 2. Said corporation may receive on deposit, for the use and benefit of the person by or for whom deposits may be made, all sums of money offered for that purpose, and manage and improve the same for the purpose and according to the directions hereinafter mentioned and provided.

SEC. 3. All deposits of money received by said corporation shall be managed and improved to the best advantage, and the income or profit thereof shall be divided by said corporation among the several persons by or for whom the said deposits shall have been made, or their legal representatives, in just proportion according to their deposits, with such reasonable deductions as may be necessary to defray the expenses of said corporation; and all such deposits may be withdrawn by the persons entitled thereto, at such reasonable times and in such manner as said corporation by its by-laws may direct; and said corporation shall have the by-laws printed, and furnish a copy thereof to every depositor of the sum of ten dollars or more at the time of the deposit.

SEC. 4. Said corporation may at their first meeting under this act, and at any subsequent meeting annually thereafter, elect by ballot any other person or persons, not exceeding thirty, including those who are at the time members, to be members of said corporation.

SEC. 5. The officers of said corporation shall consist of a president, vice president, treasurer, and such number of directors or trustees, not less than five nor more than nine, as said corporation shall determine, together with such other officers as may be found necessary for the management of its affairs; which officers, except the treasurer, shall be chosen by ballot at an annual meeting of said corporation, to be held at such times as the by-laws thereof may direct; and they shall hold their offices one year and until others are chosen and have accepted in their stead, except the treasurer, who may be removed by the president, vice president and a majority of the directors or trustees, at any time they may judge the interest of the corporation requires ; the same to be done by giving such treasurer notice of such removal in writing, under their official signatures, and the official relation of such treasurer to said corporation shall thereupon cease ; and the treasurer shall be appointed by the president, vice president and a majority of the directors or trustees, and shall hold his office during their pleasure; all of which officers shall be sworn to the faithful discharge of their duties; and the treasurer, before entering upon the dis. charge of his duties, shall give bonds to the corporation in such sum as a majority of the trustees·may require, with satisfactory sureties, which bond shall be kept good and may be increased in amount, and additional sureties required whenever a majority of the trustees so direct; and at any meeting of said corporation, duly·warned, nine members thereof, the president, vice president or treasurer being one of them, shall constitute a quorum for the transaction of business.

Sec. 6. Said corporation may hire such real estate or personal property as may be necessary for managing its affairs, or for the same purpose may take and hold real estate, and erect buildings thereon, not to exceed in value the sum of three thousand dollars; and may take and hold and dispose of any real estate whatever, which they acquire by levy, foreclosure of mortgages, or by deed, in good faith for the payment of debts, demands or liabilities previously contracted or incurred.

Sec. 7. Said corporation shall not make or issue any bill or promisory note to circulate as currency, and the president, officers and members of said corporation shall receive no compensation for their services except for money necessarily paid for such corporation, nor shall any funds be loand to any officer thereof; provided, that such reasonable allowance shall be made to the treasurer, secretary and such clerks as the business of the corpora- tion may render necessary, as the directors or trustees shall order.

SEC. 8. Said corporation m iy m ike all such by-la vs as are necessary and proper for the management of their affairs, not inconsistent with the constitution and the laws of this state.

SEC. 9. The books of said corporation shall at all times be open to the inspection of the auditor of accounts, who shall, on applic ition of at least ten depositors, in writing, make an examination of the management of the corporation, and if in the opinion of said auditor of accounts the affairs of said corporation have been improperly managed, he shall report the same to 'the next session of the legislature, and in that case the said corporation shall pay the said auditor for his services; and the treasurer of said corporation shall make an annual report to the auditor of accounts of the number of depositors, amount deposited and dividends declared, which report shall be certified and sworn to by the treasurer and at least two of the directors or trustees.

SEC. 10. Said corporation shall be located in the village of Factory Point, in Manchester, in the county of Bennington, and Robert Ames, M. S. Colburn and Ranney Howard, or either of them, are authorized to call the first meeting of said corporation, by giving written notice of the time and place of such meeting to each of said corporators, at least six days previous thereto.

SEC. 11. This act shall be subject to the general laws of this state relating to savings banks and moneyed corporations, now in force or that may hereafter be passed, and may be amended or repealed as the legislature may see fit.

SEC. 12. This act shall take effect from its passage.

Approved, November 24, 1874.

17

No. 154.—AN ACT IN AMENDMENT OF AN ACT ENTITLED "AN ACT TO INCORPORATE THE HYDE-PARK SAVINGS BANK AND TRUST COMPANY."

It is hereby enacted by the General Assembly of the State of Vermont:

SEC. 1. Section three of an act entitled "An act to incorporate the Hydepark Savings Bank and Trust Company," approved November 18, one thousand eight hundred and seventy, is hereby so amended as to extend the time during which the subscription books are therein required to be opened, until the first day of October, one thousand eight hundred and seventy-six.

SEC. 2. This act shall take effect from its passage.

Approved, November 18, 1874.

No. 155.—AN ACT TO INCORPORATE THE MERCANTILE TRUST COMPANY.

It is hereby enacted by the General Assembly of the State of Vermont:

SEC. 1.   John B. Page, Francis Slason, William Gilmore, Edwin Martindale, Frederick Chaffee, Jacob Edgerton, Henry C. Gleason, William Y. Ripley, Sidney W. Rowell, and their associates and successors, are hereby constituted a corporation and body politic by the name of the Mercantile Trust Company; and by that name may sue and be sued, have a common seal, and the same alter at pleasure, may purchase and hold real and personal estate for their own use, and such real and personal estate as may be received in the collection of debts, and may sell and convey the same; and shall have and enjoy all the privileges incident to corporations; and said corporation shall be located in the town of Rutland.

SEC. 2.   The capital stock of said corporation shall be fifty thousand dollars, with the power to increase the same to an amount not exceeding five hundred thousand dollars, which shall be divided into shares of one hundred dollars each.

SEC. 3.   In addition to the general powers and privileges of a corporation, said Mercantile Savings Bank and Trust Company shall have power:

First. To receive moneys on deposit or in trust, at such rate of interest or on such terms as may be agreed upon, the rate of interest to be allowed for deposits not exceeding the legal rate.

Second. To accept and execute all such trusts of every description, not inconsistent with the laws of this state, as may be committed to them by any person or persons whomsoever, or by any corporation, or by order of any probate court, or other court of record of this state.

Third. To take and accept, by grant, assignment, transfer, devise, or bequest, and hold, any real or personal estate, or trusts created in accordance with the laws of this state, and execute such trusts on such terms as may be declared, established or agreed upon.

Fourth. To receive upon deposit for safe keeping, stocks, bonds, and other securities; also plate, jewelry, and other valuable property; and to act as agent for the purpose of issuing, registering or countersigning the certificates of stock, or other evidences of debt, of any corporation, association, municipality, state or public authority, and for collection of interest or dividends on the same, on such terms as may be agreed upon.

Fifth. To accept from and execute trusts for married women in respect to their separate property, whether real or personal, and act as agent for them in the management of such property.

Sixth. To accept deposits where public officers or municipal or private corporations are authorized or required by law to deposit moneys in bank; and such deposits may be made by such officers or corporations with the said Mercantile Trust Company.

SEC. 4. No bond or other collateral security shall be required from the said corporation when appointed guardian, receiver, or depositary, but all investments of such character shall be at the sole risk of the said corporation; and for all losses of such moneys, or of any moneys or securities received by said corporation on deposit or in trust, the capital stock, property and effects of the said corporation shall be absolutely liable, (the act of God or the public enemies excepted); and in case of the dissolution of the said corporation, by act of law, or otherwise, the debts due from said corporation as guardian, receiver, or depositary of moneys in court, and for deposits in favor of minors, insane persons, or married women, in their own right, shall have a preference.

SEC. 5. All the business of said corporation shall be managed by a board of trustees—the number to be controlled by a vote of the stockholders—a majority of whom shall be a quorum for the transaction of business; who shall be stockholders in said corporation, each to the amount at least of one thousand dollars, and inhabitants of this state, and who shall be elected annually, at such time as the by-laws of such corporation shall provide, and shall hold their offices for one year from the time of their election and until their successors are chosen and qualified. Notice of such election shall be given by publication in a newspaper printed in the town of Rutland, for four weeks next previous to such election, and all such elections shall be made by ballot, (every stockholder being entitled to one vote for trustees for every share of the capital stock standing in his name on the books of the corporation,) by the stockholders of said corporation, who shall be present in person or by proxy, and the persons, to the number previously decided upon by a vote of the stockholders, who shall receive the greatest number of votes at such election shall be trustees; and if any two or more persons shall receive an equal number of votes, so that more than the number of persons designated as aforesaid shall, by a plurality of votes, appear to be elected, the stockholders shall proceed to ballot a second time, and by a plurality of votes determine which of said persons so having an equal number of votes shall be trustees ; and in case any vacancy shall happen by death, ·resignation, or otherwise, the vacancy shall be filled from among the stockholders by a majority of the remaining trustees. After their election, the trustees shall elect from among their number a president, and such other officers as they shall deem necessary. The said trustees shall be liable to the creditors and stockholders of said corporation for any loss which may be sustained in consequence of any unfaithfulness or remissness in the discharge of their official duties imposed by this act, and any number of such trustees may be sued in the same action by any claimant under these provisions.

Sec. 6. Said commissioners shall, upon the whole amount of stock being subscribed for, or as soon after as they shall think proper, not exceeding sixty days, call a meeting of the stockholders of said corporation at such place in Rutland as they shall think proper, by publishing a notice thereof, signed by three or more of them, in one or more newspapers printed in the county of Rutland, three weeks successively, previous to such meeting, for the purpose of electing trustees of said corporation; and said commissioners shall deliver to said trustees of said corporation, when elected, and within ten days after they shall enter upon the duties of their office, a list of all the names of persons entitled to shares in said corporation, and the number of shares to which each is entitled, and the sum by each deposited with them, also the moneys received by them on deposit on said shares; which list said trustees shall cause to be recorded in the books of said corporation, and thereupon issue certificates to such subscribers for their stock.

SEC. 7. The shares of such corporation shall be transferred only in such manner and under such regulations as shall be prescribed by the by-laws thereof; provided, no transfer shall be valid until recorded by the cashier or treasurer, or, in his absence, by one of the trustees, in a book for that purpose, nor until the person making the same shall have previously discharged all debts and liabilities due from him to said corporation.

SEC. 8. The trustees of said corporation may make such by-laws and regulations as they may deem necessary and proper, not inconsistent with this act or the laws of this state.

SEC. 9. The said corporation shall be allowed as compensation for the care of trust property, the investment and collection of the same, and for other services rendered in the execution of such trust, such sum as shall be agreed upon; and, in the absence of any agreement, such compensation as is fixed by the by-laws or regulations of said corporation in force at the time such trust is created.

SEC. 10. The trustees and other officers of said corporation may, at their discretion, pay to any minor or married woman such sums as may have been deposited by and be due him or her, the same as if such minor were of age and such married woman unmarried; and the check, receipt or acquittance of such minor or married woman shall be a full discharge for the amount for which it is given.

SEC. 11. The trustees shall have a discretionary power of investing the moneys received by them on deposit or in trust, in stocks or bonds of the United States, of the states of Maine, New Hampshire, Vermont, Massachusetts, Connecticut, Rhode Island or New York, or any of the towns, cities or counties in either of said states, or in such real or personal security as they shall deem proper; provided, that when a special direction or agreement is given or made by or with those making deposits, or leaving trust property with said corporation, as to the mode of investment thereof, the same shall be strictly followed.

SEC. 12. No trustee, officer or employe of said corporation shall be, at any one time, directly or indirectly indebted thereto for more than three per cent of its capital paid in; and for any violation of this section, any director or officer consenting thereto shall be liable to the corporation for the whole amount of such unauthorized indebtedness.

SEC. 13. This act shall not be construed to confer on said corporation any right or power to make any contract or to accept or execute any trust whatever which it would not be lawful for any individual under the general rules of law which are or shall be in force, to make, accept or execute.

SEC. 14. If at any time the capital stock paid into said corporation shall be impaired by losses or otherwise, the trustees shall forthwith repair the same by assessments upon the stockholders; and no dividends shall be made or declared upon the capital stock of said corporation until the same are actually earned and realized, over and above all losses and expenses.

SEC. 15. Any president, trustee, or other officer of said corporation, who shall misapply or divert the moneys, funds, or other trust property confided to and accepted by said corporation, from the purposes and objects prescribed by this act, or who shall participate in such misapplication or diversion, shall, on conviction thereof, be punished by imprisonment in the state prison not exceeding five years and be fined not exceeding one thousand dollars, or either of said punishments, in the discretion of the court.

SEC. 16. The persons named in the first section of this act are appointed commissioners for receiving subscriptions for shares in the capital stock of said corporation, and they shall open books for that purpose at the town of Rutland, within two years after the passage of this act, notice of which opening shall be published in two newspapers published in the said town of Rutland, three weeks in succession, the last of which shall not be more than two weeks previous to the day fixed for such opening, which notice shall be signed by at least a majority of said commissioners. Said commissioners shall be sworn to a faithful discharge of their duty, and such books shall continue open from ten o'clock A. M. till four o'clock P. M. each day, Sundays excepted, for the space of five days and thereafter until five hundred shares shall be subscribed for; and the subscribers shall, at the time of subscribing, deposit with the commissioners ten dollars on each share by them subscribed for. The commissioners, in case more than the whole amount of capital stock is subscribed for, shall allot and distribute the same among the subscribers, by deducting the excess from those subscribing the greatest number of shares, thus making subscriptions equal so far as may be without dividing shares, in such manner as they may deem most for the interest of all concerned ; and if there shall be any increase of the capital stock of said corporation as herein provided, the said increase shall be divided among the then stockholders *pro rata*, if they will accept the same; and in case the whole of such increase is not then distributed, the surplus may be divided among the then stockholders of said corporation, who will receive and pay for the same in proportion to the amount of stock held by them, or in such other manner as the board of trustees shall determine.

SEC. 17. The corporation shall not commence business, further than to organize, until at least twenty-five per cent of the whole capital stock shall have been paid into said corporation. After the shares shall have been distributed and allotted, each stockholder shall pay the whole amount remaining due on the shares held by him, at such time or times as the trustees shall appoint, of which at least ten days notice shall be given to each subscriber by mail, and by publishing the same in some newspaper printed in Rutland; and the shares of each stockholder omitting to make such payment shall be forfeited, together with all previous payments made thereon; provided, that there shall be at least fifteen thousand dollars of the capital stock paid in yearly until the whole fifty thousand dollars shall have been paid in.

SEC. 18. This corporation shall be subject to the provisions of sections twenty-five, twenty-six, twenty-seven, twenty-eight, twenty-nine, thirty, thirty-one, thirty-two, thirty-three, thirty-four and thirty-five of chapter eighty-six of the general statutes, relating to private corporations, savings banks, or other moneyed corporations.

SEC. 19. The legislature shall have power at any time

hereafter to repeal, alter or modify this act or any of its provisions.

SEC. 20. This act shall take effect from its passage.

Approved, November 24, 1874.

No. 156.—AN ACT TO AMEND AN ACT ENTITLED "AN ACT TO INCORPORATE THE MISSISQUOI SAVINGS BANK AND TRUST COMPANY."

It is hereby enacted by the General Assembly of the State of Vermont:

SEC. 1. Section sixteen of an act to incorporate the Missisquoi Savings Bank and Trust Company, approved November 15, 1872, is hereby amended by striking out the word " two " before the word years, in the fifth line of said section, and inserting in lieu thereof the word *four.*

SEC. 2. This act shall take effect from its passage.

Approved, November 18, 1874.

No. 157.—AN ACT TO INCORPORATE THE MONT- PELIER SAVINGS BANK.

SECTION	SECTION
1. Corporators; name; powers.	7. By-laws.
2. Deposits may be received.	8. Treasurer to make annual re-
3 Members, how constituted.	port.
4. Officers.	9. First meeting, how called.
5. Deposits, how invested and	10. Location.
managed.	11. Act subject to general laws.
6. May purchase and hold real	12. To take effect.
estate.	

It is hereby enacted by the General Assembly of the State of Vermont :

SEC. 1. Homer W. Heaton, James W. Brock, J. Warren Bailey, Whitman G. Ferrin, John A. Page, Charles Dewey, George W. Scott, Joel Foster, Jr., of Montpelier, and such other persons as shall be elected members of the corporation hereby constituted, at the annual meeting thereof, according to such by-laws as may be hereafter established, are hereby constituted a body politic and corporate by the name of the Montpelier Savings Bank; and by that name may sue and be sued, may have a common seal, and the same alter at pleasure, and all deeds, conveyances, bequests, covenants and agreements made by their treasurer, or other person by them authorized, shall be good and valid.

SEC. 2. Said corporation may receive on deposit, for the benefit and use of the person for whom deposits may be made, all sums offered for that purpose, and manage and improve the same for the purpose and according to the directions hereinafter mentioned and provided.

SEC. 3.   Said corporation at their first meeting, or at any annual meeting, may elect by ballot any number of persons, not exceeding in all thirty, to be members of said corporation.

SEC. 4.   The officers of said corporation shall consist of a president, vice president, treasurer and such number of trustees as the said corporation by their by-laws may direct—not less than three nor more than six—together with such other officers as may be found necessary, which officers shall be chosen by ballot according to the by-laws, and shall hold office for one year and until others are chosen, except the treasurer who may be removed by the president, vice president, and a majority of the trustees, at any time they may think the interest of the corporation requires it.   All which officers shall be duly sworn to the faithful discharge of their duties, and the treasurer shall give bonds to the corporation in such sums as the trustees shall direct.

SEC. 5.   All deposits of money received by said corporation shall be managed and improved to the best advantage, by loaning the same by order or consent of a majority of the trustees, on mortgage of real estate unencumbered and equal in value to double the amount of the loan secured thereon, except to an amount not exceeding one half of the amount on deposit in said corporation, which said sum may be invested in the purchase of stocks of the United States, or any of them, in bank stock of any bank in this state, or in any city or town, bonds of the New England states, or in undoubted personal security or otherwise, as the trustees shall direct; provided, that said stocks may be sold from time to time to such an amount as will meet the demand for deposits or other claims on said corporation, and the income and profits of said deposits shall be divided by said corporation amongst the several depositors, according to the by-laws of said corporation, after deducting the expenses of said corporation, and all such deposits as may be withdrawn according to the by-laws of said corporation; and said corporation shall have their by-laws printed, and furnish a copy to every depositor of the sum of ten dollars or more at the time of the deposit.

SEC. 6. Said corporation may purchase or hire real estate of the value of five thousand dollars, and may take, hold and dispose of all real estate that they may acquire by any foreclosure of mortgage, or by deed in good faith, for the payment of debts previously contracted.

SEC. 7. Said corporation may make all such by-laws as are necessary and proper for the management of their affairs, not inconsistent with the laws of this state.

SEC. 8. The treasurer of said corporation shall make an annual report of the number of depositors, amount deposited and dividends divided, which report shall be certified and sworn to by the treasurer and a majority of the trustees.

SEC. 9. Homer W. Heaton and John A. Page are hereby authorized to call the first meeting of the corporation, giving each member thereof six days notice in writing, of the time and place of meeting.

SEC. 10. Said corporation shall be located in Montpelier, in the county of Washington.

SEC. 11. This act shall be subject to all the general laws

of this state relating to savings banks and moneyed corporations, now in force or that may be hereafter enacted, and may be amended or repealed as the public good may require.

SEC. 12.   This act shall take effect from its passage.

Approved, November 24, 1874.

No. 158.—AN ACT TO CHANGE THE NAME OF THE NATIONAL TRUST COMPANY.

It is hereby enacted by the General Assembly of the State of Vermont:

SEC. 1.   The National Trust Company, incorporated by an act approved November 19, 1868, and located and doing business at St. Albans, shall hereafter be known and called the St. Albans Trust Company.

SEC. 2.   This act shall take effect from its passage.

Approved, November 24, 1874.

No. 159.—AN ACT IN AMENDMENT OF SECTION FIFTEEN OF AN ACT ENTITLED "AN ACT TO INCORPORATE THE NEWPORT SAVINGS BANK AND TRUST COMPANY," APPROVED NOVEMBER 15, 1872.

It is hereby enacted by the General Assembly of the State of Vermont:

SEC. 1. Section fifteen of an act entitled "An act to incorporate the Newport Savings Bank and Trust Company," is hereby amended so that the word "two," in the fifth line of said section fifteen, shall read *five*.

SEC. 2. This act shall take effect from its passage.

Approved, November 24, 1874.

No. 160.—AN ACT TO AMEND AN ACT ENTITLED "AN ACT TO INCORPORATE THE RICHFORD SAVINGS BANK AND TRUST COMPANY."

It is hereby enacted by the General Assembly of the State of Vermont:

SEC. 1. Section three of an act entitled "An act to incorporate the Richford Savings Bank and Trust Company," approved November 21, 1872, is hereby amended by striking out the words "one year," in the third line of said section, and inserting in lieu thereof the words *three years*.

SEC. 2. This act shall take effect from its passage.

Approved, November 17, 1874.

No. 161.—AN ACT INCORPORATING THE ST. JOHNSBURY LOAN AND TRUST COMPANY.

It is hereby enacted by the General Assembly of the State of Vermont:

SEC. 1. The subscribers to the capital stock of the corporation hereby established, their associates and successors, are hereby constituted a corporation and body politic by the name of the St. Johnsbury Loan and Trust Company; and by that name may sue and be sued, have a common seal, and the same alter at pleasure, may purchase and hold real and personal estate for their own use, and such as may be received in the collection of debts, and may sell and convey the same, and shall have and enjoy all the privileges incident to corporations; and said corporation shall be located in the village of St. Johnsbury.

SEC. 2. The capital stock of said corporation shall be divided into shares of one hundred dollars each, and after the organization of the company as hereinafter mentioned, the capital stock thereof may be increased to an amount not exceeding the sum of five hundred thousand dollars, under such regulations as said corporation may prescribe.

SEC. 3. In addition to the general powers and privileges of a corporation, the St Johnsbury Loan and Trust Company shall have power :

First. To receive moneys, gold and silver, on deposit or in trust, and issue certificates of deposit therefor, at such rate of interest or on such terms as may be agreed upon, the rate of interest to be allowed for deposits not exceeding the legal rate ; also to buy and sell exchange and coin and draw bills of exchange on any country, and issue letters of credit.

Second. To accept and execute all such trusts of every description, not inconsistent with the laws of this state, as may be committed to them by any person or persons whomsoever, or by any corporation, or by order of any probate court, or other court of record in this state.

Third. To take and accept, by grant, assignment, transfer, devise or bequest, and hold any real or persona estates or trust created in accordance with the laws of this state, and execute such trusts on such terms as may be declared, established or agreed upon.

Fourth. To accept from and execute trusts for married women in respect to their separate property, real or personal, and act as agent for them in the management of their property.

Fifth. To accept deposits where public officers or municipal or private corporations are authorized or required by law to deposit money in bank; and such deposits may be made by such officers or corporations with said St Johnsbury Loan and Trust Company.

Sixth. To receive for safe]keeping, stocks, bonds, and other valuable property, upon such terms as may be agreed upon.

SEC. 4. No bond or other collateral security shall be required from the said corporation when acting as receiver or depository, but all investments of such character shall be at the sole risk of said corporation; and for all losses of such moneys, or of any moneys or securities received by said corporation on deposit or in trust, the capital stock, property and effects of the said corporation shall be absolutely liable, (the act of God or the public enemy only excepted); and in case of the dissolution of said corporation, the debts due from said corporation as receiver or depository of moneys in court, and for deposits in favor of minors, insane persons, or married women in their own right, shall have a preference.

SEC. 5. The business of said corporation shall be managed by ten trustees, a majority of whom shall be a quorum for the transaction of business, who shall be stockholders to the amount of one thousand dollars in said corporation and inhabitants of this state, and who shall be elected annually in the month of January, at such times as the by-laws of said corporation shall provide, and shall hold their offices for one year from the time of their election and until their successors are chosen and qualified. Notice of such election shall be given by publication in a newspaper printed in St. Johnsbury, at least three weeks prior to such election, and all such elections shall be made by ballot, (every stockholder being entitled to one vote for every share of capital standing in his name on the books of said corporation,) by the stockholders of said corporation, who shall be present in person or by proxy, a majority of the votes cast being necessary to an election ; and in case any vacancy shall happen by death, resignation, or otherwise, the vacancy shall be filled from among the stockholders by a majority of the remaining trustees. After their election, the trustees shall elect from their number a president, cashier, who shall be the treasurer, and such other officers as may be required by the by-laws of such corporation. The said trustees shall be liable to the creditors and stockholders of said corporation for any loss which may be sustained in consequence of any incompetency, unfaithfulness, or remissness in the discharge of their official duties imposed by this act.

Sec. 6. The shares of said corporation shall be transferred only in such manner and under such regulations as shall be prescribed by the by-laws thereof; provided, no transfer shall be valid until recorded by the cashier, or in his absence, by one of the trustees, in a book for that purpose, nor until the person making the same shall have previously discharged all debts and liabilities due from him to said corporation.

Sec. 7. The trustees of said corporation may make such by-laws and regulations as they deem necessary and proper, not inconsistent with the laws of this state.

Sec. 8. The said corporation shall be allowed as a compensation for the care of trust property, the investment and collection of the same, and for other services rendered in the execution of each trust, such sum as shall be agreed upon; and in the absence of any agreement, such compensation as is fixed by the by-laws or regulations of said corporation in force at the time such trust is created:

SEC. 9. The trustees and other officers of said corporation may, at their discretion, pay to any minor or married woman such sums as may have been deposited by and be due to him or her, the same as if such minor were of age and such married woman unmarried; and the check, receipt or acquittance of such minor or married woman shall be a full discharge for the amount for which it is given.

SEC. 10. The trustees shall have a discretionary power of investing the moneys received by them on deposit, or in trust, in such real or personal security as they may deem proper; provided, that when a special direction is given by, or agreement made with those making the deposits, or having trust property with said corporation, as to the mode of investment thereof, the same shall be strictly followed.

SEC. 11. No trustee, or other officer of said corporation shall be, at any one time, directly or indirectly indebted thereto for more than five per cent of its capital paid in; and for any violation of this section, any director or officer consenting thereto shall be liable to the corporation for the whole amount of such unauthorized indebtedness.

SEC. 12. This act shall not be construed to confer on said corporation any right or power to make any contract or to accept or execute any trust whatever which it would not be lawful for any individual under the general rules of law which are or shall be in force, to make, accept or execute.

SEC. 13. If at any time the capital stock paid into said

corporation shall be impaired by losses or otherwise, the trustees shall forthwith repair the same by assessments upon the stockholders, and no dividends shall be made or declared upon the capital stock of said corporation until the same are actually earned and realized over and above all losses and expenses.

SEC. 14. Any trustee or other officer of said corporation who shall misapply or divert the moneys, funds or other trust property confided to and accepted by said corporation, from the purposes and objects prescribed by this act, or who shall participate in such misapplication or diversion, shall, on conviction thereof, be punished by imprisonment in the state prison not exceeding five years, and be fined not exceeding one thousand dollars, or either of said punishments, in the discretion of the court.

SEC. 15. Luke Buzzell, Henry Fletcher, Gates B. Bullard, N. M. Johnson, David Goodall, Charles Rogers, Jr., George E. Goodall, Otis G. Hale, Orville Lawrence, Jacob McNiel, are hereby appointed commissioners to receive subscriptions to the capital stock of said corporation; and they shall open books for that purpose at the village of St. Johnsbury within one year after the passage of this act, notice of which opening shall be published in all the newspapers published in the county of Caledonia at least three weeks before such time of opening such books, which notice shall be signed by a majority of said commissioners. Said commissioners shall be sworn to a faithful discharge of their duty, and such books shall continue open from ten o'clock A. M., until four o'clock P. M., daily, for the space of one week, when said commissioners shall call a meeting of the subscribers to said capital stock, to be holden in said St. Johnsbury, at such hour and on such day as they may deem expedient, by giving ten days personal notice to each subscriber, when such corporation may organize by the election of a board of trustees. Five per cent of the capital stock of said corporation shall be paid in, in cash, at the time of the subscription thereof, the balance at the time of the first meeting for the election of a board of trustees; and upon the organization of said company, the same shall be delivered by said commissioners to the board of trustees. Any increase of the capital stock of said corporation at any time, shall be divided among the stockholders at the time of such increase *pro rata*, if they will accept the same. Said corporation shall receive no moneys or other property on deposit or in trust, until fifty thousand dollars of the capital stock of said corporation shall have been paid in, in cash. The trustees chosen at the meeting of the subscribers to said capital stock, as mentioned in this section, shall hold their offices for one year and until their successors shall be chosen and qualified.

SEC. 16. This corporation shall be subject to all the provisions of sections twenty-five to thirty-five inclusive, of chapter eighty-six of the general statutes, relating to private corporations, savings banks, or other moneyed corporations.

SEC. 17. The legislature may alter, amend or repeal this act as the public good may require; and the same shall take effect from its passage.

Approved, November 24, 1874.

No. 162.—AN ACT TO INCORPORATE THE UNION SAVINGS BANK AND TRUST COMPANY.

It is hereby enacted by the General Assembly of the State of Vermont:

SEC. 1. Orville Sinclair, J. B. Small, —— Reynolds, L. B. Platt, L. B. Platt, Jr., —— Stevens, B. B. Smalley, and their associates and successors, are hereby constituted a corporation and body politic by the name of the Union Savings Bank and Trust Company; and by that name may sue and be sued, may have a common seal, and the same alter at pleasure; may purchase and hold real and personal estate for their own use, and such real and personal estate as may be received in the collection of debts, and may sell and convey the same; and shall have and enjoy all the powers and privileges incident to corporations; and said corporation shall be located in the town

Colchester or the city of Burlington in the county of Chittenden.

SEC. 2. The capital stock of said corporation shall be fifty thousand dollars, with the power to increase the same to an amount not exceeding five hundred thousand dollars, which shall be divided into shares of one hundred dollars each.

SEC. 3. In addition to the general powers and privileges of a corporation, the said Union Savings Bank and Trust Company shall have power:

First. To receive moneys on deposit or in trust, at such rate of interest or on such terms as may be agreed upon, the rate of interest to be allowed for deposits not exceeding the legal rate.

Second. To accept and execute all such trusts of every description, not inconsistent with the laws of this state, as may be committed to them by any person or persons whomsoever, or by any corporation, or by order of any probate court, or other court of record in this state.

Third. To take and accept, by grant, assignment, transfer, devise, or bequest, and hold any real or personal estate, or trusts created in accordance with the laws of this state, and execute such trusts on such terms as may be declared, established or agreed upon.

Fourth. To receive upon deposit for safe keeping, stocks, bonds, and other securities; also plate, jewelry, and other valuable property; and to act as agent for the purpose of issuing, registering or countersigning the certificates of stock, or other evidences of debt, of any corporation, association, municipality, state or public authority, and for collection of interest or dividends on the same, on such terms as may be agreed upon.

Fifth. To accept from and execute trusts for married women in respect to their separate property, whether real or personal, and act as agents for them in the management of such property.

Sixth. To accept deposits where public officers or municipal or private corporations are authorized or required by law to deposit money in bank; and such deposits may be made by such officers or corporations with the said Union Savings Bank and Trust Company.

SEC. 4. No bond or other collateral security shall be required of the said corporation when appointed guardian, receiver, or depositary, but all investments of such character shall be at the sole risk of the said corporation; and for all losses of such moneys, or of any moneys or securities received by said corporation on deposit or in trust, the capital stock, property and effects of said corporation shall be absolutely liable, (the act of God and public enemies excepted); and in case of the dissolution of the said corporation, by act of law or otherwise, the debts due from said corporation as guardian, receiver, or depositary of moneys in court, and for deposits in favor of minors, insane persons, or married women in their own right, shall have a preference.

SEC. 5. All the business of said corporation shall be managed by seven trustees, a majority of whom shall be a quorum for the transaction of business, who shall be stockholders in said corporation, each to the amount of at least five hundred dollars, and inhabitants of this state, and who shall be elected annually, at such time as the by-laws of said corporation shall provide, and shall hold their offices for one year from the time of their election and until their successors are chosen and qualified. Notice of such election shall be given by publication in a newspaper printed in the county of Chittenden for four weeks next previous to such election, and all such elections shall be made by ballot, (every stockholder being entitled to one vote for trustees for every share of capital stock standing in his name on the books of the corporation,) by the stockholders of said corporation who shall be present in person or by proxy, and the seven persons who shall receive the greatest number of votes at such election shall be trustees; and if any two or more persons shall receive an equal number of votes, so that more than seven persons shall by a plurality of votes appear to be elected, the stockholders shall proceed to ballot a second time, and by a plurality of votes determine which of said persons, so having an equal number of votes, shall be trustees; and in case any vacancy shall happen by death, resignation, or otherwise, the vacancy shall be filled from among the stockholders by a majority of the remaining trustees. After their election, the trustees shall elect from among their number a president and vice president, and such other officers as they may deem necessary. The said trustees shall be liable to the creditors and stockholders of said corporation for any loss which may be sustained in consequence of any incompetency, unfaithfulness or remissness in the discharge of their official duties imposed by this act, and any number of such trustees may be sued in the same action by any claimant under these provisions.

SEC. 6. Said commissioners shall, upon the whole amount

of stock being subscribed for, or as soon after as they shall think proper, not exceeding sixty days, call a meeting of the stockholders of said corporation at such place in the town of Colchester, or city of Burlington, as they shall think proper, by publishing a notice thereof, signed by a majority of them, in one or more newspapers printed in the county of Chittenden, three weeks successively, previous to such meeting, for the purpose of electing seven trustees of said corporation; and said commissioners shall deliver to said trustees of said corporation, when elected, and within ten days after they shall enter upon the duties of their office, a list of all the names entitled to shares in said corporation, and the number of shares to which each is entitled, and the sum by each deposited with them, also the moneys received by them on deposit on said shares; which list said trustees shall cause to be recorded in the books of said corporation, and thereupon issue certificates to such subscribers for their stock.

Sec. 7. The shares of such corporation shall be transferred only in such manner and under such regulations as shall be prescribed by the by-laws thereof; provided, no transfer shall be valid until recorded by the cashier or treasurer, or, in his absence, by one of the trustees, in a book for that purpose, nor until the person making the same shall have previously discharged all debts and liabilities due from him to said corporation.

Sec. 8. The trustees of said corporation may make such by-laws and regulations as they deem necessary and proper, not inconsistent with this act or the laws of this state.

Sec. 9. The said corporation shall be allowed as compensation for the care of trust property, the investment and collection of the same, and for other services rendered in the execution of such trust, such sums as shall be agreed upon; and, in the absence of any agreement, such compensation as is fixed by the by-laws or regulations of such corporation in force at the time such trust is created.

SEC. 10. The trustees and other officers of said corporation may, at their discretion, pay to any minor or married woman such sums as may have been deposited by and be due to him or her, the same as if such minor were of age and such married woman unmarried; and the check, receipt or acquittance of such minor or married woman shall be a full discharge for the amount for which it is given.

SEC. 11. The trustees shall have a discretionary power of investing the moneys received by them on deposit or in trust, in stocks or bonds of the United States, or the states of Maine, New Hampshire, Vermont, Massachusetts, Connecticut, Rhode Island or New York, or any of the towns, cities or counties of either of said states, or in such real or personal security as they may deem proper; provided, that when a special direction or agreement is given or made by or with those making deposits, or leaving trust property with said corporation, as to the mode of investment thereof, the same shall be strictly followed.

SEC. 12. No trustee, officer or employe of said corporation shall be, at any one time, directly or indirectly indebted thereto for more than five per cent of its capital paid in, and no loan shall be made such trustee, officer, or employe upon a pledge of the stock of said corporation standing in his or her name, and only upon the same kind and classes of security as loans to non-stockholders; and for any violation of this section, any director or officer consenting thereto shall be liable to the corporation for the whole amount of such unauthorized indebtedness.

SEC. 13.   This act shall not be construed to confer on said corporation any right or power to make any contract or to accept or execute any trust whatever which it would not be lawful for any individual under the general rules of law which are or shall be in force, to make, accept or execute.

SEC. 14.   If at any time the capital stock paid into said corporation shall be impaired by losses or otherwise, the trustees shall forthwith repair the same by assessments upon the stockholders; and no dividends shall be made or declared upon the capital stock of said corporation until the same are actually earned and realized, over and above all losses and expenses.

SEC. 15.   Any president, trustee, or other officer of said corporation, who shall misapply or divert the moneys, funds, or other trust property confided to and accepted by said corporation, from the purposes and objects prescribed by this act, or who shall participate in such misapplication or diversion, shall, on conviction thereof, be punished by imprisonment in the state prison not exceeding five years and be fined not exceeding one thousand dollars, or either of said punishments, in the discretion of the court.

SEC. 16.   The persons named in the first section of this act are appointed commissioners for receiving the subscriptions for shares in the capital stock of said corporation, and they shall open books for that purpose in the town of Colchester or city of Burlington, within two years after the passage of this act, notice of which opening shall be published in a newspaper published in said Chittenden county, three weeks in succession previous to the day fixed for such opening, which notice shall be signed by at least a majority of said commissioners. Said commissioners shall be sworn to a faithful discharge of their duties, and such books shall continue open from ten o'clock A. M. till four o'clock P. M. each day, Sundays excepted, for the space of five days and thereafter until five hundred shares shall be subscribed for; and the subscribers shall, at the time of subscribing, deposit with the commissioners ten dollars on each share by them subscribed for. The commission-ers, in case more than the whole amount of capital stock is subscribed for, shall allot and distribute the same among the subscribers, by deducting the excess from those subscribing the greatest number of shares, thus making the subscriptions equal so far as may be without dividing shares, in such manner as they may deem most for the in-terest of all concerned ; and if there shall be any increase of the capital stock of said corporation as herein provided, the said increase shall be divided among the then stock-holders *pro rata*, if they will accept the same; and in case the whole of such increase is not thus distributed, the surplus may be divided among the then stockholders of said corporation, who will receive and pay for the same in proportion to the amount of stock held by them, or in such other manner as the board of trustees shall deter-mine.

SEC. 17. The corporation shall not commence business, further than to organize, until at least twenty-five per cent of the whole capital stock shall have been paid into said corporation. After the shares shall have been dis-tributed and allotted, each stockholder shall pay the whole amount remaining due on the shares held by him, at such time or times as the trustees shall appoint, of which at least ten days notice shall be given to each subscriber by mail, and by publishing the same in some newspaper printed in the county of Chittenden; and the shares of each stock holder omitting to make such payment shall be forfeited, together with all previous payments made thereon ; provided, there shall be at least ten thousand dollars of the capital stock paid in yearly until the whole fifty thousand dollars shall have been paid in.

SEC. 18. This corporation shall be subject to all the provisions of sections twenty-five, twenty-six, twenty-seven, twenty-eight, twenty-nine, thirty, thirty-one, thirty-two, thirty-three, thirty-four and thirty-five of chapter eighty-six of the general statutes, relating to private corporations, savings banks, or other moneyed corporations.

SEC. 19. The legislature shall have power at any time hereafter to repeal, alter or modify this act or any of its provisions.

SEC. 20. This act shall take effect from its passage.

Approved, November 24, 1874.

No. 163.—AN ACT TO AMEND AN ACT ENTITLED "AN ACT TO INCORPORATE THE EAGLE RAILROAD AND SLATE COMPANY," APPROVED DECEMBER 6, 1853.

It is hereby enacted by the General Assembly of the State of Vermont:

SEC. 1.   The corporation created and constituted by the name of the Eagle Railroad and Slate Company, by an act entitled an act to incorporate the Eagle Railroad and Slate Company, approved December. 6, 1853, shall hereafter be known and designated by the name of the Eagle Slate Company; and by that name said corporation may sue and be sued, and all acts heretofore done and hereafter to be done by said corporation, under the name of the Eagle Slate Company, shall be as valid and effectual in every respect as if said corporation had so been named in its said act of incorporation.

SEC. 2.   Sections two and six of the said act are hereby repealed.

SEC. 3.   The said Eagle Slate Company may from time to time issue and dispose of the bonds of said company, secured by mortgage on the real and personal estate of said corporation or of any part thereof, at an interest of seven per cent per annum, payable semi-annually for each year the same shall remain outstanding; which mortgage or mortgages, when recorded in the office of the town clerk of the town or towns in which such property is situated, shall be good and sufficient to hold the property mortgaged without any further act.

SEC. 4.   This act shall take effect from its passage.

Approved, November 12, 1874.

19

No. 164.—AN ACT TO INCORPORATE THE MIDDLE-TOWN TELEGRAPH COMPANY.

It is hereby enacted by the General Assembly of the State of Vermont:

SEC. 1. D. Doolittle, L. Copeland, A. W. Gray, L. Gray, A. A. Greene, I. N. Gray, D. G. Adams, and their associates and successors, are hereby constituted a corporation and body politic by the name of Middletown Telegraph Company, for the purpose of establishing a telegraph line from Middletown to Poultney; and by that name may sue and be sued, may have a common seal, and the same may alter at pleasure, may hire or purchase with cash, stock or otherwise, such real and personal property, rights and privileges as said corporation, or its directors, if thereto authorized by its by-laws, may deem desirable and necessary for the prosecution of its business; and may hold, sell, and convey, let, lease, and improve the same or any part thereof, as the business or benefit of said company may require; and shall have and enjoy all the rights, powers, privileges and franchises incident to corporations.

SEC. 2. The first meeting of said corporation shall be held at such time and place as shall be designated by either three of the corporators named, by giving notice to each of the others, and at least six days previous to such meeting; at which, or at any other legal meeting of the corporation, such corporation may make, alter or amend such by-laws, rules and regulations, not inconsistent with the constitution and laws of this state or of the United States, for the election, appointment and duties of such officers, and for conducting the affairs of said corporation, as may be deemed necessary.

Sec. 3. The capital stock of said corporation is hereby fixed at one thousand dollars, and shall be divided into shares of ten dollars each; and said capital stock may be increased from time to time, to an amount not exceeding in the whole three thousand dollars, whenever a majority in interest of the stockholders shall by vote decide so to do. The mode of transfer of said stock may be fixed by said corporation, and said stock may be issued and disposed of by said corporation at its discretion.

Sec. 4. Said corporation shall not contract debts to an amount exceeding three fourths of the capital stock actually paid in, and if the indebtedness of the company shall at any time exceed that amount, the directors shall be personally liable to the creditors for such excess; and no part of the capital stock shall at any time be withdrawn or reduced until the indebtedness of the company is all paid.

Sec. 5. At each meeting of the stockholders of said company, all questions shall be determined by a majority of votes, counting one vote for each share represented, and absent stockholders may vote by proxy, duly authorized in writing, signed by the person or persons represented, or their duly constituted attorney therefor, and filed with the clerk.

SEC. 6. This act shall be subject to the control of future legislatures to alter, amend or repeal as the public good may require, and also subject to the general statutes relating to private corporations.

SEC. 7. This act shall take effect from its passage.

Approved, November 12, 1874.

No. 165.—AN ACT TO INCORPORATE THE CAMBRIDGE MOUNT MANSFIELD TURNPIKE COMPANY.

SECTION

1. Corporators; name; purpose; powers, rights and privileges.
2. Limitation of powers.
3. Capital stock; shares; transfer; organization; limitation of indebtedness.
4. Commissioners to receive subscriptions; to open books and give notice; to call meetings for organization; first

SECTION

meeting when and how called; officers; annual meetings.
5. Surveys.
6. By-laws; power of directors.
7. Privileges of corporation.
8. Lands may be purchased; proceedings in case of disagreement as to price.
9. Tolls and toll gates.
10. Subject to future legislation; to take effect.

It is hereby enacted by the General Assembly of the State of Vermont:

SEC. 1. Such persons as shall hereafter become stockholders in this company shall be a body corporate by the name of the Cambridge Mount Mansfield Turnpike Company, for the purpose and with the right to build a turnpike road, not to exceed six rods in width, from some point at or near the residence of Widow Charles Gallup, in Cambridge, in the county of Lamoille, or from such other point as shall be deemed most expedient, on a zig-zag line to the Lake of the Clouds, so-called, near that part of Mount Mansfield known as the Chin, and shall have all the rights and privileges incident to such corporations.

Sec. 2. If the corporation created by this act shall not within five years commence the building of said road, then the rights and privileges granted by this act shall be null and void.

Sec. 3. The capital stock of this company shall be ten thousand dollars, which may be increased to an amount sufficient to complete the road; and said capital stock shall be divided into shares of fifty dollars each, and shall be deemed personal property, and may be transferred and sold in the manner which said corporation may by their by-laws prescribe, and the said company may organize whenever four thousand dollars of said capital stock shall have been subscribed; and if the indebtedness of said corporation shall at any time exceed one half of the capital stock actually paid in, the directors and stockholders shall be personally liable for such excess to the creditors of said corporation.

Sec. 4. Elias Chadwick, R. L. Flagg, W. H. Griswold, William Melendy, Daniel W. Cutting, W. H. Parker, Clarence D. Gates, of Cambridge, in the county of Lamoille, Hon. Carolus Noyes and Hon. Nathaniel Parker, of Burlington, in the county of Chittenden, James M. Hotchkiss, of Fairfax, and Fred Carpenter, of Georgia, in the county of Franklin, shall be commissioners, who shall within one year from the passage of this act open books for receiving subscriptions to the capital stock of this company, at some convenient place in Cambridge, county of Lamoille, and in such other places and at such times as they may deem expedient, giving two weeks notice thereof in the Lamoille Newsdealer, a newspaper printed at Hydepark, in said Lamoille county, and shall call all meetings of said corporation necessary for due organization of the same. As soon as the capital stock of four thousand dollars shall be subscribed, the commissioners shall call a meeting of the stockholders by giving two weeks notice thereof as aforesaid, or by mailing a written notice to each stockholder, to choose five directors, and each stockholder to have as many votes as he has shares; and the said commissioners shall certify the names of those elected, and deliver the books of subscription to such directors, and the time and place of holding the first meeting of the directors shall be fixed by said commissioners. The directors shall elect from their number a president, and the directors and officers so elected shall hold their offices one year and until others are elected in their places. The time and place of holding the annual meeting shall be appointed by the directors, and two weeks notice thereof shall be given in either manner as aforesaid.

SEC. 5. The directors may cause such surveys to be made as they may deem necessary, previous to the location of said road, and when said road shall be finally located, the directors shall certify the same under their hands, which certificate and survey shall be recorded in the town clerk's office in the town of Cambridge, in the county of Lamoille; and which road so surveyed and certified shall be deemed the line on which said road shall be built.

SEC. 6. Three directors shall constitute a quorum, and shall be competent to transact all the business of the corporation, and shall have power to prescribe by-laws and regulations for the proper management and disposition of the stock, property and effects of the corporation, the transfer of shares, the conduct of their affairs, and all other matters appertaining to the corporation, and shall have power to appoint a treasurer and clerk of the corporation.

SEC. 7. The said corporation may enter upon and take possession of all such lands as may be necessary for the construction and maintenance of said turnpike road, and may receive and hold all voluntary grants of lands which may be made to them.

SEC. 8. All lands thus entered upon and used by said corporation, which are not voluntarily granted to them, shall be purchased of the owner or owners thereof, and in case the parties shall disagree as to the price of the lands, it shall be the duty of any judge of the county court in the county of Lamoille, on proper notice to the parties, to appoint three disinterested commissioners, who shall determine the damages which the owner or owners of the lands so entered upon may have sustained, and upon the payment of such damages, with the expenses attending the appraisal, then the corporation shall be deemed possessed of such lands.

SEC. 9. Said corporation shall have power to erect one or more toll gates on said road, locate and change their location at pleasure, and may regulate the tolls and charges to be collected of persons traveling on and using said road.

SEC. 10. This act shall be subject to any such future legislation as the public good may require, and shall take effect from its passage.

Approved, November 23, 1874.

No. 166.—AN ACT TO INCORPORATE THE NOTCH TURNPIKE COMPANY.

SECTION
1. Corporators; name; purpose.
2. Capital stock; shares; to be deemed personal property; company may organize when five thousand dollars is subscribed.
3. Commissioners to receive subscriptions; first meeting, when and how called; each share entitled to one vote; officers; tenure of office of.
4. Annual meetings.
5. Limitation of benefits conferred by this act.
6. Directors may cause surveys

SECTION
to be made; certificate of same to be recorded.
7. What constitutes a quorum; by-laws.
8. May enter upon, receive and hold lands.
9. Lands purchased of owners and disagreement as to price, how determined. .
10. Toll gates and tolls.
11. Corporation may borrow money and issue bonds and notes; limitation of amount.
12. Subject to future legislation.
13. To take effect.

It is hereby enacted by the General Assembly of the State of Vermont:

SEC. 1. Such persons as shall hereafter become stockholders in this company shall be a body corporate by the name of the Notch Turnpike Company, for the purpose and with the right of building a turnpike road, not to exceed six rods in width, from some point at or near Charles Burt's sawmill, in the town of Stowe, in the county of Lamoille, to some point at or near Stevensville, in the town of Underhill, in the county of Chittenden, by the most direct and feasible route, and shall have all the rights and privileges incident to such corporations.

SEC. 2. The capital stock of this company shall be fifty thousand dollars, and shall be divided into shares of twenty-five dollars each, and shall be deemed personal property, and may be transferred and sold in the manner which said corporation may by its by-laws prescribe, and the said company may organize whenever five thousand dollars of the capital stock shall be subscribed.

SEC. 3. W. H. H. Bingham, E. C. Mower, Dan Cady and Lemuel B. Smith, of Stowe, in the county of Lamoille, and C. W. Reynolds, M. E. Hapgood and William M. Naramore, of Underhill, C. M. Spaulding, E. H. Lane and L. F. Wilbur, of Jericho, E. F. Whitcomb, Josiah Tuttle and M. A Bingham, of Essex, A. J. Stevens, Charles Lafountain and J. B. Small, of Colchester, Lawrence Barnes, H. P. Hickok, V. P. Noyes, F. C. Kennedy, Henry Loomis, L. B. Platt, and E. W. Peck, of the city of Burlington, in the county of Chittenden, shall be commissioners, and shall within two years from the passage of this act open books for receiving subscriptions to the capital stock of said company at convenient places in the counties of Lamoille and Chittenden, and shall give two weeks notice of the time and place of opening such books by publishing the same in one newspaper in each of said counties, and may call meetings for the due organization of the company. When five thousand dollars of the capital stock shall have been subscribed, the commissioners shall call a meeting of the stockholders, by giving two weeks notice thereof by publication in one or more newspapers in each of said counties, or by mailing a written notice to each stockholder, of the time and place of meeting, to chose nine directors, and each stockholder shall be entitled to as many votes as he has shares of stock, and the said commissioners shall certify the names of the directors so chosen or elected, and shall deliver to them the books of subscription, and the time and place for the first meeting of said directors shall be fixed by the said commissioners. A majority of the commissioners shall constitute a quorum for the transaction of business. The directors shall elect from their number a president, and may also elect a treasurer, and such other officers as may be deemed necessary to the proper management of the affairs of the company, and such officers shall hold their offices for one year and until others are chosen in their places.

SEC. 4. Meetings of the stockholders shall be held at least once in each year, and may be called at any time by a vote of the directors. The time and place of holding all meetings of the stockholders shall be fixed by the directors, and the same notice shall be given as before provided for the first meeting of the stockholders.

SEC. 5. If the corporation created by this act shall not within five years commence building said road, this act shall be null and void.

SEC. 6. The directors may cause such surveys to be made as they may deem necessary, previous to the location of said road; and when said road shall be finally located, the directors or a majority of them shall certify the same under their hands, which certificate shall be recorded in the town clerk's office of the towns of Stowe and Underhill aforesaid, and such location shall be deemed the line on which said road shall be built.

SEC. 7. Five directors shall constitute a quorum, and shall be competent to transact all the business of the corporation, and shall have power to prescribe by-laws and regulations for the proper management and disposition of the stock, property and effects of the corporation, the transfer of shares, the conduct of its affairs, and all other matters pertaining to the corporation.

SEC. 8. The said corporation may enter upon and take possession of all such lands as may be necessary for the construction and maintenance of said turnpike road, and may receive and hold all voluntary grants of land which may be made to them.

SEC. 9. All lands thus entered upon and used by said corporation, which are not voluntarily granted to them, shall be purchased of the owner or owners thereof; and in case the parties shall be unable to agree upon the price of the lands taken, the company hereby incorporated, or the person owning the lands taken, may apply to the county court of the county in which said land is situated, by petition in writing, describing the lands to be taken, served on the opposite party in the same manner as writs of summous, which shall appoint three disinterested commissioners, who shall determine the damage sustained by said owner or owners of said land, and report the same to the court, whose report when accepted by the court shall be final; and upon payment of such damages, with the expenses attending the appraisal, the corporation shall have the right to enter upon and take such lands.

SEC. 10. Said corporation shall have power to erect and maintain one or more toll gates at such points as they may deem proper, and may change the location of the same at pleasure, and may fix the rate of tolls to be collected from persons traveling upon said road; provided, however, that the legislature may at any time reduce said tolls in case they be deemed exorbitant.

SEC. 11. Such corporation shall have the right to borrow money and issue its bonds or negotiable notes, bearing interest at seven per cent, to an amount not exceeding the amount of its capital stock actually paid in.

SEC. 12. This act shall be subject to such future legislation as the public good may require.

SEC. 13. This act shall take effect from its passage.

Approved, November 24, 1874.

———

No. 167.—AN ACT TO INCORPORATE AN ASSOCIATION CALLED THE VERMONT ASSOCIATION FOR THE PROTECTION AND PRESERVATION OF FISH AND GAME.

It is hereby enacted by the General Assembly of the State of Vermont:

SEC. 1. That M. S. Colburn, W. W. Henry, George Ballard, H. N. Newell, E. J. Phelps, B. B. Smalley, M. Goldsmith, Martin G. Evarts, M. C. Edmunds, C. F. Orvis, W. Y. W. Ripley, L. P. Norton, A. J. Potter, Ralph Graves, George G. Smith, F. S. Stranahan, J. W. Newton, E. S. Peck, Carrol S. Pitkin, W. H. Lord, W. C. Clement, A. W. Higgins, H. A. Sawyer, J. C. Guild, John Pierpoint, William L. McAuly, Henry Fairbanks, their associates and successors, are hereby constituted a body politic by the name of the Vermont Association for the Protection and Preservation of Fish and Game; and for such purposes may have a common seal and the same alter at pleasure, may sue and be sued, hold and convey real and personal property to an amount not to exceed twenty-five thousand dollars, and receive by gift or bequest any property, real or personal, that may be placed in their hands for the purposes afore-said, and in all respects have and enjoy all the privileges incident to such corporations.

SEC. 2. The first meeting of said corporation may be held at such time and place as may be designated by any three of the corporators, by their giving notice to the other corporators personally, or by publishing the same in three weekly papers printed at Montpelier, Rutland and Burlington, at least two weeks previous to the time appointed for such meeting.

SEC. 3. This association may make a constitution and by-laws, not inconsistent with the laws of this state or the United States, for its government, and for the election and admission of associates, and shall annually elect such officers as they shall deem necessary to manage and control the affairs and concerns of said association.

SEC. 4. This act shall be subject to the control of the legislature to alter or amend as the association and the public good shall require.

SEC. 5. This act shall take effect from its passage.

Approved, November 20, 1874.

No. 168.—AN ACT TO INCORPORATE THE VILLAGE OF BARTON.

It is hereby enacted by the General Assembly of the State of Vermont:

SEC. 1. All that part of Barton, in the county of Orleans, enclosed within the following boundaries, to wit:

Beginning on Crystal Lake, at the south-east corner of land belonging to the estate of William P. May, late of Barton, deceased, and running northerly on the east line of said land to land owned by T. C. Cobb, thence north-easterly on the line of said Cobb's land to land owned by —— Judkins, thence on the line of said land to land owned by Edward Barnard, thence on northerly side of said Barnard's land to land owned by William W. Grout, thence on northerly line of said Grout's land to land owned by John G. Hall and J. V. Hall, to land owned by Gry E. Rowell, thence on the northerly line of said Rowell's land to land owned by S. R. Corey, thence on the northerly and westerly line of said Corey's land, so as to include land owned by Merrick Mansfield, to land owned by John Bean, thence on northerly and westerly line of said Bean's land to land owned by Hiram Baxter, thence on westerly line of said Baxter's land to land owned by Cyrus Eaton, thence on said Eaton's westerly line to land owned by W. H. Martin, thence on westerly line of said Martin's land to Roaring Brook Park, thence on westerly line of said Park across the West Glover road to land owned by William O. Brown, thence along the westerly, southerly and easterly lines of said Brown's land to the south-east corner of land owned by Horatio Nye, thence in a straight line to the nearest point of land owned by Reuben Dewey, thence along the southerly and easterly lines of said Dewey's land to the cemetery, thence along the westerly and southerly lines of the cemetery, and across the highway, to a point on the easterly boundary of said highway in a right line with the south line of said cemetery, and from thence in a straight line to the place of beginning,— all surface measure,—shall hereafter be known by the name of the village of Barton; and by that name may have

perpetual succession, and be capable of suing and being
sued, may prosecute and defend in any court, may have
a common seal, and the same alter at pleasure, and shall
be capable of purchasing, holding and conveying real and
personal estate for the use of said village; and may, at
any annual or special meeting warned for that purpose, as
herein provided, lay a tax upon the polls of the inhabitants, and the ratable estate within the same, whether residents or non-residents, for any of the purposes herein
mentioned, and the trustees shall make out a rate-bill accordingly and deliver the same to the collector, who shall
have the same power to collect such tax as the collector
of town taxes, and may in like manner levy on and sell
property to satisfy the same, and for want thereof may
commit any person to jail against whom he has such a tax.

SEC. 2.   Said corporation shall have power to make such
prudential by-laws, rules and regulations as they shall
from time to time deem proper; to alter, repeal or amend
the same; such in particular as relate to their streets,
sidewalks, alleys, public highways, commons and parks,
the cleaning, repairing, improving the same; such as relate
to slaughter-houses and nuisances generally; such as
relate to a watch, and the lighting of the streets of said
village, the restraining of any cattle, horses, sheep, swine,
or geese, from running at large in said village; to establish
and regulate a market; to suppress and restrain disorderly
and gaming houses, and all descriptions of gaming, and
for the destruction of all instruments and devices used
for that purpose; to compel the owner or occupant of any
unwholesome, noisome, or offensive house or place to
remove or cleanse the same from time to time, as may be
necessary for the health or comfort of the inhabitants of

said village; to regulate the manufacture and keeping of gunpowder, ashes, and all other combustible or dangerous materials; to prevent immoderate riding or driving in the streets, and cruelty to animals; to regulate the erection of buildings, and prevent encumbering the streets, sidewalks and public alleys with firewood, lumber, carriages, boxes, or other things, and provide for the care, preservation and improvement of public grounds; to provide a supply of water for the protection of the village against fire, and for other purposes, and to regulate the use of the same; to compel all persons to remove from the sidewalks and gutters adjacent to the premises owned or occupied by them, all snow, ice, dirt, and garbage, and to keep such sidewalks and gutters clean; to license inn-keepers, keepers of saloons or victualing-houses, and auctioneers, under such regulations and for such sums of money as the trustees may prescribe; to regulate or restrain the use of rockets, squibs, fire-crackers, or other fire-works, in the streets or commons, and to prevent the practicing therein of any amusements having a tendency to injure or annoy persons passing thereon, or endanger the security of property; to regulate the making of alterations and repairs of stove-pipes, fire-places and other things from which damage by fire may be apprehended; and also to regulate the use of buildings in crowded localities for hazardous purposes; to provide for the preservation of buildings from fires by precautionary measures and inspections, and to establish and regulate a fire-department and fire-companies, and other matters deemed necessary for the proper regulation of the affairs of said village; provided, that no such by-laws shall be inconsistent with the constitution or laws of the state or the United States. And said corporation shall have power to impose such reasonable fine, penalty

20

or forfeiture for the breach of any by-laws by them established, as they may judge reasonable, which may be prosecuted for and recovered in an action of debt before any court proper to try the same, in which action it shall be deemed sufficient to declare generally, setting forth the particular by-law for a breach of which said suit is brought; and all fines, penalties and forfeitures so recovered shall be paid into the treasury of the village, to be expended for the benefit and improvement of the village, as may seem best to the board of trustees.

SEC. 3. Every person who resides within the limits of said village, and is a legal voter in town meeting in the town of Barton, shall be entitled to vote in any village meeting.

SEC. 4. At every annual meeting of said village, the qualified electors of said village shall, by ballot if called for, elect from among their number a moderator, a clerk, a treasurer, a collector of taxes, five trustees, three fire-wardens, and an attorney.

SEC. 5. It shall be the duty of the moderator to preside at all the meetings of said village, and he shall have the same power as a moderator of town meetings.

SEC. 6. It shall be the duty of the clerk to keep fair and accurate records of all the proceedings of said corporation, and he shall give copies of the same when required, with power to certify to the same. It shall be his duty to warn special meetings of said corporation, agreeably to the direction of the trustees, or a majority of them, and all annual meetings, by posting notice of the time and place of such meetings in at least three public places in said village, at least ten days previous to said time of meet-

ing, together with a statement of the business to be transacted. Any meeting of said corporation may be adjourned,
and any business may be transacted at such adjourned
meeting, which might, under the warning, have been transacted at the original meeting, as well as any other business, notice of which shall be given at such original meeting before the adjournment of the same.

SEC. 7. The treasurer and collector shall perform for
said corporation the same duties required by law respectively of a town treasurer and a collector of town taxes,
and shall have the same powers, shall proceed in the same
manner, be subject to the same liabilities, and give like
bonds to said corporation for the faithful performance of
their respective duties.

SEC. 8. The trustees shall have the general care and
management of the prudential interests of said village;
shall make out all taxes, and direct the expenditures of
all moneys belonging to said village, and shall draw all
orders upon the treasurer, and generally shall perform all
duties legally enjoined upon them by said corporation;
and all powers vested in said trustees may be performed
by a majority of them. The trustees, in case of the
death, removal or disability of any of the officers mentioned in this act, may perform their respective duties
until others are elected.

SEC. 9. All the territory embraced within the limits of
said village is hereby constituted a highway district of
the town of Barton, and all the highway taxes assessed
upon the polls and ratable estate therein shall be paid in
money; and the selectmen of the town of Barton shall
make out a tax-bill therefor, and deliver the same seasonably, as required by law, with a warrant for its collection,

to the collector of said village, who shall collect the same
as other taxes of said village are collected, and pay three
fourths of the same over to the treasurer of said village,
and the remaining one fourth of said tax to the town
treasurer; which money shall be drawn from said village
treasury by the trustees, and shall be expended by them
in building, constructing, sustaining, and repairing the
streets, highways, walks, alleys and lanes of said village;
and no surveyors of highways for said highway district
shall be required or chosen by said town.

SEC. 10. The trustees of said village may lay out, alter,
maintain and discontinue any street, road, lane, alley, or
walk in said village, and appraise and settle the damages
therefor, causing their proceedings to be recorded in the
town clerk's office in said town; provided, that any person
aggrieved by their proceedings shall have the like opportunity for applying to the county court for the county of
Orleans, to obtain redress, as is or may be allowed by law
to those aggrieved with the proceedings of selectmen in
similar cases. Said trustees in making, altering, or repairing sidewalks, shall have power, subject to the ordinances and by-laws of said village, on giving twelve days
notice to the parties of the time and place of hearing, to
assess the owners of lands adjoining such sidewalk as the
said trustees shall judge such lands to be benefited
thereby; and when they shall have made any such assessment, they shall make a report thereof, setting forth their
doings in that respect; which report they shall cause to
be recorded in the town clerk's office in said Barton,
and when so recorded, the amount so assessed shall be
and remain a lien, in the nature of the tax, upon the lands
so assessed, until the same shall be paid. From such

assessment there shall be the same right of appeal to the county court, and the same proceedings in respect to such appeal as is before provided in this section, and the final decision of the county court in the matter of such appeal shall, when the record thereof is duly recorded as aforesaid, be a lien upon the lands so assessed as above mentioned; but such appeal shall not delay the making, altering, or repairing such sidewalk; and if the owner of such lands shall neglect, for the space of six months after the final decision of said trustees, or in case of appeal to the county court, to pay to the village treasurer the amount of said assessment, the trustees shall issue their warrant for the collection of the same, directed to the village collector of taxes, who shall have authority to sell at public auction so much of said land as will satisfy said assessment and all legal fees, and who shall proceed in the same manner as collectors of town taxes are required by law to proceed in selling real estate at auction for the collection of town taxes.

Sec. 11. The trustees of said village shall have the sole power of granting licenses and vacating the same, within the limits of said village, agreeably to the by-laws, rules and ordinances thereof that the selectmen have by chapter ninety-five, and by section twenty-two of chapter one hundred and nineteen of the general statutes; and all moneys received for such licenses shall belong to the village treasury, and be paid into the same.

Sec. 12. The fire wardens of said village shall be present at all fires, having some distinguishing badge, fixed upon by the corporation; and said wardens, in time of fire, are hereby empowered to demand reasonable assistance r om the inhabitants of said village or any of them, and

all persons who may be present at such times are hereby
required to assist in extinguishing and preventing the
spreading of such fire, and to remove goods and effects out
of any house or other building endangered by such fire;
and the majority of said fire wardens present at any fire are
hereby further empowered to cause to be pulled down or removed such buildings as they may think necessary for the
purpose of preventing the progress or spreading of said
fire, and for that purpose may command the assistance of
any person in said village; they are also empowered, by
force if necessary, to suppress any tumults and disorders
at said fire, and all persons present are required to yield
strict obedience to said wardens and all orders given by
them; and if any person shall neglect or refuse to obey
the orders of said fire wardens or either of them, in time
of fire in said village, in any manner authorized in this
act, such offender shall, upon conviction before any
justice of the peace, forfeit and pay a fine not exceeding
fifty dollars, with costs of prosecution, to the treasurer of
said corporation.

SEC. 13. The trustees of said village may organize one
fire and hook and ladder company in said village, for the
purpose of preventing fires, and at the expense of said
village may purchase a fire engine and other necessary
implements; provided, the corporation shall so direct by
vote at a meeting duly called for that purpose.

SEC. 14. The trustees may make a grand list for said
village at any time prior to voting a tax, on the following
basis: the town grand list of Barton, comprised within the
limits of said village, shall constitute such grand list, and
the trustees shall deduct therefrom all real estate lying

and being without the limits of said village, as near as may be, and such list when completed shall be final and conclusive upon all concerned.

SEC. 15. No member of said village shall be deemed thereby incompetent to act as judge, justice of the peace, juror, sheriff, or constable in any cause or proceeding in which said corporation shall be interested.

SEC. 16. The annual meeting of said corporation, for the choice of officers, and for the transaction of any business specified in the warning of said meeting, shall be holden in the village of Barton, on the first Monday of January, each year. The first meeting of said corporation shall be warned by any two justices of the peace within said village, by posting notices of said meeting, as hereinbefore provided for the calling of like meetings by the clerk.

SEC. 17. This act shall take effect from its passage, and shall at all times be under the control of the legislature of this state to alter or repeal.

SEC. 18. At the first meeting of the legal voters of said village of Barton, to be holden as provided in section sixteen of this act, the justices warning said meeting shall insert in such warning an article as follows: "To see if the legal voters of the village of Barton will accept and approve of the act of incorporation of said village." And if a majority of the legal voters present at such meeting are in favor thereof, then this act shall be in full force, otherwise of no effect.

Approved, November 21, 1874.

No. 169.—AN ACT TO AMEND THE ACT TO INCOR-
PORATE THE VILLAGE OF BRATTLEBORO, AP-
PROVED OCTOBER 29, 1872.

*It is hereby enacted by the General Assembly of the State
of Vermont:*

SEC. 1. Section seventeen of said act is so amended
that the same shall read as follows:

When any person shall be dissatisfied with the decision
of said bailiffs in the award of damages for land taken for
a sewer or drain, or in any assessment for contribution
for the same, such persons may petition the county court
for Windham county for a re-assessment of such damages
or contribution, and any number of persons aggrieved
may join in the petition. Such petition shall be served on
the clerk of such village within sixty days next after the
said award of damages, or said assessment for contribution, shall be filed in said clerk's office.

SEC. 2. Sections twenty-seven, twenty-nine and thirty-
one of said act are hereby amended by striking out the
words, "waste pipes," whenever they may occur in said
sections, and inserting in lieu thereof the words, *distribut-
ing pipes.*

SEC. 3. This act to take effect from its passage.

Approved, November 18, 1874.

No. 170.—AN ACT IN AMENDMENT OF AND IN AD-
DITION TO AN ACT APPROVED NOVEMBER 26,
1872, ENTITLED "AN ACT IN AMENDMENT OF
AN ACT TO INCORPORATE THE CITY OF BUR-
· LINGTON," APPROVED NOVEMBER 22, 1864, AND
OF THE SEVERAL AMENDMENTS THEREOF
HERETOFORE ENACTED.

SECTION

1. Duties of city clerk defined.
2. Powers of · police officers; fees.
3. Powers and duties of superintendent of streets; to be under control of standing committee of board of aldermen on streets, who shall be street commissioners; duties of street commissioners; appeals from their decisions may be taken to county court; proceedings there; special powers of street commissioners; assessments made by same, how collected and paid.
4. City judge; may appoint clerk; fees of; temporary vacancy in office of city judge, occasioned by absence or disability, how filled; jurisdiction of judges; appeals, when not allowable; salary and fees of city judge; criminal prosecutions before, by whom brought; fees of city attorney in such cases; clerk to take receipt from officer to whom mittimus is delivered; costs before, how audited and paid; no trial by jury except in civil actions; city judge unable to attend, clerk to continue case; death or absence of judge not a cause for discontinuance; case then to be disposed of by his successor; petition to set aside judgment, how and when received; limitation of time for filing such petition; city judge, in sign-

SECTION

ing citation, to take recognizance for costs; may set aside said judgment and stay proceedings, in his discretion; to have same power over its records and proceedings as county court; vacancies in office of, how filled; further special powers of city judge; clerk to be the recording officer thereof.

5. Duties of inspectors of elections.
6. Exhibitions of common showmen and shows, to be regulated (by authorities); to regulate the running at large of certain animals, and prescribe penalties therefor; to cause removal of obstructions from sidewalks; may grant licenses; to regulate and alter grades of streets and direct construction of sidewalks; proceedings under this section: to manage and control public places, parks and commons; to regulate or prohibit putting up signs or awnings.
7. Taxes, how assessed and collected; limitation of city credit.
8. All taxes, except state and county, to be assessed by city council; how collected and paid; duties of city council and treasurer, thereto pertaining.
9. Subject to future legislation.
10. To take effect.

It is hereby enacted by the General Assembly of the State of Vermont:

Sec. 1. Section six of said act is hereby amended so as to read as follows :

The city clerk shall perform for the city the same duties devolving by law upon town clerks, except so far as the same are rendered unnecessary by this charter, and shall receive the same fees therefor. He shall be clerk of the city council and of the board of aldermen. He shall be sworn to the faithful performance of his duties, and his records, copies and certificates, shall be legal evidence in all courts, and for all purposes, as those of town clerks are. He shall have the exclusive charge and custody of the records and papers of the city, which shall not be taken out of or away from his office, unless upon the order or process of a court of competent jurisdiction.

Sec. 2. Section eight of said act is hereby amended by adding after the word " city," in the thirteenth line of said section, so as to read as follows :

All police officers shall have authority to serve anywhere within the state and return process in criminal causes returnable within the city : and for such duties there shall be taxed and allowed the fees provided by law for a sheriff, for similar services, which fees shall belong to the city, and be paid into the city treasury whenever such policeman shall be under pay from the city.

Sec. 3. Section nine of said act is hereby amended so as to read as follows :

The superintendent of streets, subject to the orders and ordinances of the city council, shall have the immediate care and supervision of the streets and public sewers of the city, and it shall be his duty to see that the same are properly constructed and kept in suitable and sufficient repair, and in the performance of such duties, shall have all the power and authority conferred by law upon highway surveyors and street commissioners of towns. He shall be under the general direction and control of the standing committee of the board of aldermen on streets and highways, which said standing committee shall consist of three members of such board, to be appointed by the board of aldermen annually in the month of April, and who shall hold their office for the term of one year from the first Monday in April, and until their successors shall be chosen and qualified; and said members of such standing committee shall constitute the board of street commissioners, and it shall be the duty of said board of street commissioners to see that all streets and highways, laid out and established in said city, are properly constructed, and when in their judgment the public good requires shall cause such streets and highways to be worked and graded the entire width thereof, and made in such a manner as they shall judge will best accommodate the public. Said board shall at all times be subject to the ordinances and orders of the city council. The street commissioners, so appointed, shall have the same power to lay out, alter and discontinue streets and highways as is vested by law in selectmen of towns; and all proceedings in respect to laying out, altering or discontinuing highways in said city, shall be had in the same manner as is prescribed by law in respect to such matters in towns, except that the street commissioners shall, in said city, act in the place of selectmen; and from all their acts, or omissions, or refusals to act in such respect, appeals may be taken to the county court in the same manner, and conducted with the same proceedings, as is provided by law for appeals from the decision of selectmen in such matters, except that in the appointment of commissioners by the county court in connection with any appeal to said court from any decision of the street commissioners, made under the authority of this act, no person shall be disqualified for appointment by said court as commissioner, by the fact that he is a resident or tax payer in said city.

Said street commissioners, in laying out or altering highways, shall have power, subject to the ordinances and by-laws of the city council, on giving twelve days notice of the time and place of hearing to the parties interested, in the manner provided by section ninety-three of chapter twenty-four of the general statutes, to assess the owners of lands adjoining such highway, so much of the expenses of opening, making or altering such highway, including land damages, as the said commissioners shall judge such lands will be benefited thereby; and if the highway has not been, at the time of making such assessment, actually opened, made or altered, as the case may be, the said commissioners shall estimate the probable expense of such opening, making or altering of the same, and make the aforesaid assessment upon such estimate. In case of assessment, the commissioners shall embrace in the statement of their decision in regard to the laying out or altering of the highway, a full statement of all assessments made by them, especially describing the lands so assessed, and such statement they shall cause to be recorded in full by the city clerk, in the city clerk's office; and when so recorded, the amount so assessed shall be and remain a lien, in the nature of a tax, upon the lands assessed, until the same shall be paid, except in cases of appeal from such assessment, or of appeal under section forty-one of chapter twenty-four of the general statutes. From such assessment there shall be the same right of appeal to the county court, and the same proceedings in respect to such appeal, as is before provided in this section ; and the final decision of the county court in the matter of such appeal shall, when the record thereof is duly recorded in the city clerk's office, as aforesaid, be a lien upon the lands so assessed as aforesaid. But such an appeal from such assessment, or an appeal from the allowance of land damages, shall not delay the opening, making or altering of such highway ; and if the owners of such land, so assessed, shall neglect for sixty days after the recording of the final decision of the said street commissioners, as aforesaid, in case there shall be no appeal from such decision ; and in case of appeal to the county court within sixty days after the recording of the final decision of said court, as aforesaid, to pay to the city treasurer the amount of said assessment, the city treasurer shall issue his warrant to the constable of the city for the collection thereof; and such constable shall have authority to sell at public auction so much of said land as will satisfy said assessment and all legal fees ; and he shall proceed in the same manner as collectors of town taxes are required by law to proceed in selling real estate at auction for the collection of town taxes. In all cases of appeal under section forty-one of chapter twenty-four of the general statutes, the question of assessment upon the owners of adjoining lands shall also pass to the county court, and shall be referred to and be reported upon by the commissioners to be appointed by such court, and shall be adjudicated by said court.

The street commissioners are authorized, subject to the orders and ordinances of the city council, to establish, construct and maintain public sewers in the city, and they may assess the owners of lands or buildings adjoining the streets through which such sewers may be established opposite such lands or buildings, so much of the expenses of constructing such sewers, as the said commissioners shall judge such lands or buildings to be benefited thereby, and the street commissioners are also authorized and empowered to establish, construct and maintain public sewers, in and through the lands of individuals and corporations, on making compensation for lands taken therefor, in the same manner as is prescribed by law in the laying out and establishing of highways. And they may assess the owners of lands through which such sewers may be established and constructed, in the same manner, and to the same extent, as is hereinbefore provided in respect to public sewers, established and constructed in the streets of the city; and the same proceedings shall be had, and the same rights of appeal shall exist, as in the case of the laying out and establishing of highways, and the same lien shall attach, and be enforced in the same manner in respect to such assessments as is in this act provided in respect to assessments by the street commissioners upon adjoining land owners in case of laying out or making highways.

Whenever a petition in writing shall be presented to the board of aldermen, signed by the owner or owners of a majority of the frontage upon any street, lane or alley in said city, or of any portion of such street, lane or alley, particularly describing such street, lane or alley, or portion thereof, and praying that the same may be graded, paved or macadamized, curbed and guttered, or that either of such improvements may be made, the city coun-il shall forthwith order and direct the street commission-ers to cause such street, lane or alley, or such portion thereof as shall be specified in such petition, or order of said city council, to be graded, paved or macadamized, as the case may be, and curbed and guttered, all at the ex-pense and cost of all the owners of lands or buildings adjacent to, or abutting upon such street, lane or alley, or part thereof, specified and described in such petition or order of said city council. And the street commis-sioners on giving twelve days notice of the time and place of hearing, to the parties interested, in the manner provided in section ninety-three of chapter twenty-four of the general statutes, shall assess the cost or expense thereof upon all the lands and buildings fronting upon or adjacent to the street, lane or alley, or part thereof, spec-ified and described in such petition or order, graded, paved or macadamized, curbed and guttered, as aforesaid, according to the frontage of such lands or buildings upon such street, lane or alley, or part thereof. And said street commissioners shall make up a statement of all such as-sessments made by them, particularly describing the lands or buildings assessed, and such statement they shall forthwith cause to be recorded in the city clerk's office, and when so recorded shall be and remain a lien, in the nature of a tax upon the lands or buildings assessed, until the same shall be paid.

It shall be the duty of the city clerk to place said lists of assessments in the hands of the city treasurer for col-lection, as soon after he shall have recorded the same as may be. The city treasurer shall thereupon, forthwith notify, in writing, the owner or owners of lands or buildings so assessed, their agents or attorneys, stating therein the amount of such assessment, and all such assessments shall be paid to the city treasurer, within sixty days after the same shall have been filed for record in the city clerk's office,and if the owner or owners,of any such lands or buildings so assessed as aforesaid, shall neglect, refuse or omit to pay any such assessment to the city treasurer, within the time aforesaid, the city treasurer shall issue his warrant to the constable of the city for the collection thereof, and such constable shall proceed to collect the same, in the manner hereinbefore prescribed in this section, for the collection and enforcement of assessments made in cases of the laying out or altering of highways.

Sec. 4. Section eleven of said act, is hereby amended so as to read as follows:

Sec. 11. A city judge shall be annually elected from among 'the freemen of the city, on the first Tuesday of March. The city judge shall be judge of the city court, which shall be a court of record, and shall have a seal. The city judge shall appoint a clerk of the city court, and may remove him at pleasure. The clerk of said court shall be entitled to receive the sum of fifty cents for recording each case in said court, and the same fees for copies of records, as are allowed by law to clerks of county courts, and such additional compensation as may be allowed him by the city judge out of his salary. The city court shall be open at all times, and shall be held by the city judge, except that in case of his absence from the city, or inability to serve, the board of aldermen may appoint from among the justices of the peace in said city, some one of them to act in his place and hold said court during such absence or disability; and such justice of the peace, so acting and holding said court, shall have and exercise all the powers of the city judge.

The city court shall have jurisdiction of all actions of a civil nature, including replevin and trespass on the freehold, if either of the parties reside in said city at the time of the commencement of the action, or if neither party reside in the state at such time, where the debt, damages, or value of the goods and chattels replevied or other matter in demand, does not exceed five hundred dollars, but nothing herein contained shall affect the original jurisdiction of the county court, as now provided by law; provided, that the provisions of section thirty-three of chapter thirty-one of the general statutes, in regard to the town in which writs in certain suits therein described shall be made returnable, shall apply to said city court. The city court may try and determine all prosecutions for such criminal offenses committed within the county of Chittenden as are not punishable by death or imprisonment in the state prison, except offenses within the jurisdiction of a justice of the peace to try and determine, which are committed without said city, by a respondent residing without said city. The city court is empowered to cause to be apprehended and committed to prison, or bound over with sufficient sureties for trial by the county court, all persons charged with crimes committed in said county, exceeding its jurisdiction to try. The city court shall have exclusive original jurisdiction of all complaints and prosecutions for violations of city ordinances and by-laws. In all prosecutions in which, by law, a

21

sentence of imprisonment in the county jail may be rendered, the city court may, in its discretion, render a sentence of imprisonment at hard labor in the city house of correction, for a term not exceeding six months. In all criminal causes before said court, there shall be the same right of appeal to the county court as is secured by law in criminal causes before a justice of the peace, and such appeal shall be taken in the same manner, and under the same regulations, as in criminal causes before a justice of the peace. From the judgment of the city court in all civil cases, excepting as hereinafter provided, an appeal may be taken to the county court, under the same regulations as are provided for appeals from the judgment of a justice of the peace in civil actions. No appeal shall be allowed in either of the following cases :

First. When judgment was rendered by nonsuit default.

. *Second.* In actions where neither the *ad damnum* in the plaintiff's writ, nor the sum demanded by the declaration, nor the specifications or exhibits of the plaintiff on trial, shall exceed the sum of fifty dollars, excepting actions for fine or penalty, actions of trespass on the freehold, actions in which the legality of the assessment or collection of any tax is concerned, and actions where the defendant pleads in offset any *bona fide* demand or demands exceeding the sum of fifty dollars, and actions where the defendant *bona fide* pleads the authority of any court, civil or military, in excuse or justification ; or where the defendant shall *bona fide* plead, in excuse or justification, that he was acting as public officer, under or by virtue of any tax-bill or military warrant; except that either party, in any action for the recovery of any subscription to the capital stock of any corporation, may appeal, and in all cases where the title to land is concerned, either party may appeal.

Third. In actions of replevin for property, the value whereof, as fixed by the appraisers, does not exceed twenty dollars.

Fourth. In criminal prosecutions where the respondent is acquitted.

In all prosecutions for criminal offenses within the jurisdiction of the city court to try and determine, and in all civil cases before said court, exceptions to the decisions of said court, upon questions of law, may be taken to the supreme court in the same manner and under the same regulations as provided by law for exceptions from the county court to the supreme court in criminal and civil cases respectively. But no such exceptions shall be allowed when an appeal is taken to the county court.

When any person shall be in actual confinement in the jail of Chittenden county, by virtue of a complaint for any crime or misdemeanor alleged to have been committed in said county, the city court shall, upon the application of such person, order the state's attorney of said county to file an information against such person; and said court shall have the same powers, and perform the same duties, and under the same regulations, as are prescribed in sections eighty-six, eighty-seven and eighty-nine of chapter thirty of the general statutes, for cases where such application is made to the supreme court of said county.

The city judge shall receive a salary of three hundred dollars per annum, to be paid by the state treasurer, and, in addition, shall be entitled to the fees taxed for him as costs in the city court, according to law, and shall also receive a fee of one dollar and fifty cents in full of all fees, in naturalization cases, to be paid by the person naturalized, and such naturalization shall be in accordance with the statutes of this state.

In all causes, both civil and criminal, before the city court, the city judge, and parties, shall be entitled to tax and receive double the costs allowed by law to justices of the peace, and parties respectively, in suits or prosecutions before justices of the peace.

The city judge shall also be entitled to tax and receive the sum of one dollar, for each bill of exceptions allowed and signed by him; he shall also fix the amount to be paid to the clerk of the city court, as his additional compensation, from, and out of his salary as city judge. Criminal prosecutions before said court may be brought by the state's attorney, city attorney, and any grand juror in said county; but all prosecutions for a breach of any city ordinance shall be brought solely by the city attorney; but in case of the absence of the city attorney from the city, or by reason of his inability to serve, prosecutions for breach of city ordinances may be brought by a city grand juror, in the city court; and prosecutions for criminal offenses may be brought by the city attorney before justices of the peace; and the city attorney shall, in all cases, be subject to all and the same penalties and liabilities for any neglect or violation of official duty, as are or shall be imposed by law upon state's attorneys for similar offenses. The city attorney shall be entitled to tax and receive, in addition to the fees provided by law for town grand jurors, the sum of three dollars for every prosecution or complaint in said city court, for a breach of any city ordinance; and in all other prosecutions in said court for criminal offenses, excepting those under chapter ninety-four of the general statutes, respecting the traffic in intoxicating drinks, or any amendments thereof or additions thereto, the prosecuting officer shall be entitled to tax and receive the same fees provided by law for town grand jurors, and in addition thereto, the sum of one dollar and fifty cents for each trial in which the respondent shall be convicted. All fines, penalties and forfeitures recovered in said court shall be paid to the city judge, and by him into the city treasury, excepting in cases where, by law, express provision to the contrary is made; and when any mittimus shall be issued by the city court in any cause where a fine shall have been imposed and made payable to said city, or where a penalty shall have been imposed, in which said city is interested, the clerk of the court shall take from the officer to whom the mittimus shall be delivered, a receipt therefor, and immediately transmit or deliver the same to the city treasurer; and whenever any justice of the peace in said city shall issue a mittimus in any cause, where the fine or penalty imposed by him is payable to, or in which the city may be interested, he shall take from the officer to whom such mittimus shall be delivered, a receipt therefor, and immediately transmit or deliver the same to the city treasurer. In criminal causes in said court, the costs shall be audited and paid as is provided by law for costs in crim-

inal causes before a justice of the peace. In all prosecutions for nuisances, the city court shall have power, subject
to such restrictions as may be prescribed by the city council,
in a summary manner to order such nuisance to be abated
and removed, and to issue such warrants as shall be necessary to carry such orders into effect.

Said city court shall have all the powers granted by law
to justices of the peace in the county of Chittenden, and
the judge of said court shall be authorized to perform the
duties required by law to be performed by justices of the
peace; and all existing provisions of law applicable to proceedings before justices of the peace, and the effect thereof,
shall apply to said city court, except that in trials by jury,
it shall be the duty of the city judge to instruct the jury
on questions of law, and that there shall be no trial by
jury in said court except in civil actions, and with the further exception, and that writs of *mesne* and final process,
and mittimusses, returnable to said court, may be signed
either by the city judge or the clerk of said court, and that
all affidavits under sections seventy-six and seventy-seven of
chapter thirty-three of the general statutes, may be filed
either with the judge or the clerk of said court; provided,
that all hearings under section seventy-eight of said chapter
thirty-three shall be had before the city judge. Whenever
the city judge shall be unable to attend at the time appointed for the trial of any cause, the clerk of the court shall continue the same for a period not exceeding three weeks; and
the death, resignation, removal from the city, permanent
inability to serve, or expiration of the term of office, on the
part of the city judge, shall not cause a discontinuance or

transfer to another jurisdiction of any cause pending in said city court, but the same shall continue pending in said city court, and be tried and disposed of by his successor in office. And when any judgment shall have been rendered by said court in any action upon default, and the defendant or any trustee therein shall have been unjustly deprived of his day in court, by fraud, accident or mistake, or such defendant shall have been unjustly deprived of a hearing in the assessment of damages in any action, or when a party or trustee shall have been prevented from entering an appeal from the judgment of said court, by fraud, accident or mistake, the city court may on the petition of the person aggrieved, in its discretion, and on such terms and conditions as such court shall judge reasonable, reverse and set aside such judgment and proceed to hear, try and determine such action, and make all necessary orders therein, in the same manner as if no judgment had been rendered; and shall be entitled to the same fees as on the trial.

No petition shall be sustained under the foregoing provisions unless brought within two years next after the rendition of such judgment, and when brought, the same verified by oath, with a citation annexed thereto, signed by the city judge, shall be served upon the adverse party, at least six days, and not more than thirty days, before the time appointed in such citation for trial.

The city judge, on signing such citation, shall take sufficient surety by way of recognizance to the adverse party, which shall be minuted on such citation, conditioned, that if the petitioner shall fail to prosecute his petition to effect, or finally to recover in such action, he will pay to the adverse party all intervening damages and costs that shall have accrued to him by reason of such petition being preferred.

The city judge, from a consideration of the facts set forth in such petition and verified as aforesaid, may in his discretion, order a stay of proceedings on such judgment, whether execution shall have issued or not, until a final decision shall be made on such petition.

And the city court shall have the same power over its judgments, records and proceedings as is now vested in the county court by statute or common law, and may exercise in connection therewith, all the powers of courts of record at common law.

In case of death, resignation, removal from the city, or permanent inability to serve, on the part of the city judge, his office shall be filled by the board of aldermen from among the legal voters of the city. The city judge shall have power to take affidavits and depositions to be used in any court in the state, and also to take acknowledgments of deeds or other conveyances of lands, or any estate or interest therein.

And the city judge is further authorized and empowered to perform all the duties required to be performed by judges of the supreme court under and by sections thirty-four, thirty-five and thirty-six of chapter thirty-six of the general statutes, and shall have and exercise in such cases all the powers conferred upon judges of the supreme court by said sections.

The clerk of said court shall be the recording officer thereof, and shall furnish to any person, on demand and tender of the legal fees, certified copies of any of the records, proceedings or minutes of such court, under the seal thereof.

SEC. 5. Section eighteen of said act is hereby amended so as to read, after the twenty-first line thereof, as follows:

Such inspectors of election shall, immediately after any election for representative of the city and senators to the general assembly, and also of member of congress, and of presidential electors, whenever elections for such shall have been held in said city, certify the result of such election in their respective wards, to the city clerk, who shall make a record thereof.

SEC. 6. Number three of section twenty of said act, is hereby amended so as to read as follows:

3. To regulate the exhibitions of common showmen and shows of every kind not interdicted by law, and to regulate, restrain or license itinerant venders and peddlers.

Number thirteen of said section twenty of said act, is hereby amended so as to read as follows:

13. To restrain or regulate the running at large of cattle, horses, swine, sheep and goats, and to regulate or restrain the running at large of dogs. And in addition to the tax now imposed by the laws of this state upon the owners or keepers of dogs, to impose upon or require of the owner or keeper of any dog or dogs, such additional tax or a license fee for the keeping thereof, and prescribe such penalties in default thereof as may be deemed necessary. And all moneys received hereunder, shall be paid into the city treasury and belong to said city.

Number sixteen of said section twenty, is hereby amended so as to read as follows:

16. To compel all persons to remove from the sidewalks and gutters in front of the premises owned or occupied by them, all snow, ice, dirt and garbage, and to keep such sidewalks and gutters clean, and to compel the owners or occupants of any land or premises in the city, to cut and remove from the streets and sidewalks in front of such land or premises, all grass, thistles and weeds growing, or being thereon, under such regulations as may be prescribed therefor.

Number seventeen of said section twenty, is hereby amended so as to read as follows:

17. To license inn-keepers, keepers of saloons, victualing houses, billiard saloons and auctioneers, under such regulations as shall be prescribed therefor; and all moneys paid for such licenses shall belong to the city, and be paid into the city treasury.

Number twenty-two of said section twenty of said act, is hereby amended so as to read as follows:

22. To regulate, establish and alter the grade of streets, and the grade and width of sidewalks, and the construction thereof, and to prescribe the material to be used therein; and also, to provide, order and direct that the sidewalks upon such streets as the city council shall designate, shall be constructed at the expense of the owner or owners of the land or buildings, adjacent thereto. And in case any such owner or owners shall neglect, refuse or omit to construct such sidewalk in the manner, within the time, and of the material prescribed by the city council, the street commissioners are

hereby authorized and empowered to construct the same, and to assess the lands or buildings of such owner or owners so neglecting, refusing or omitting as aforesaid, adjacent to, or abutting on any such sidewalk, so constructed by said street commissioners, the cost or expense thereof,—such assessments to be apportioned among the owners of such lands or buildings, fronting as aforesaid, according to their frontage upon such sidewalk, to be made in the manner and in accordance with the provisions of section three of this act, relating to the making assessments for the laying out or altering of highways. Such assessments when made and recorded in the office of the city clerk of said city, shall be and remain a lien upon such lands or buildings, in the nature of a tax, and may be enforced and collected in the manner prescribed for the collection of assessments in said section three.

Section twenty of said act is hereby further amended, by adding after the twenty-seventh clause in said section, the following two clauses, numbered respectively twenty-eight and twenty-nine, to wit:

28. To manage and control the public places, parks and commons in said city, and to regulate the use of the same by the public, and to prevent and punish trespasses or willful injuries to, or upon any fountain, shade or ornamental tree or shrub, building or structure placed therein, by or under the orders of the city council, in such a manner as shall not be inconsistent with the laws of this state.

29. To regulate, or prohibit the suspending or putting up of any sign or awning in or over any street, lane, alley, common or other public place in the city; and whenever the

public good may require, to order and direct that any such sign or awning heretofore erected or suspended as aforesaid, shall be taken down or removed.

SEC. 7. Section twenty-four of said act, is hereby amended so as to read as follows:

Sec. 24. The mayor shall assess on the grand list of the city, all state and county taxes. The highway tax for the city shall be collected in money. Warrants for the collection of state and county taxes shall be signed by the mayor or a justice of the peace in the city. The city council may, in addition to the taxes required by law to be raised upon the grand list of the city, annually assess upon such grand list a tax for city purposes, which shall not exceed two hundred cents upon the dollar thereof, exclusive of the tax for the support of schools, except when authorized by the legal voters of the city in general meeting assembled. And said city council may also annually assess upon the grand list of the city, a tax not exceeding fifteen cents on the dollar thereof, the proceeds of which said tax shall be applied to the sinking fund, for the redemption of the bonded debt of the city. The money raised by taxation, from fines and from other lawful sources, shall constitute the entire sum from which appropriations and payment are to be made, according to law, by or under the authority of the city council; and the credit of the city, other than by temporary loans, not exceeding seventy-five cents on the dollar of the grand list of the city for the time being, shall not be pledged except by authority of the legal voters of the city.

SEC. 8. Section twenty-eight of said act, is hereby amended so as to read as follows:

Sec. 28. All taxes, except state and county taxes, shall be assessed by the city council; and whenever any tax shall be asses-ed by the city council, the tax-bill shall be delivered to the city treasurer, to whom the taxes so assessed shall be paid; and if at the expiration of one month and eight days from the time said tax-bill shall have been delivered to said treasurer, any taxes shall remain unpaid, the treasurer shall make up a tax-bill, of all taxes which remain unpaid, for the collection of all such taxes so remaining unpaid, and annex a warrant to the said tax-bill, adding to each unpaid tax five per cent, which warrant shall be returnable to such city treasurer in sixty days from its date, and shall be addressed and delivered to the constable of the city; and it shall be the duty of such constable to collect all taxes legally imposed, contained in such tax-bill and warrant, including such five per cent, and pay the same to the city treasurer on or before the time when such warrant is made returnable, subject to such abatement of such taxes as may be made by the board for the abatement of taxes. The city council may extend the time for the collection and payment of such taxes and five per cent, and the return of any such warrant by such constable, from time to time, as in their judgment shall be proper, not exceeding one year in the whole. Such constable shall have the same power and authority in the collection of such taxes and five per cent, and shall proceed in the same manner therein, and be under the same duties and liabilities, and have the same privileges in respect thereto, as the general laws of the state now or may hereafter prescribe in regard to the collection of taxes by constables or collectors of taxes in towns, and he shall be entitled to the same fees for the service of such warrant on the respective delinquent tax payers named therein, and the collection of such taxes and five per cent, as collectors of taxes are by law now entitled to, when they levy on persons or estate, and such fees shall be collected by such constable of such delinquent tax payers, and shall be the only compensation of such constable for the collection and payment to the city treasurer, of such taxes and five per cent. Public notice of the fact shall be given by the city treasurer when any tax shall be assessed by the city council and the tax bill delivered to him, by publication in all the daily and weekly newspapers published in said city for the period of eight days immediately succeeding the time when such tax-bill shall have been delivered to the city treasurer, and in such notice the time shall be named, when, according to this section, all unpaid taxes on such tax-bill will be placed in the hands of the constable for collection, as aforesaid.

Sec. 9. This act shall be a public act, and may be altered, amended or repealed by the general assembly, whenever the public good may require.

Sec. 10. This act shall take effect from its passage.

Approved, November 24, 1874.

No. 171.—AN ACT TO INCORPORATE THE VILLAGE OF DANBY, IN THE COUNTY OF RUTLAND.

It is hereby enacted by the General Assembly of the State of Vermont:

SEC. 1. All that territory within the following bounds in the towns of Danby and Mount Tabor, in the county of Rutland, to wit: Beginning at a point in the highway leading from Danby Boro, so-called, to Wallingford where the lane leading to the dwelling house of Henry Wilber diverges from said highway, thence south on the west line of said highway to the south line of lands of Mrs. H A. Griffin; thence west on Mrs. Griffin's south line to the southwest corner thereof, thence north on the west line of said Mrs. Griffin's land to lands of E. A. Smith, thence west and south on the south and east lines of said Smith's land to land of Charles H. Congdon, thence on said Congdon's west line to lands of Willard Baker; thence south on the west line of said Willard Baker's land to Mill Brook; thence down the channel of Mill Brook to the west line of Daniel Kelley's wood lot; thence south and east on the line of said Kelley's wood lot to the land of David A. Kelley, thence east on the south line of David A. Kelley's land to the highway, thence south on the west line of said highway to the south line of land of Mary A. Sowle, thence on the south and east lines of Mary A. Sowle's land to the south line of lands of Nathan L. Baker, thence east on said Baker's south line to lands of John B. Griffith, thence on the west and south lines of said Griffith's land to Otter Creek; thence down the channel of Otter Creek to Charles H. Griffith's south line; thence east on said Griffith's south line to the southeast corner of said Griffith's land, thence north on said Griffith's east line and in the continuance thereof to lands of John B. St. Marrs, thence east and north on the lines of St. Marr's land to the Lapham Branch, so-called, thence up said branch to the east line of Charles II. Congdon's land, thence north on said Congdon's east line to the northeast corner of said Congdon's land, thence west on Congdon's north line to the place of beginning—shall hereafter be known by the name of the Village of Danby; and by that name may have perpetual succession, sue and be sued, and prosecute and defend in any court, may have a common seal and the same alter at pleasure, and shall be capable of purchasing, holding and conveying real and personal estate for the use of said village, and may at any annual or special meeting warned for that purpose, as herein provided, lay a tax upon the polls of the inhabitants and the ratable estate within the same, whether of residents or non-residents, for any of the purposes herein mentioned, and the trustees shall make out a rate-bill accordingly and deliver the same to the collector, who shall have the same power to collect such tax as the collector of town taxes, and may in like manner levy on and sell property to satisfy the same, and for want thereof may commit any person to jail against whom he has such a tax.

Sec. 2. Said corporation shall have power to make such prudential by-laws, rules and regulations as the inhabitants thereof shall from time to time deem proper; to alter, repeal or amend the same; such in particular as relate to their streets, sidewalks, alleys, public highways, sewers, commons and parks, the cleaning, repairing, improving the same; such as relate to slaughter-houses, and nuisances generally; such as relate to a police force, and the lighting of the streets of said village, the restraining of any cattle, horses, sheep, swine or geese from running at large in said village; to establish and regulate a market; to suppress and restrain disorderly and gaming houses, and all descriptions of gaming, to compel the owner or occupant of any unwholesome, noisome, or offensive house or place to remove or cleanse the same from time to time, as may be necessary for the health or comfort of the inhabitants of said village; to prohibit or regulate the manufacture and keeping of gunpowder, coal, ashes, and all other combustible or dangerous materials; to prevent immoderate riding or driving in the streets, and cruelty to animals; to regulate the erection of buildings, and prevent encumbering the streets, sidewalks and public alleys with firewood, lumber, carriages, boxes, or other things, and provide for the care, preservation and improvement of public grounds; to provide a supply of water for the protection of the village against fire, and for other purposes, and to regulate the use of the same; to compel all persons to remove from the sidewalks and gutters adjacent to the premises owned and occupied by them, all snow, ice, dirt, and garbage, and

to keep such sidewalks and gutters clean; to license inn-
keepers, keepers of saloons or victualing-houses, and auctioneers, under such regulations and for such sums of money
as the trustees may prescribe; to regulate or restrain the
use of rockets, squibs, fire-crackers, or other fire-works, in the
streets or commons, and to prevent the practicing therein of
any amusements having a tendency to injure or annoy persons passing thereon, or endanger the security of property;
to regulate the making of alterations and repairs of stove-
pipes, fire-places and other things from which damage by
fire may be apprehended; to provide for the preservation
of buildings from fires by precautionary measures and inspections, and to establish and regulate a fire-department
and fire-companies, and other matters deemed necessary
for the proper regulation of the affairs of said village; provided, that no such by-laws shall be inconsistent with the
constitution or laws of this state or the United States.
And said corporation shall have power to impose such reasonable fine, penalty or forfeiture for the breach of any by-
laws by them established, as they may judge reasonable,
which may be prosecuted for and recovered in an action of
debt before any court proper to try the same, in which action it shall be deemed sufficient to declare generally, setting forth the particular by-law for a breach of which said
suit is brought; and all fines, penalties and forfeitures so
recovered shall be paid into the treasury of the village,
to be expended for the benefit and improvement of the village, as may seem best to the board of trustees.

Sec. 3. Every person who resides within the limits of
said village, and is a legal voter in town meeting in either
of the towns of Danby or Mount Tabor, shall be entitled
to vote in any village meeting.

SEC. 4. At every annual meeting of said village, the qualified voters of said village shall, by ballot if called for, elect from among their number a moderator, a clerk, a treasurer, a collector of taxes, five trustees, and three fire wardens.

SEC. 5. It shall be the duty of the moderator to pre-side at all meetings of said village, and he shall have the-the same power as a moderator of town meetings.

SEC. 6. It shall be the duty of the clerk to keep fair and accurate records of all proceedings of said corpora-tion, and he shall give copies of the same when re-quired, with power to certify to the same. It shall be the duty of the clerk to warn special meetings of said corpora-tion, when directed by a majority of the trustees, or on petition of any ten legal voters, and all annual meetings, without direction or petition, by posting notices of the time and place of said meetings in at least three public places in said village, at least ten days previous to said time of meet-ing, together with a statement of the business to be trans-acted, which business may be transacted at said meeting, or at any meetings, to which the same may be adjourned.

SEC. 7. The treasurer and collector of taxes shall per-form for said corporation the duties corresponding to the duties of town treasurers and collectors of town taxes, and shall have the same powers, shall proceed in the same manner, and be subject to the same liabilities, and give the same bonds to said corporation for the faithful perform-ance of their respective duties.

SEC. 8. The trustees shall have the general care and management of the prudential interests of said village; shall be the general administrative officers thereof, shall have the charge and control of highways, sewers, side-walks, and shall perform, all and singular, the powers given to said corporation, not specially reposed in some other officers or body; shall make out all taxes and rate-bills voted by said corporation, direct the expenditure of all moneys belonging to said village, and draw all orders upon the treasurer thereof, and generally shall perform all duties legally enjoined upon them by said corporation; and all powers vested in said trustees may be performed by a majority of them.

SEC. 9. The territory embraced within the limits of said village in the town of Danby shall constitute a high-way district of said town, and the territory embraced within the limits of said village in the town of Mount Tabor shall constitute a highway district in that town, and the highway taxes assessed upon the polls and ratable estate of said village, shall be paid, worked out and ex-pended on the highways in said village, under the direction and control of the trustees; and the selectmen of the towns of Danby and Mount Tabor respectively shall make out a rate-bill therefor and deliver the same to said trustees, who shall collect, lay out and expend the same upon the highways of said village, and said village may vote such further sum as may be deemed expedient for building sidewalks, repairing streets or making improvements thereto, and no highway surveyor shall be chosen by either of said towns for said village or any part thereof; and any contract now in force between either of said towns and any person as to keeping its highways in repair, shall re-main in full force the same as it would be and remain if this act had not passed.

SEC. 10. The trustees of said village shall have the

solo power of granting licenses and vacating the same within the limits of the said village, agreeably to the by-laws, rules and ordinances thereof, for any and all purposes that said village may grant licenses, and for all purposes for which selectmen may grant the same in towns, under the laws of this state.

SEC. 11. It shall be the duty of the fire wardens of said village to be present at fires therein, and direct as to the extinguishing thereof, and preventing the spread of fires, the removal of goods from houses on fire, or in imminent danger of being consumed; and they are empowered to pull down or cause to be removed, such buildings as they shall judge necessary to prevent the progress or spreading of said fire, and they are hereby empowered to demand reasonable assistance from any and all persons present, in the performance of their duties, and all persons present at any fire in said village shall give strict and prompt obedience to all legal and reasonable orders given by any fire warden; and said fire wardens shall, while in the performance of their duties at any fire in said village, have all the powers of a constable in suppressing tumults and breaches of the peace taking place in their presence.

SEC. 12. The trustees of said village shall carry out all votes of said corporation in organizing fire companies, hook and ladder companies, and purchasing engines and apparatus for extinguishing fires.

SEC. 13. The grand list of the polls of the inhabitants and ratable estate within said village, as made out by the listers of the towns of Danby and Mount Tabor respectively, shall be the grand list of said village, and the trustees shall make a copy of said list and file the same in the office of the clerk of said village, within ten days after the same shall be completed and filed in the town clerks' offices.

Sec. 14.   No inhabitant or tax payer of said village shall be deemed thereby incompetent to act as judge, justice of the peace, juror, sheriff, or constable, in any cause or proceeding in which said corporation shall be interested.

Sec. 15.   The annual meeting of said corporation, for the choice of officers, and for the transaction of any business specified in the warning of said meeting, shall be holden in said village on the first Monday in January, in each year.   The first meeting of said corporation shall be warned by any two justices of the peace in the county of Rutland, by posting notices of said meeting, as hereinbefore provided for the calling of meetings by the village clerk.

Sec. 16. · At the first meeting of the legal voters of said village of Danby, to be holden as heretofore provided, the justices warning said meeting shall insert in such warning an article as follows: " To see if the legal voters of the village of Danby will accept and approve of the act of incorporation of said village."   And if a majority of the legal voters present at such meeting are in favor thereof, then this act shall be in full force, otherwise of no effect.

Sec. 17.   This act shall take effect from its passage.

Approved, November 24, 1874.

No. 172.—AN ACT IN ADDITION TO AN ACT EN-
TITLED AN ACT TO INCORPORATE THE VIL-
LAGE OF FAIRHAVEN, APPROVED OCTOBER 31,
1865.

It is hereby enacted by the General Assembly of the State of Vermont :

SEC. 1.   The village of Fairhaven, in its corporate capacity, is hereby authorized and empowered to procure a
supply of pure water for public and private uses in said
village ; and for that purpose it may take and hold, by
purchase or otherwise, such ponds, springs, streams, water
sources and waters thereof, and such lands under and
around the same, within the limits of the town of Fairhaven, as may be necessary for the purposes aforesaid.

SEC. 2.   The said village corporation, for the purpose of
using the water taken as aforesaid, may build and construct dams and reservoirs, lay pipes and aqueducts, and

connect the same with pipes and reservoirs which may hereafter be laid or constructed by said village corporation, to convey the water taken as aforesaid to the reservoirs of said village and the buildings and dwelling houses therein, and may take, by purchase or otherwise any lands which may be necessary therefor, in said town of Fairhaven, and may also lay pipes along and across the highways of said town, and in and across the streets, alleys and lanes of said village.

SEC. 3. Said village corporation shall, within sixty days after taking any springs, streams, ponds, water sources or lands under the provisions of this act, file in the office of the town clerk of said town of Fairhaven, a description of the same sufficiently accurate for identification at all times.

SEC. 4. The said village corporation shall be liable to pay all damages that shall be sustained by any person or persons in their property by the taking of any lands, springs of water, water sources, streams or ponds, by the construction of any dams or reservoirs, or the laying of any pipes, hydrants or aqueducts, or other works for the purposes aforesaid; and if such person shall be dissatisfied with the sum offered or tendered to him by the trustees of said village for his damages in the premises, such person may petition the county court for the county of Rutland for the appointment of three commissioners to assess his damages in the premises; which petition shall be served on one of the trustees of said village, within sixty days next after the filing of the description of the property so taken as aforesaid in the town clerk's office of said town, as required by the third section of this act.

SEC. 5. Such proceedings shall be had in said Rutland county court, on said petition, as are provided by law for the re-assessment of damages for land taken for highways, excepting that the notice required to be given by said commissioners shall be given to one of the trustees of said village.

SEC. 6. The trustees of said village, until otherwise provided by its by-laws or ordinances, shall have the control and management of the aqueduct, when laid, as provided in this act, by said village, and may from time to time grant permits to use the water from said aqueduct, upon such terms and conditions, and for such compensation or rent, as shall from time to time be prescribed by rules and regulations hereafter established by said village corporation.

SEC. 7. Said village corporation is hereby authorized and empowered to adopt, make, establish, amend or repeal ordinances, by-laws, rules and regulations for the management and control of said aqueduct, and to impose such fine, penalty or forfeiture for the breach thereof, not exceeding twenty-five dollars for any one offense, as may be judged reasonable by said corporation, which may be recovered as provided in section two of the act incorporating said village.

SEC. 8. Any person who shall divert the water or any part thereof from the sources which shall be taken by said village corporation, pursuant to the provisions of this act, or shall maliciously corrupt the same or render it impure, or who shall willfully destroy or injure any dam or reservoir, aqueduct, pipe or hydrant, or the property held, owned or used by said corporation for the purposes of this act, shall pay three times the amount of actual damages to said corporation, to be recovered in an action on the case, founded on this statute; and any such person, on conviction of either the malicious or willful acts aforesaid, shall be punished by a fine not exceeding one hundred dollars, and by imprisonment in the county jail for the county of Rutland for a term not exceeding six months.

Sec. 9. If any person shall use any of the water from said aqueduct without the permission of the trustees of said village, or such other officers duly authorized by the by-laws or ordinances of said village to give permission therefor, an action of trespass on the case may be maintained against him by said village for the recovery of damages therefor, with full costs, and such damages shall in no case be less than the rates prescribed for the use of the same amount of water by said corporation.

Sec. 10. Said village corporation is also hereby authorized and empowered, by vote at any legal meeting called for that purpose, to borrow money to lay and construct said aqueduct, and pay all the other necessary expenses connected therewith, as contemplated by the provisions of this act, and to issue its bonds or notes therefor, signed by the trustees of said village and countersigned by the treasurer thereof, and bearing interest at a rate not exceeding seven per cent, payable semi-annually, with coupons for such interest thereto attached, which bonds shall be payable at such time or times and at such place as said village corporation may direct.

Sec. 11. Should the said village corporation, for a period of one year from the date of the approval of this act, fail or neglect to acquire the necessary water source, pond, streams of water or springs, and commence the construction of said aqueduct, then Samuel W. Bailey, C. C. Knights, E. L. Allen, E. H. Phelps and A. N. Adams, their associates and successors, who are hereby constituted a corporation under the name of the Fairhaven Aqueduct Company, with all the powers incident to corporations, shall have all the powers, rights and privileges given to and conferred upon the village of Fairhaven aforesaid, by this act, and all the rights, powers and privileges hereby granted to said village shall thereafter cease and vest exclusively in said Fairhaven Aqueduct Company, which is hereby authorized and empowered to [supply] said village with pure water for public and private use, in accordance with the terms and provisions of this act.

SEC. 12. This act shall be taken and deemed to be a public act, and shall at all times be under the control of the legislature to amend or repeal as the public good may require.

SEC. 13. This act shall take effect from its passage.

Approved, November 21, 1874.

No. 173.—AN ACT TO AMEND AN ACT TO INCORPORATE THE VILLAGE OF LUDLOW, APPROVED NOVEMBER 17, 1866, AND TO EXTEND ITS POWERS.

SECTION
1. Power of trustees to establish and discontinue streets, &c., with proviso; owners of adjoining property may be assessed; right of appeal; col-

SECTION
lection of taxes; trustees shall have power to grant and revoke licenses; to take effect.

It is hereby enacted by the General Assembly of the State of Vermont:

SEC. 1. Section fifteen of an act entitled "An act to incorporate the village of Ludlow," approved November 17, 1866, is hereby amended so as to read as follows, viz:

The trustees of said village may lay out, alter, maintain and discontinue any street, road, lane, alley, walk or sidewalk in said village, and appraise and settle the damages therefor, causing their proceedings to be recorded in the town clerk's office in said town; provided, that any person aggrieved by their proceedings, shall have like opportunity for applying to the county court for the county of Windsor, to obtain redress, as is or may be allowed by law to those aggrieved with the proceedings of selectmen in similar cases. Said trustees, in making, altering or repairing sidewalks, shall have power, subject to the ordinances and by-laws of said village, on giving twelve days notice to the parties of the time and place of hearing, to assess the owners of lands adjoining such sidewalk, so much of the expense of making, altering or repairing such sidewalks as the said trustees shall judge such lands to be benefited thereby. And when they shall have made any such assessment, they shall make a report thereof, setting

forth their proceedings in that respect, which report they shall cause to be recorded in the town clerk's office in said Ludlow, and when so recorded, the amount so assessed shall be and remain a lien, in the nature of the tax, upon the lands so assessed, until the same shall be paid. From such assessment there shall be the same right of appeal to the county court, and the same proceedings in respect to such appeal, as is before provided in this section, and the final decision of the court in the matter of such appeal shall, when the record thereof is duly recorded as afore-said, be a lien upon the lands so assessed as above mentioned. But such appeal shall not delay the making, altering or repairing such sidewalk, and if the owner of such lands shall neglect for the space of six months after the final decision of said trustees, or in case of appeal to the county court, to pay to the village treasurer the amount of said assessments, the] trustees shall issue their warrant for the collection of the-same, signed by such authority as tax-warrants are required by law to be signed, directed to the village collector of taxes, who shall have authority to sell at public auction so much of said land as will satisfy said assessment and all legal fees, and who shall proceed in the same manner as collectors of town taxes are required by law to proceed in selling real estate at auction for the collection of town taxes. The trustees shall have the same power of granting licenses and vacating the same within the limits of said village, which the selectmen have, by virtue of the general statutes, in the town, and all moneys received therefor shall belong to the village treasury and be paid into the same. This act shall take effect from its passage.

Approved, November 24, 1874.

No. 174.—AN ACT AMENDING AN ACT INCORPORATING MIDDLEBURY VILLAGE.

SECTION
1. Boundaries; name; powers, rights and privileges.
2. Annual meeting; officers; warning.
3. Trustees may call special meetings.
4. Officers to be sworn and give bonds.
5. Duties of clerk.
6. Trustees to make and deliver to collector all tax-bills; other duties of trustees.
7. Trustees may lay out and alter streets, when.
8. May appoint police officers; powers of.
9. By-laws; list of same.
10. Money not to be paid out ex-

SECTION
cept by direction of trustees; auditors to be appointed.
11. Taxes may be assessed, when and how.
12. Highway districts; highway taxes, how assessed and collected.
13. Vacancies, how filled.
14. Water department.
15. Water rents.
16. How established and collected.
17. May be ordered paid in advance.
18. Water commissioners.
19. Duties and powers of.
20. Water bonds, how issued; record of.
21. When to take effect.

It is hereby enacted by the General Assembly of the State of Vermont:

SEC. 1. The inhabitants of that part of the town of Middlebury embraced within the following limits, commencing on the east bank of Otter Creek at the lower falls, near the foundry, thence running easterly to and including the dwelling house built by George Hammond, thence southerly to a point where the turnpike and creek roads intersect, thence westerly to a ledge in the road a few rods south of the dwelling house of George Porter, thence north to Weybridge line, thence east to center of Otter Creek, thence north to place of beginning,—are hereby incorporated and made a body corporate and politic under the name of the Village of Middlebury; and by that name may sue and be sued, prosecute and defend in any court, may have a common seal, and alter the same at pleasure, may take, hold, purchase and convey real and personal estate, and generally shall have, exercise and enjoy all such rights, immunities, powers and privileges as are incident to public corporations.

SEC. 2. The inhabitants of said village, qualified by law to vote in town meeting, shall meet at the court house or other suitable place on the first Wednesday in January, annually, at which meeting shall be chosen a moderator, clerk, seven trustees, treasurer, collector, auditor and water commissioner, and any other business specified in the warning of such meeting; which warning shall be signed by the clerk, naming such other business as the trustees may direct, and shall be posted up in three or more public places in said village, at least ten days before the time of holding such meeting.

SEC. 3. The trustees are hereby authorized to call special meetings of said corporation as the interest of the same may require, causing the same to be warned by the clerk in the manner heretofore specified for warning annual meetings; and any meeting may be adjourned from time to time as said corporation may judge proper, and any business may be transacted at such adjourned meetings, although not specified in the original warning, provided notice of such business shall be given in the usual manner of warning meetings, by giving ten days notice.

SEC. 4. All the officers, before they enter upon the duties of their respective offices, shall be sworn to the faithful discharge of the duties thereof, and the treasurer and collector shall, before assuming their duties, give bonds to said corporation in such sum and with such sureties as

said trustees shall direct, conditioned for the faithful performance of the duties of their offices respectively.

SEC. 5. It shall be the duty of the clerk of said village
to keep fair records of all the proceedings of said corporation, and to give copies of the same when required, and
he shall receive such fees as town clerks are entitled by
law to receive for like services; also to warn all meetings
of said corporation, agreeably to the directions of the
trustees. He shall also perform all other duties required
by this act, and such as are usually performed by village
clerks.

SEC. 6. It shall be the duty of the trustees to make
out and deliver to the collector an assessment or rate-bill
of all taxes which shall be laid by said corporation, to see
that all the by-laws of said corporation are duly executed,
and to direct, prosecutions for all breaches of the same,
and generally to take care of all the prudential concerns
of, and perform all duties which shall be legally enjoined
on them by said corporation. They shall also appoint from
time to time such number of fire wardens as the corporation may by their by-laws direct, and the same remove
at pleasure. They are authorized to organize one or more
fire companies, with such powers and regulations as the
said corporation by their by-laws may provide; but no
such fire company shall exercise any powers until the
same shall be recorded by the clerk of said village. All
powers vested by this act in said trustees may be exer-
cised by a majority of them, and in case of the incapacity
of the clerk, the trustees may warn meetings of said corporation by signing the warning and posting it in the
usual manner.

SEC. 7. The trustees of said village shall have exclu.
sive power to control, lay out, establish, alter and discon.
tinue streets, highways, lanes and alleys, with the grounds
and walks of the same, within the limits of said village,
and a survey of the same shall be recorded in the village
records, and they shall so lay out, establish, alter and dis.
continue such streets, highways and alleys, when so direct.
ed by said village at a meeting legally held for that pur.
pose, or by vote of said trustees at a regular meeting of
said board, when requested by five or more freehold proprietors of premises adjoining the proposed improvement;
provided, that nothing in this section shall be construed
to supersede the jurisdiction of the supreme or county
court in the premises.

SEC. 8. The trustees shall have power to appoint five
police officers, and on special occasions may temporarily
increase the number, whose names shall be recorded by
the clerk of the village, and they shall hold their office un.
til duly discharged, or others appointed. Said police shall
have the same power to serve criminal processes within
said village that a constable now has, and shall have power to arrest all persons who may be disturbing public
meetings, or any disorderly or drunken person, and confine
the same in the jail in said village not exceeding twenty-
four hours, and the person so arrested shall be dealt with
as if arrested on a complaint and warrant; and said police
shall perform such other duties and have such other powers as said village may vote.

SEC. 9. Said village shall have power to make, establish,
alter, amend or repeal ordinances, regulations and by-laws
for the following purposes, and to inflict penalties for the
breach thereof:

23

1st.   To establish and regulate a market.

2d.   To suppress and restrain disorderly and gaming houses, and all descriptions of gaming.

3d.   To regulate the exhibition of shows of every kind not prohibited by law.

4th.   To abate and remove nuisances.

5th.   To regulate alterations and repairs of stove-pipes, furnaces, fire-places and other things for which damage by fire may be apprehended.

6th.   To prevent immoderate riding or driving in the streets, and cruelty to animals.

7th.   To regulate the erection of buildings, and prevent encumbering the streets, sidewalks and alleys with fire-wood, lumber, carriages, boxes or other things, and provide for the care and improvement of public grounds.

8th.   To restrain the running at large of cattle, horses, swine, sheep, dogs and geese.

9th.   To provide a supply of water for the protection of the village against fire, and for other purposes, and to regulate the use of the same.

10th.   To compel all persons to keep the sidewalks adjacent to their premises clean.

11th.   To license inn-keepers, saloons or eating houses, and auctioneers.

12th.   To regulate or restrain the use of fireworks of all kinds, in the streets or commons.

13th.   To prescribe the powers and duties of watchmen of said village, and to provide for lighting the streets.

14th.   To regulate the grade of streets, the grade and width of sidewalks, and the construction thereof.

15th.   To prohibit and punish willful injuries to trees planted for shade, ornament, convenience or use, and to prevent and punish trespass or willful injuries to or upon public buildings, squares, commons, cemeteries or other property.

16th. Said corporation may make and establish, amend or repeal any other by-laws, rules and ordinances which it may deem necessary for the well being of said village, and not repugnant to the constitution or laws of this state. All which by-laws and ordinances shall be recorded in the office of the clerk of said village, and the clerk's certificate that such by-laws and ordinances were adopted at a legal meeting of said village, shall be *prima facie* evidence of such fact in any court in this state, and such certificate shall also be received in evidence in all courts in this state; and such corporation may impose a fine not exceeding fifty dollars for the breach of any by-law, rule, or ordinance, which fines, together with all other fines imposed by this act, may be recovered before any justice of the peace within and for the county of Addison, in an action on the case, declaring generally for the breach of such by-law, rule, or ordinance, or section of this act.

SEC. 10. No money shall be expended by any person for or in behalf of said village except by the direction of the trustees, and no money shall be paid out of the village treasury except upon orders signed by a majority of the trustees, who shall keep a full and true record and account of all orders drawn and expenditures made by them, and shall make report thereof at each annual meeting; and said village may appoint one or more auditors to audit and settle the accounts of any or all its officers, or may settle the same in such other manner as it may direct.

SEC. 11. The said village may at any annual meeting, or special meeting called for that purpose, lay a tax on the polls of the inhabitants of said village, and the ratable estate within the same, for any of the purposes heretofore mentioned, and the trustees shall make out a rate-bill accordingly, and deliver the same to the collector, who shall have the same power to collect such tax as the collector of town taxes, and may in like manner sell property to satisfy the same, and for want thereof commit any person to jail against whom he may have such tax.

Sec. 12. All the territory embraced within the limits of said village is hereby constituted a highway district of the town of. Middlebury, and all the highway taxes assessed on the poils and ratable estate therein shall be paid in money, and the selectmen of the town shall make out a tax-bill therefor and deliver the same, with a warrant for its collection, to the collector of said village, who shall collect the same as other taxes are collected, and pay the same over to the treasurer of said village, which money shall be drawn from the treasury by the trustees, and shall be expended by them in building, maintaining and repairing the streets, highways, walks, alleys and lanes of said village; and no surveyor of highways for said village shall be appointed by said town, and said village shall not be liable to build or repair any bridge across Otter Creek.

Sec. 13. Whenever there shall be a vacancy in any of the offices of said village, from any cause whatever, the village may fill such vacancy at any legal meeting. The trustees may make temporary appointments for such vacancies, and the persons thus appointed shall hold their office until the village shall elect others in their place.

SEC. 14. The corporation of said village shall have power to organize and establish a water department in order to supply said village with water for the fire department, domestic and other purposes, and may purchase and hold all necessary real and personal estate for that purpose, and may issue their corporation bonds to secure any present or future indebtedness for establishing and operating their water works.

SEC. 15. To aid in supporting the water department of said corporation, and to insure the annual interest on the water bonds of said corporation, and to provide for their final payment, the said corporation shall establish rates of annual rents, to be charged and paid at such times and in such manner as may be determined by said corporation for the supply of water to the inhabitants of said village, and they may from time to time modify, amend, increase or diminish such rents, and extend them to any description of property or use as the said corporation may deem proper.

SEC. 16. Such water rents as shall be established upon lots, buildings, factories, furnaces, steam engines, stores, shops, stables and other property, shall be collected from the owner of the property so supplied, unless otherwise provided in the lease of the water; and such rents shall be in the nature of a tax, and be a lien and charge upon such buildings, lots and other property so supplied, and may be collected in the same manner as any corporation tax.

SEC. 17. The water rents may be ordered to be paid in advance, and all necessary provisions and orders may be made by the corporation relating to the supply or stoppage of water as they may deem necessary to insure such advance payments.

SEC. 18. Said corporation, at its next or some future annual meeting, shall elect by ballot a board consisting of three water commissioners, who shall hold their office as follows: the first commissioner shall hold his office three years, the second two years, the third one year, and at every subsequent annual meeting there shall be elected one water commissioner to fill the vacancy occasioned by the then expiring term, who shall hold his office three years from his election, and until his successor shall be chosen as above provided.

SEC. 19. The water commissioners, under the direction of the corporation, shall have the supervision of the water department, shall make and establish all necessary rules and regulations for the government and operations of the water works, and may draw orders upon the treasury for the necessary expenses of the same, may appoint a superintendent and remove the same at pleasure, may establish rates for the use of the water and provide for the collection of the same, and generally take charge of the water department, subject to the control of the corporation.

SEC. 20. Every bond issued by said corporation in pursuance of this act shall be signed by the chairman of the board of trustees, and the treasurer, and shall have the certificate of the clerk of said corporation that said bond is one of the series authorized by the corporation, and the records of the corporation shall be so kept as to show the issue of the bonds, the amounts and dates of the same, and the time when due, and the time of payment.

SEC. 21. This act shall take effect when the Middle.
bury village corporation, at a legally warned meeting, shall
accept the same, and when so accepted, all former acts
relating to said corporation are repealed.

Approved, November 24, 1874.

No. 175.—AN ACT IN AMENDMENT OF AN ACT TO INCORPORATE THE VILLAGE OF NORTHFIELD.

*It is hereby enacted by the General Assembly of the
State of Vermont:*

SEC. 1. The boundaries of the village of Northfield
shall not be so defined as to include within the limits of
said village the real estate owned and occupied by Lyman
W. Wright, and said real estate shall not constitute a part
of the highway or school district embraced in the limits of
said village.

SEC. 2. This act shall take effect from its passage.

Approved, October 28, 1874.

No. 176.—AN ACT IN ADDITION TO AN ACT EN-
TITLED AN ACT IN ADDITION TO AN ACT
INCORPORATING THE VILLAGE OF RUTLAND,
APPROVED NOVEMBER 16, 1858.

It is hereby enacted by the General Assembly of the State of Vermont:

SEC. 1. All sums of money due the village of Rutland, for water supplied to tenements, buildings and lots in said village, shall be called water rents, and the same shall be due and payable in advance, on the twentieth day of June in each year, and if the same are not paid on or before the twentieth day of July following, five per cent thereof shall be added thereto, as a penalty for not paying the same when due.

SEC. 2. All such water rents shall be collected from the owners of the tenements, buildings and lots wherein the water is used, or to be used, for which the same are due, and such water rents shall be a tax and a lien upon such tenements, buildings and lots, and shall be collected in the same manner as other taxes of said village; and the owners of such tenements, buildings and lots shall be subject to the same liabilities therefor as for other village taxes.

SEC. 3. The water commissioners of said village shall, between the twentieth day of July and the first day of August in each year make out a list of the water rents due said village, with, five per cent thereof added thereto, as provided in the first action of this act, in which list they shall set down, in three separate columns, according to the best information in their power:

First. In the first column, the name of the owner of the tenements, buildings 'or lots, chargeable with water rents under the provisions of this act.

Second. In the second column, the name of the street or avenue, and the number or description of the tenement, building or lot chargeable with water rents as aforesaid.

Third. In the third column, the amount of water rent due for water used, or to be used, in such tenement, building or lot.

And the water commissioners, or a majority of them, shall certify that the same is a true list of the water rents due said village, at the date thereof, and shall attach thereto a warrant for the collection of said water rents, signed by a justice of the peace in and for the county of Rutland, which shall be in the same form as is now prescribed by statute for warrants for the collection of town and other taxes, and shall be directed to the collector of taxes for said village ; and the water commissioners shall deliver such list of water rents, with the warrant for the collection of the same thereto attached, to such collector of taxes, who shall proceed to collect the same as is provided in this act, and all moneys collected thereon by him shall be paid to the water commissioners of said village.

SEC. 4. The owners of tenements, buildings and lots on the twentieth day of June in each year shall be the persons, or parties, from whom all water rents for the year then next ensuing shall be collected, agreeably to the provisions of this act; provided, however, that should the ownership of any tenement, building, or lot change after the twentieth day of June in any year, and no water be used therein until after that date, then the water rents therefor shall be collected of the owner or owners thereof at the date of the commencement of the use therein; and all water rents due after the twentieth day of June in any year, if not paid to the water commissioners, shall, with interest thereon from the time the same shall be and become due to the twentieth day of June next following, and a penalty of five per cent thereof added thereto, be included in the list of water rents for said village, issued next after the same shall have become due; and all water rents omitted by mistake, or through ignorance thereof, from any list, may with interest thereon from the time the same shall have become due to the twentieth day of June next after the discovery of such omission, and a penalty of five per cent thereof added thereto, be included in the list of water rents for said village, issued next after the discovery of such omission; provided, that the date of such list shall be within three years from the time such water rents shall have become due.

SEC. 5. Every water commissioner for said village, hereafter elected, before enterin upon the duties of the office shall give a bond to said village, with sufficient surety, to be approved of by the treasurer of said village, in the penal sum of six thousand dollars, with the condition to faithfully perform the duties of water commissioner for

said village during his term of office, and to account to
and with said village for all moneys which shall be received by him belonging to said village, which bond shall
be kept by such treasurer for said village. And the office
of any water commissioner, failing to give such bond for
the space of one week after his election, shall become
vacant, and may be filled as is now or may hereafter be
provided by law.

This act shall take effect from and after its passage.

Approved, November 23, 1874.

No. 177.—AN ACT AUTHORIZING THE VILLAGE OF RUTLAND TO BORROW MONEY FOR THE PURPOSE OF PAYING ITS INDEBTEDNESS.

It is hereby enacted by the General Assembly of the State of Vermont:

SEC. 1. The village of Rutland may at its next annual
meeting, or at any special meeting called for that purpose
between now and then, by vote, authorize the board of trustees of said village to borrow money, not exceeding twenty-five thousand dollars in amount, for the purpose of paying the matured notes or bonds of said village, and such
as shall hereafter mature, issued on the first day of July,
A. D. 1868, pursuant to a vote of said village of Rutland,
at a meeting thereof holden on the twentieth day of May, A.

D. 1868, and also any other matured indebtedness of said village ; and should said village so vote to borrow money as aforesaid, it is hereby authorized and empowered to issue its notes or bonds therefor, with interest coupons attached, at a rate not exceeding seven per cent per annum from date, which said notes or bonds shall be signed by the treasurer of said village of Rutland, and countersigned by the clerk thereof, and duly registered, and shall be made payable at such time or times as said village may direct.

SEC. 2. This act shall take effect from its passage.

Approved, November 20, 1874.

No. 178.—AN ACT AUTHORIZING THE BELLOWS FALLS WATER COMPANY TO DISTRIBUTE ITS CAPITAL STOCK TO ITS MEMBERS.

SECTION
1. Company may distribute and divide its capital stock.
2. Must be so authorized at a legal meeting.

SECTION
3. Debts and claims may be collected, and avails divided.
4. To take effect.

It is hereby enacted by the General Assembly of the State of Vermont:

SEC. 1. The Bellows Falls Water Company are hereby authorized to divide and distribute its capital stock, in part or in whole, among its stockholders, in proportion to their several individual interests in the same, such distribution to be made in such manner and at such times as the company may elect.

SEC. 2.   Before such distribution shall be made, the said company, at a meeting duly warned and holden for that purpose, shall direct and authorize the same to be made.

SEC. 3.   Nothing in this act shall be construed to prevent said company from holding any debts, claims or securities they may have by reason of the sale of their property and franchise to the Bellows Falls village corporation, but the same may be held and collected in accordance with the terms of the contract between the said water company and the said Bellows Falls village corporation; and the said water company are authorized to distribute the avails thereof at such times and in such manner as they may deem best.

SEC. 4.   This act shall take effect from its passage.

Approved, November 17, 1874.

No. 179.—AN ACT TO AUTHORIZE THE REMOVAL OF OBSTRUCTIONS FROM THE LAMOILLE RIVER, NORTH OF HARDWICK LINE.

SECTION
1. Names of persons authorized to remove obstructions; powers and privileges.
2. Rights of parties aforesaid.
3. Proceedings in case of disagreement as to damages.
4. Selectmen may be called upon in certain cases, to give no-

SECTION
tice in writing of time and place of hearing.
5. Parties may recover toll and damages on this statute.
6. Subject to future legislation; limitation of force.
7. To take effect.

*It is hereby enacted by the General Assembly of the State
of Vermont :*

Sec. 1. J. W. Simpson of Craftsbury, H. S. Tolman of
Greensboro, in Orleans county, and J. R. Delano of Hardwick, in Caledonia county, their associates and assignees,
are hereby empowered and authorized to remove and clear
out rocks, flood wood and other obstructions from the bed
and banks of the Lamoille river, from its source to Hardwick line, so as to make the same navigable for the runnin
of logs, ties, wood, timber or other lumber, and to receive
toll from such as shall so run logs, ties, timber or other
lumber down said river, and to enter upon the bed of said
river or its tributaries for the purpose of removing obstructions, and to make booms in said river or streams, and
slips and aprons in any dam on said river, without injury
to the water power thereof, by paying or tendering all
damage caused thereby, also the damage sustained to any
mill dam or other property along said stream or its tributaries, by reason of running logs, ties, wood or other
lumber down the stream in the manner hereinafter provided.

Sec. 2. The parties aforesaid, and other parties running
logs, ties, wood or other lumber, shall have the right to
occupy land on the margin of said river for the purpose of
banking logs or other property that shall be floated, and
the damage occasioned thereby shall be adjusted in the
manner hereinafter provided.

Sec. 3. In case the parties aforesaid shall at any time
be unable to agree with any person in the settlement of
the damages mentioned in the first and second sections of
this act, either party shall have the right to call upon the

selectmen of the town where the property is situated which is claimed to have been damaged, who shall forthwith give reasonable notice to all the parties interested, in writing, of the time and place of hearing all parties, and the decisions of said selectmen shall be final: provided, that if either of said selectmen shall be disqualified by reason of relationship or interest, then the other two shall act as aforesaid; and provided, if two of said selectmen shall be disqualified as aforesaid then, either party may apply to any three justices in the county qualified by law to judge between the parties, and said justices shall proceed as aforesaid to settle damages.

SEC. 4.　In case the parties aforesaid cannot agree with any person or persons in relation to toll, then either party shall have the right to call upon the selectmen of the towns of Craftsbury or Greensboro, who shall forthwith give reasonable notice, in writing, to all parties interested of the time and place of hearing them in the premises, and their decision shall be final.

SEC. 5.　Said parties shall have an action on this statute to recover any toll awarded to them by the selectmen aforesaid, in any court qualified by law to judge between the parties, and the same right of action is hereby given to any person who shall be awarded damages under the provisions of this act.

SEC. 6.　This act shall be in force fifteen years, but shall at all times be subject to future legislation as the public good may require.

SEC. 7.　This act shall take effect from its passage.

Approved, November 12, 1874.

No. 180.—AN ACT TO INCORPORATE THE MOOSE RIVER IMPROVEMENT COMPANY.

It is hereby enacted by the General Assembly of the State of Vermont:

SEC. 1.   Daniel Colby, David Hopkins of St. Johnsbury, Isaac R. Houston of Victory, and Orville Lawrence of Waterford, and their associates and successors, are hereby constituted a corporation and body politic by the name of the Moose River Improvement Company ; and by that name may sue and be sued, may have a common seal, may purchase, hold, rent and convey personal and real estate not exceeding in value fifty thousand dollars, for the purpose of clearing Moose River and its tributaries of obstructions, of building reservoirs, sluices, canals, locks and booms in said river or its tributaries, also slips and aprons on any dam, without impairing the water power thereof, that may be necessary to make Moose River and its tributaries in a condition for floating logs, or manufactuing lumber or such other commodities as may come within their province, and for the transaction of all business connected therewith, including the manufacture of lumber and the right to occupy land on the margin of the streams for banking logs or other property, by paying or tendering all damages caused thereby; also the damages done to any mill, dam or other property along said stream or its tributaries, by reason of running logs, ties, wood or other lumber down said streams; provided, that in no case shall the water be raised in said river or its tributaries, by reason of dams, reservoirs or locks, so as to damage any highway, said damages to be assessed as hereinafter pro-vided.

SEC. 2. The capital stock of said company shall not be less than ten thousand dollars, nor exceed fifty thousand dollars, and the shares thereof shall not be less than twenty-five dollars, nor exceed one hundred dollars each.

Sec. 3. Said corporation's business affairs shall be managed by a board of directors, not exceeding five in number, who shall be stockholders, and shall be annually chosen by the stockholders in said corporation, at such time and place as they shall from time to time appoint.

SEC. 4. Said company shall not organize until five thousand dollars of its capital stock shall be subscribed, nor shall said company contract any debt until twenty-five per cent of the capital stock so subscribed shall have been paid in, nor shall said company at any time contract debts exceeding in amount three fourths of the capital actually paid in, and if such indebtedness shall exceed that amount, the directors and stockholders shall be personally holden to the creditors for such excess, and no part of the capital stock so paid in, shall be diverted from the business of said company.

24

Sec. 5. This corporation shall be entitled to receive toll from any other person or persons, who shall float logs, lumber or other property in said Moose River or its tributaries, after the same have been cleared of their obstructions. And in case this corporation shall at any time be unable to agree with any person or persons in the settlement of damages, as mentioned in the first section of this act, then either party shall have the right to call upon the selectmen of the town where the property is situated which is claimed to have been damaged, who shall forthwith give reasonable notice, in writing, to all the parties interested, of the time and place of hearing them in the premises, and shall proceed to assess such damages ; provided, that if either of said selectmen shall be disqualified by reason of relationship or interest, then the other two shall act as aforesaid ; and provided, that if two of said selectmen shall be disqualified as aforesaid, then either party may apply to any three justices of the peace in the county, qualified by law to judge between the parties, and said justices shall proceed as aforesaid, and assess said damages. In case this corporation cannot agree with any person or persons in relation to toll, then either party shall have the right to call upon the selectmen of their town, and in case of their disqualification, as in case of damages, either party may apply to any three justices of the peace of the county, qualified by law to judge between the parties, who shall forthwith give reasonable notice, in writing, to all persons interested, of the time and place of hearing them in the premises, and shall assess said toll ; provided, that in any case where the damages or toll awarded by the selectmen or justices of the peace, as the case may be, shall exceed the sum of fifty dollars, either party shall have the right of appeal to the next term of the county court to be held in and for the county of Essex, in the action for the recovery of such damage or toll. But in any case where the damages or toll awarded does not exceed fifty dollars, the decision of the selectmen or justices of the peace, as the case may be, shall be final.

SEC. 6. In case the parties named in this act shall at any time neglect or refuse, twenty days after request, to construct a slip or apron in any dam on said river, or its tributaries, then the party who is liable to sustain injury from such neglect or refusal to construct such slip or apron, shall have the right to call upon the selectmen of the town where such dam is situated, who shall determine whether, and if so when, such slip or apron shall be constructed, and their decision shall be final.

SEC. 7. If the said parties for the space of twenty days after the time fixed by the decision of the selectmen, deciding that they shall construct such slip or apron, shall neglect or refuse to construct the same, the owner of such dam shall have the right to construct such slip or apron, and shall have the right, (in case he cannot agree with said parties as to the price he shall be paid therefor,) to call upon said selectmen to fix the price that said owner or owners shall be paid, and their decision shall be final.

SEC. 8. The provisions of this act, with reference to the disqualification of any of said selectmen, by reason of interest or relationship, as mentioned in section five, and the substitution of three justices of the peace, and all provisions relative to notice, shall apply to sections six and seven of this act.

SEC. 9. Said parties shall have an action on this statute to recover any toll awarded to them by the selectmen, or justices of the peace aforesaid, in any court qualified by law to judge between the parties, and the same right of action is hereby given to any person or persons who shall be awarded damage under this act.

SEC. 10. The first meeting of said company shall be held in Victory, at such time and place as the majority of the persons named in this act may agree upon; and at such meeting, and at all other legal meetings, may make, alter and amend such by-laws, rules and regulations for the management of its affairs, not repugnant to the constitution and laws of this state, as the majority may direct, may fix the amount of the capital stock, divide the same into shares, and provide for the transfer thereof.

SEC. 11. This act shall be under the control of future legislatures to alter, amend or repeal as the public good may require, and shall be subject to the provisions of all statutes, so far as the same are applicable to this corporation.

SEC. 12. This act shall take effect from its passage.

Approved, November 24, 1874.

No. 181.—AN ACT TO AUTHORIZE THE REMOVAL OF OBSTRUCTIONS FROM WILLOUGHBY RIVER.

SECTION
1. Authority conferred to remove obstructions; purpose; powers and privileges.
2. Right to occupy land for certain purposes guaranteed.
3. Settlement for damages, how adjusted.
4. Right of appeal to justices of

SECTION
the peace for settlement of damages.
5. Right of action to recover toll or damages.
6. Authority herein granted may pertain to either party named.
7. Limitation of this act.
8. To take effect.

It is hereby enacted by the General Assembly of the State of Vermont:

SEC. 1. Elisha Foster and Joseph H. Evans of Brownington, in the county of Orleans, their associates and assigns, are hereby empowered and authorized to remove and clear out rocks, flood-wood and other obstructions from the bed and banks of Willoughby River, from its source at the outlet of Willoughby Lake in Westmore, in the county of Orleans, to Evansville, so-called, in the town of Brownington, in said county of Orleans, so as to make the same navigable for the running of logs, ties, wood, timber or other lumber down said river, and to enter upon the bed of said river, or its tributaries, for the purpose of removing obstructions and to make booms in said river or its tributaries, and slips and aprons on any dam in said river, without injury to the water power thereof, by paying or tendering all damages caused thereby in the manner hereinafter stated; also the damage sustained to any mill dam or other property along said stream, or its tributaries, by reason of running logs or ties, wood or other lumber, down said stream.

SEC. 2. The parties aforesaid, and other parties running wood, ties or other lumber, shall have the right to occupy land on the margin of said river for the purpose of banking logs or other property that shall be floated on said stream, and the damage occasioned thereby shall be adjusted in the manner hereinafter provided.

SEC. 3. In case the parties shall at any time be unable to agree with any person in the settlement of the damages mentioned in the first and second sections of this act, either party may call upon the selectmen of the town where the property is situated which is claimed to have been damaged, who shall forthwith give reasonable notice, in writing, to all the parties interested, of the time and place of hearing such claim for damage, and shall proceed to assess the same; provided, that said selectmen shall be disqualified if they are related to either party, or have any interest in the result of said hearing, and in that case the other two shall act as aforesaid; and provided also, if two of the said selectmen shall be disqualified as aforesaid, then either party may apply to any three justices of the peace in the county of Orleans, qualified by law to judge between the parties, and said justices shall proceed as aforesaid to settle the damages.

SEC. 4. In case the parties aforesaid cannot agree in relation to the amount of toll to be paid by persons floating lumber in said river, then either party shall have the right to call upon any three justices of the peace within said county of Orleans, qualified by law to judge between the parties, who shall forthwith give reasonable notice, in writing, to all parties interested, of the time and place of hearing them in the premises, and shall proceed to assess the same; provided, that in any case where the damages or toll awarded by the selectmen or justices of the peace as the case may be, shall exceed the sum of fifty dollars, either party shall have the right of appeal in the action for the recovery of such damages or toll; but in every case where the damages or toll awarded does not exceed fifty dollars, the decision of the selectmen or justices of the peace shall be final.

SEC. 5. Said parties shall have an action on this statute to recover any toll awarded to them by the justices as aforesaid, in any court qualified by law to judge between the parties; and the same right of action is hereby given to any person who shall be awarded damages under the provisions of this act.

SEC. 6. If either of the parties named in the first section of this act shall, upon the request of the other, decline to take part and share in the improvements contemplated in this act, then the other may make said improvements in his own right, and shall be individually entitled to all the benefits of this act.

SEC. 7. This act shall be in force fifteen years, but shall at all times be subject to future legislation as the public good may require.

SEC. 8. This act shall take effect from its passage.

Approved, November 24, 1874.

MISCELLANEOUS.

No. 182.—AN ACT CHANGING THE SHIRE TOWN IN THE COUNTY OF ORLEANS.

It is hereby enacted by the General Assembly of the State of Vermont:

SEC. 1. Hiland Hall of Bennington, Redfield Proctor of Rutland, and Nathaniel Parker of Burlington, (and in case any of the above named from any cause cannot or will not serve, Heman Carpenter of Northfield, and Wheelock G.'Veazey of Rutland, in the order named, are authorized to act in the place of any such,) are hereby constituted a committee for the purpose of making an examination and selecting the best location, on the line of the Connecticut and Passumpsic Rivers Railroad, between the village of North Derby, in the town of Derby, and South Barton, in the town of Barton, for the court house and other county buildings in the county of Orleans; provided, that said committee may select the best place in said

county for said county buildings, and if they think Irasburgh the best location in said county, said buildings shall
be left there; provided, that said committee shall not act
under their appointment until a majority of the legal voters
of said county of Orleans, present in town meeting and
voting, shall accept the provisions of this act by voting yes.
And it is hereby made the duty of the selectmen of the
several towns in said Orleans county, to insert in the
warning for their annual March meeting in 1875, an article by which the question of accepting of the provisions
of this act may be submitted to a vote, by written or printed
ballots, *yes* or *no*, as follows : for removal or against removal; and the town clerk of each town shall take and
keep a check-list of the name of each person voting upon
the question in their respective towns.   It shall be the
duty of the town clerk of each town in said county, within ten days after said meeting, to certify the vote of his
town upon said question to the county clerk of said
county, and to the chairman of said committee appointed
under the provisions of this act; and if a majority of the
votes cast in all of said towns shall be in favor of removal,
then said committee shall proceed to act under their commission, but not otherwise.

Sec. 2.   Said committee shall, in the month of June, A.
D. 1875, proceed to make such examination and select
said location, and said committee shall determine what
sum the town where said location is fixed shall contribute
toward the erection of new county buildings, and shall
take satisfactory security to the county for the payment
thereof; and having so fixed said location and taken such
security for any sum so required to be paid, shall, on or
before the first day of July next, report their decision to

the governor, and within fifteen days thereafter the governor shall certify the same to the judges of the Orleans county court.

Sec. 3. The judges of Orleans county court shall, upon being so certified of the location, proceed as soon as may be to purchase suitable grounds for a court house, jail and other necessary county buildings, and take conveyances thereof to said county of Orleans, and shall immediately erect a suitable court house, jail and other public buildings and offices necessary for the use of said county thereon; and for any expense thereby incurred may draw orders upon the county treasury to an amount not exceeding twelve thousand dollars.

Sec. 4. The judges of the Orleans county court are also empowered to sell and convey, or otherwise dispose of all lands, buildings and other property at Irasburgh belonging to said county, (except such lands, buildings and other property now at Irasburgh and used by the county of Orleans, as the town of Irasburgh or any person has donated and given to said county, to hold for use or otherwise, and all such lands, buildings and other property, after the county shall cease to use the same at Irasburgh, shall become the sole property of the town of Irasburgh or such person,) or remove said buildings, any part thereof, or any such other property, save as above excepted, in such manner as they shall judge most for the interest of said county, and apply the avails thereof toward the erection of said new county buildings, or pay the same into the county treasury.

Sec. 5. The courts in and for said county shall continue to be holden at Irasburgh until and including the

January term of the county court, A. D. 1876, but thereafter all sittings of the supreme court, county court, and court of chancery, shall be holden at the place to be so fixed upon and determined by said committee.

SEC. 6. This act shall take effect when the town where such buildings are located shall give security to the county of Orleans, to be approved by the Hon. T. P. Redfield, one of the judges of the supreme court, that the erection of the same shall, in no event, cost said county to exceed the sum of twelve thousand dollars.

Approved, November 24, 1874.

No. 183.—AN ACT ANNEXING GOSHEN GORE TO THE TOWN OF PLAINFIELD.

SECTION
1. Goshen Gore, adjoining Plainfield, annexed to Plainfield.
2. When to take effect, with proviso.
3. Grand list of said gore annexed to grand list of Plainfield.

SECTION
4. If Plainfield accept this act, treasurer not to make out tax, as provided in section three of an act approved December 1, 1862.

It is hereby enacted by the General Assembly of the State of Vermont:

SEC. 1. Goshen Gore, adjoining Plainfield, is hereby annexed to the town of Plainfield.

SEC. 2. This act shall take effect on the third Tuesday of March, A. D. 1875; provided, however, this act shall not take effect unless the said town of Plainfield shall at the next annual March meeting vote to accept of such annexation; and it is hereby made the duty of the selectmen of the town of Plainfield to insert in the warning of such March meeting an article in regard to acting upon such question.

SEC. 3. The grand list of said Goshen Gore, so far as it relates to the appraisal of real estate as made·out by the commissioner appointed for that purpose by the governor, for the year 1874, is hereby annexed to the appraisal of real estate of the town of Plainfield for the year 1874; and it is hereby made the duty of the listers of the town of Plainfield for the year 1875, to annex the appraisal of the real estate of such gore aforesaid, to the grand list of the town of Plainfield, and the grand list when so made shall be the basis of taxation and the grand list upon which all taxes shall hereafter be assessed, until a new appraisal shall be made in said town; provided, the town of Plainfield vote to accept of the provisions of this act.

SEC. 4. In case the town of Plainfield vote to accept the provisions of this act, the treasurer of this state shall not thereafter make out any tax on said lands as provided in section three of an act approved December 1, 1862, relating to taxing the lands in the several gores in this state.

Approved, November 24, 1874.

No. 184.—AN ACT IN RELATION TO THE TWO PARISHES IN THE TOWN OF WESTMINSTER.

It is hereby enacted by the General Assembly of the State of Vermont:

SEC. 1. An act approved November 17, 1870, entitled an act to repeal an act entitled an act in alteration of an act entitled an act to divide the town of Westminster into two parishes, passed October 31, 1798, is hereby repealed and the act that was repealed is re-enacted.

SEC. 2. This act shall not take effect until said town of Westminster, at a legal meeting thereof, duly warned for that purpose, shall, by a vote of a majority of the legal voters present at such meeting, give their assent to and confirm the same.

Approved, November 12, 1874.

No. 185.—AN ACT PROVIDING FOR THE PAYMENT OF WITNESSES AND EXPENSES BEFORE LEGIS-LATIVE COMMITTEE.

SECTION	SECTION
1. Fees for summoning witnesses, and fees to be paid to witnesses in certain cases.	2. Auditor directed to draw an order in payment thereof. 3. To take effect.

It is hereby enacted by the General Assembly of the State of Vermont:

SEC. 1. The same fees and expenses as are now allowed for summoning witnesses to appear before the county courts of this state, shall be allowed for summoning witnesses to appear before the committee on railroads, to whom was referred House Bill No. 138, entitled " An act making provision for regulating the 'rates for the transportation of freight, passengers or cars on certain railroads therein named," and to the witnesses so summoned there shall be allowed and paid the same fees and expenses as are now allowed by the provisions of an act entitled " An act relating to the expenses before legislative committees," approved November 26, 1872.

SEC. 2. The auditor of accounts is hereby authorized and directed, on presentation of the proper certificate of the sergeant-at-arms, to draw his order upon the state treasurer, payable to the sergeant-at-arms, for such sum as shall be sufficient to pay the amount provided for in section one of this act.

SEC. 3. This act shall take effect from its passage.

Approved, November 24, 1874.

No. 186.—AN ACT FOR THE BETTER PRESERVA- TION OF THE MONUMENT OF NATHANIEL CHIPMAN, AT TINMOUTH.

It is hereby enacted by the General Assembly of the State of Vermont:

SEC. 1. A sum of money not exceeding one hundred and fifty dollars is hereby appropriated for the purpose of erecting an iron fence around the monument to Nathaniel

Chipman, in the cemetery in the town of Tinmouth, said sum to be drawn from the treasury and expended under the direction of Judah H. Round, Cyrus Cramton, George Caperon, Redfield Proctor and R. Buell, who are hereby appointed commissioners for that purpose.

SEC. 2.   This act shall take effect from its passage.

Approved, November 12, 1874.

No. 187.—AN ACT TO AMEND AN ACT AUTHORIZING THE GOVERNOR TO CONTRACT FOR STATUES OF JACOB COLLAMER AND ETHAN ALLEN, APPROVED NOVEMBER 27, 1872.

It is hereby enacted by the General Assembly of the State of Vermont:

SEC. 1.   Section one of an act entitled an act authorizing the governor to contract for statues of Jacob Collamer and Ethan Allen, approved November 27, 1872, is hereby amended so as to read as follows:

The governor of this state is authorized and requested to contract in behalf of the state, with such person as he shall deem proper, for a statue in marble of the late Jacob Collamer, and with Larkin G. Mead for a statue in marble of Ethan Allen, and said statues when completed, to be placed in the national statuary hall in Washington.

SEC. 2.   This act shall take effect from its passage.

Approved, October 28, 1874.

No. 188.—AN ACT IN ADDITION TO AN ACT APPROVED NOVEMBER 26, 1872, ENTITLED AN ACT FOR THE BETTER PRESERVATION OF THE MONUMENT ERECTED ON THE HUBBARDTON BATTLE GROUND.

It is hereby enacted by the General Assembly of the State of Vermont:

SEC. 1. A sum of money not exceeding three hundred dollars is hereby further appropriated for the purpose of erecting a fence about the monument on the Hubbardton battle ground, in the town of Hubbardton, in the county of Rutland; said sum to be drawn from the treasury and expended under the direction of Seneca Root and Chauncey S. Rumsey of Hubbardton, and Ferrand F. Parker of Castleton in said county, who are hereby appointed commissioners for that purpose.

SEC. 2. This act shall take effect from its passage.

Approved, November 18, 1874.

No. 189.—AN ACT LAYING A TAX ON THE COUNTY OF BENNINGTON.

SECTION	SECTION
1. Tax of three cents assessed.	3. Selectmen to deliver tax-bills; time of payment.
2. Treasurer to issue his warrants.	4. To take effect.

It is hereby enacted by the General Assembly of the State of Vermont:

25

SEC. 1. There is assessed a tax of six cents on the dol-lar on the lists of polls and ratable estate of the several towns in the county of Bennington, for the year 1874, for the purpose of meeting the deficiency in the treasury of said county, and repairing the county buildings of said county.

SEC. 2. The treasurer of said county is hereby directed, on or before the first day of January, 1875, to issue war-rants to the first constable of the several towns in said county, for the collection of said tax in the same manner as by law state taxes are required to be collected.

SEC. 3. The selectmen of the several towns in said county shall make out and deliver to the first constables of their respective towns, in the month of January, 1875, a tax-bill for the collection of said tax in the same manner as is required by law for the collection of state taxes, and pay to the treasurer of said county the amount of said tax, on or before the first day of June, 1875.

SEC. 4. This act shall take effect from its passage.

Approved, November 24, 1874.

No. 190.—AN ACT LAYING A TAX ON THE COUNTY OF CALEDONIA.

It is hereby enacted by the General Assembly of the State of Vermont:

SEC. 1.   There is hereby assessed a tax of two cents on the dollar on the list of the polls and ratable estate of the inhabitants of Caledonia County, for the year A. D. 1874, to pay the indebtedness of said county, and paying the current expenses of the same.

SEC. 2.   The treasurer of said county is hereby directed, on or before the tenth day of December, A. D. 1874, to issue his warrants to the first constables of the several towns in said county, for the collection of the tax hereby assessed, to be collected in the same manner as by law state taxes are required to be collected.

SEC. 3.   The selectmen of the several towns in said county shall make out and deliver to the first constable of their respective towns, in the month of December, A. D. 1874, a tax-bill for the collection of said tax in the same manner as is required by law for the collection of state taxes, and the first constable of the several towns in said county shall collect and pay into the treasury of said county the amount of said tax, on or before the first day of March, A. D. 1875.

SEC. 4.   Instead of the credit mentioned in section sixty-four of chapter eighty-four of the general statutes, the treasurer of the county shall credit each constable one fortieth part of the sum contained in the warrant by him issued to such constable, who shall be accountable for so much of said fortieth part so credited as shall not be allowed by way of abatements to such constable.

SEC. 5. Whatever balance may remain in the treasury of said county after paying its debts, and not wanted for immediate payment of current expenses of said county, the treasurer is hereby authorized, with the consent and approval of the county judges, to place the same at interest, for the benefit of the county.

SEC. 6. This act shall take effect from its passage.

Approved, October 21, 1874.

No. 191.—AN ACT LAYING A TAX ON THE COUNTY OF CHITTENDEN.

It is hereby enacted by the General Assembly of the State of Vermont:

SEC. 1. That a tax of three per cent be levied on the polls and ratable estate of the several towns and the city of Burlington, in the county of Chittenden, for the purpose of paying the county indebtedness and current expenses of said county.

SEC. 2. The selectmen of the several towns, and the board of aldermen of the city of Burlington, shall, during the month of January, 1875, assess a tax of three per cent on the polls and ratable estate of their respective towns and the city of Burlington; and the collectors of the several towns and the city of Burlington shall collect the same and pay it into the county treasury on or before the first day of June, A. D. 1875.

SEC. 3. This act shall take effect from its passage.

Approved, November 5, 1874.

No. 192.—AN ACT LAYING A TAX ON THE COUNTY OF FRANKLIN.

SECTION
1. Tax of fifteen cents assessed.
2. Commissioners appointed.
3. Treasurer to issue his warrant; selectmen to issue tax-bills.
4. Commissioners may borrow money.

SECTION
5. Towns in this county must vote to accept this act; manner.
6. Meeting, how warned; article to be inserted.
7. To take effect.

It is hereby enacted by the General Assembly of the State of Vermont :

SEC. 1. There is hereby assessed a tax of fifteen cents on the dollar of the polls and ratable estate in the several towns of the county of Franklin for the year eighteen hundred and seventy-five; and a like tax of fifteen cents on the dollar of the polls and ratable estate in said towns for the year eighteen hundred and seventy-six, for the purpose of completing and furnishing the court house of said county, and for paying the indebtedness and current expenses of said county.

SEC. 2. Victor Atwood, L. H. Hapgood, C. D. Rublee, S. H. Soule, Fletcher Tarbell, James M. Hotchkiss and

Henry Comings are hereby constituted and appointed commissioners for the purpose of completing and furnishing said court house, and are hereby authorized to expend for said purpose a sum not exceeding the amount to be raised by the taxes aforesaid.

SEC. 3. The treasurer of said county is hereby directed, on or before the first day of June in each of said years, to issue his warrants to the first constables of the several towns of said county, for the collection of the taxes mentioned in the first section of this act, in the same manner as by law state taxes are required to be collected, and there shall be credited to said constable in lieu of that provided by section sixty-four, chapter eighty-four, of the general statutes, one fortieth part of the sum named in said warrants, and such constables shall be accountable for so much of said fortieth part as shall not be allowed by way of abatements, and the selectmen of the several towns aforesaid, shall make out and deliver to the first constables of their respective towns, in the month of June of each of said years, a tax-bill for the collection of said tax in the same manner as is required by law in case of state taxes; and said constables shall collect and pay to the treasurer of said county the amount of said taxes for each of the years aforesaid, on or before the first day of September of the year for which said tax is assessed.

SEC. 4. The commissioners aforesaid are hereby authorized to borrow money, not exceeding the sum to be realized from the taxes aforesaid, and may pledge the credit of the county therefor, to be expended by them for the purpose of carrying into effect the provisions of this act.

SEC. 5. This act shall not take effect for the pu⌐
of charging said county with the tax aforesaid, u⌐
the same be accepted by the said county of Frankli
the manner following, that is to say: There shall be
in the several towns of said county on the sixteenth
of January, A. D. 1875, a meeting of the legal vote⌐
said towns, for the purpose of voting upon the ac⌐
ance of this act, and at said meetings the votes shal
by ballot, and said ballots shall be in the form follow
"For a tax," or "Against a tax"; and the clerks o⌐
several towns shall, immediately after said meeting, t⌐
mit to the county clerk of said county the ballots w
shall be cast at said meetings, and the county clerk
thereupon proceed to canvass said ballots and certify
same to the commissioners named in this act, and if
said canvass it shall appear that a majority of all
votes are in favor of the tax, then said county sha⌐
deemed to have accepted this act, and thereupon
act shall immediately take effect for all purposes of thi⌐

SEC. 6. It is hereby made the duty of the selec⌐
of the several towns aforesaid, to warn said meeting
posting a notice thereof in the manner prescribed by
for warning town meetings, and shall insert therein
following article in substance, that is to say: "To s⌐
the voters of the town of (inserting the name o⌐
town) will vote to accept the provisions of an act o⌐
legislature of this state, entitled "An act laying ⌐
on the county of Franklin," approved November
A. D. 1874.

SEC. 7. This act shall take effect from its passage

Approved, November 23, 1874.

No. 193.—AN ACT LAYING A TAX ON THE COUNTY OF GRAND ISLE.

It is hereby enacted by the General Assembly of the State of Vermont:

SEC. 1.   There is hereby assessed a tax of four cents on the dollar on the list of polls and ratable estate in the several towns in the county of Grand Isle, for the year one thousand eight hundred and seventy-four, for the purpose of meeting the deficiency in the treasury of said county, and paying the current expenses of the same.

SEC. 2.   The treasurer of said county is hereby directed, on or before the first day of January, A. D. 1875, to issue warrants to the first constables of the several towns in said county, for the collection of said tax, in the same manner as by law state taxes are required to be collected.

SEC. 3.   The selectmen of the several towns in said county shall make out and deliver to the first constable of their respective towns, in the month of January, A. D. 1875, a tax-bill for the collection of said tax, in the same manner as is required by law for the collection of state taxes, and the first constable shall collect and pay to the treasurer of said county the amount of said tax on or before the first day of June, A. D. 1875.

SEC. 4.   This act shall take effect from its passage.

Approved, November 24, 1874.

No. 194.—AN ACT TO REPEAL AN ACT ENTITLED
AN ACT TO PROVIDE FOR BUILDING A JAIL
IN THE COUNTY OF RUTLAND, APPROVED NO-
VEMBER 21, 1867.

*It is hereby enacted by the General Assembly of the
State of Vermont:*

SEC. 1. An act entitled an act providing for the building a jail in the county of Rutland, approved November
21, 1867, is hereby repealed.

Approved, November 24, 1874.

No. 195.—AN ACT LAYING A TAX ON THE GRAND
LIST OF THE REAL ESTATE OF HARRIS GORE
IN WASHINGTON COUNTY.

SECTION	SECTION
1. Tax of five hundred cents assessed on real estate.	establish highways; proceedings in relation thereto.
2. Committee to superintend expenditures.	4. Commissioner to issue tax-bill.
3. Commissioner of gore may	5. To take effect.

*It is hereby enacted by the General Assembly of the State
of Vermont:*

SEC. 1. There is hereby assessed a tax of five hundred
cents on the dollar of the grand list of real estate of 1874,
now on file in the county clerk's office in Washington
county, of Harris Gore, in the county of Washington, pay-

able in money, on or before the first day of June next, for the purpose of making and repairing highways and bridges in said gore.

Sec. 2. Richard L. Martin of Harris Gore, J. E. Hollister of East Montpelier, and Orman L. Hoyt of Plainfield, are hereby appointed a committee to superintend the expenditure of said tax.

Sec. 3. The commissioner for said gore shall have the right, and it is hereby made his duty upon proper application, to lay out and establish highways in said gore, and to cause a record thereof to be made in the county clerk's office of the county of Washington. And his doings in the premises shall be governed by and be in accordance with the statutes regulating the laying out of roads and highways by selectmen in their several towns. And the land owners shall have the same right to appeal from the said commissioner's appraisal of land damages that land owners in towns now have in the case of the appraisal of land damages in like case by selectmen, and the method of procedure shall be the same as in like case of appraisal by selectmen.

Sec. 4. The commissioner for said gore shall make and issue his tax-bill for the tax aforesaid, in due form of law and commit the same to the collector for said gore, who shall collect the same and pay it over to said committee, and said commissioner shall audit the accounts of said committee, and the collection of said tax by said collector, and his decision in the premises shall be final.

Sec. 5. This act shall take effect from its passage.

Approved, November 5, 1874.

No. 196.—AN ACT IN AMENDMENT OF AN ACT APPROVED NOVEMBER 5, 1874, ENTITLED "AN ACT LAYING A TAX ON THE GRAND LIST OF THE REAL ESTATE OF HARRIS GORE IN WASHINGTON COUNTY."

It is hereby enacted by the General Assembly of the State of Vermont :

SEC. 1. The first section of said act is hereby amended so as to read as follows :

Sec. 1. There is hereby assessed a tax of five hundred cents on the dollar of the grand list of real estate of 1874, now on file in the county clerk's office in Washington county, of Harris Gore, in the county of Washington, payable in money on or before the first day of June next, for the purpose of making and repairing highways and bridges, and paying land damages therefor, in said gore.

SEC. 2. This act shall take effect from its passage.

Approved, November 24, 1874.

No. 197.—AN ACT RELATING TO THE ASSESSMENT OF TAXES IN THE TOWN OF TOPSHAM.

It is hereby enacted by the General Assembly of the State of Vermont :

SEC. 1. All town and school district taxes hereafter to be assessed on the grand list of the town of Topsham for the year 1874, shall be assessed on the grand list of said town as completed by the listers after the last quinquennial appraisal of the real estate in said town.

SEC. 2. This act shall take effect from its passage.

Approved, November 24, 1874.

No. 198.—AN ACT TO ENABLE THE PROPRIETORS AND PEW-OWNERS OF THE OLD METHODIST MEETING-HOUSE AT THE VILLAGE OF BARTON LANDING, IN BARTON, TO DISPOSE OF THE SAME.

SECTION	SECTION
1. Pew-owners authorized to sell and dispose of; proceedings; meeting.	3. Pews to be appraised; how.
	4. Value of pews to be deposited by owners before sale; proviso.
2. Officers of meeting; who may vote.	5. To take effect.

It is hereby enacted by the General Assembly of the State of Vermont :

SEC. 1. The pew-owners and proprietors of the " Old Methodist Episcopal Meeting-House," so called, situated in the village of Barton Landing, in Barton, and in the county of Orleans, are hereby authorized and empowered to make such disposition of said meeting-house as a majority of the pew-owners and proprietors shall direct at a meeting warned for the purpose in the manner hereinafter named: If the quarterly conference of the Methodist Episcopal Church, at said village of Barton Landing, shall, at any regular meeting of said conference, vote to authorize and request the clerk of said conference to call a meeting of the pew-owners and proprietors of said meeting-house to act upon the disposition of said house, or if a majority of the pew-owners and proprietors of said house shall unite, in writing, requesting the clerk of said quarterly conference to call such meeting, then the said clerk shall call said meeting by posting notices of such meeting in three public places in said town of Barton, at least twenty days before such meeting, and publishing the same in the Barton Monitor, or such paper as may be printed at Barton, for two weeks successively, the last of which publication shall not be more than four weeks nor less than one week preceding said meeting. Two thirds of the members of said quarterly conference must vote in favor of calling such meeting; but if such vote is declared, or if the majority of the pew-owners and proprietors shall unite, in writing, as aforesaid, then it shall be obligatory upon the said clerk to call such meeting at once in the manner heretofore specified, and naming in said call the hour and place of said meeting.

SEC. 2. The preacher in charge of said church shall preside at said meeting, or in his absence a chairman *pro tempore* may be elected; the clerk heretofore named, or in his absence a secretary *pro tempore*, shall keep a true record of the proceedings of said meeting. At such meeting each owner or proprietor of a pew or pews who shall be present or represented by proxy legally constituted, shall be entitled to one vote for each pew so owned by him. And if at such meeting, held pursuant to the provisions of this act, or at a regularly adjourned meeting of the same, the pew-owners representing a majority of the pews in said house shall vote to sell or otherwise dispose of said house, then said meeting shall elect three appraisers, who shall be disinterested men, to appraise such pews or parts of pews as are hereinafter mentioned, and said meeting shall by vote fix a day, which shall not be less than ten nor more than twenty days from the time of such meeting, when said appraisers shall meet to perform the duties imposed upon them by the provisions of this act. At the day so fixed upon, at one o'clock in the afternoon, the said appraisers shall attend at said house, and after hearing the parties interested who may be present, shall appraise the pews or parts of pews of all such pew-owners as shall not then, or at any time prior thereto, in writing, have consented and agreed to the disposition of said house, as made by said meeting.

SEC. 4.   Before selling or in any way disposing of said house, the pew-owners who have assented to such disposition, in writing, as aforesaid, shall deposit with the stewards of the Methodist Episcopal Church at said Barton Landing the appraised value of all pews or parts of pews the owners of which have not so consented, in writing, to such disposition; provided, however, that the pew-owners and proprietors may, if they choose, elect any person to receive such deposit by a majority vote at the meeting of said pew-owners and proprietors.   The funds so deposited with said stewards, or with such person as shall have been duly elected as aforesaid, shall be held in trust for said non-consenting pew-owners and proprietors, to be paid to them, their representatives, agents, or assignees, on demand and without interest.

SEC. 5.   This act shall take effect from its passage.

Approved, November 12, 1874.

No. 199.—AN ACT TO ENABLE THE PEW-OWNERS AND PROPRIETORS OF THE METHODIST MEET-ING-HOUSE IN BERLIN TO DISPOSE OF THE SAME.

SECTION	SECTION
1. Pew-owners to dispose of same; meeting to be called for that purpose.	3. If meeting vote to dispose of same, proceedings.
2. Organization; each pew-owner to have one vote for each pew owned by him.	4. Deposit to be made with town treasurer before sale.
	5. To take effect.

It is hereby enacted by the General Assembly of the State of Vermont:

SEC. 1. The pew-owners and proprietors of the Methodist meeting house situated in Berlin, county of Washington, are hereby authorized and empowered to make such disposition of said church and the site as a majority of the pew-owners and proprietors shall direct, at a meeting warned for that purpose by three of the pew-owners or proprietors, by posting notices in three public places in said town of Berlin, at least twelve days before such meeting, in the manner and subject to the restrictions herein contained.

SEC. 2. The meeting so called shall be organized by the election of a chairman to preside in said meeting, and a secretary, who shall keep a true record of all the proceedings in said meeting; and at such meeting each owner of a pew or pews shall be entitled to one vote for each pew by him owned.

SEC. 3. If at such meeting, held pursuant to the provisions of this act, a majority of the pew-owners, repre-

senting a majority of the pews, shall decide to sell or otherwise dispose of such church and site, such meeting shall
by vote fix the day, which shall not be less than twelve
nor more than eighteen days from the time of such meeting, on which day, at ten o'clock in the forenoon, three appraisers, appointed by the selectmen of Berlin, shall attend
at such meeting-house, and after hearing the parties interested who may be present, shall appraise the pews or
parts of pews of all such pew-owners as shall not, in
writing, have agreed to the disposition of said meeting-
house in such way as the majority vote may have determined.

SEC. 4.   Before selling, or in any way disposing of said
meeting-house, the pew-owners assenting to such disposition, shall deposit with the treasurer of said town of Berlin the appraised value of all pews, the owners of which
shall not have given their assent, in writing, to such sale or
disposition, by said treasurer to be paid to the parties entitled thereto on demand, without interest; and said treasurer shall be liable for the money so deposited with him
to the several persons entitled thereto.

SEC. 5.   This act shall take effect from its passage.

Approved, November 24, 1874.

No. 200.—AN ACT TO ENABLE THE BAPTIST CHURCH OF NEW HAVEN AND WEYBRIDGE TO DISPOSE OF THEIR PARSONAGE.

It is hereby enacted by the General Assembly of the State of Vermont:

SEC. 1. The members of the Baptist Church, known as the Baptist Church of New Haven and Weybridge, in the county of Addison, are hereby authorized and empowered to sell and convey, in any legal and proper manner, the lots or parcels of ground which have been held and occu. pied by them as a parsonage, and the proceeds thereof may be appropriated by them to promote the objects of benevolence now sustained by that denomination in this state.

SEC. 2. This act shall take effect from its passage.

Approved, October 28, 1874.

No. 201.—AN ACT TO AMEND SECTIONS ONE AND THREE OF AN ACT ENTITLED "AN ACT TO ENABLE THE PROPRIETORS AND PEW-OWNERS OF THE OLD WHITE CHURCH IN ORWELL, COUNTY OF ADDISON, TO DISPOSE OF THE SAME," APPROVED NOVEMBER 21, 1872.

SECTION
1. Pew-owners may vote to sell, at meeting called for that purpose; notice of, how given.

SECTION
2. Manner of sale.

It is hereby enacted by the General Assembly of the
State of Vermont:

SEC. 1.   Section one of an act entitled an "Act to enable
the proprietors and pew-owners of the Old White Church
in Orwell, county of Addison, to dispose of the same,"
approved November 21, 1872, is hereby amended so as
to read as follows:

The resident pew-owners and proprietors of the Old
White Church, so called, situated in the center village in
Orwell, in the county of Addison, are hereby authorized
and empowered to make such disposition of said church
as a majority of the pew-owners, residing in said Orwell,
shall direct, at a meeting warned for that purpose by the
pew-owners in said church, representing a majority of the
pews owned by persons residing in said town of Orwell,
who shall sign such call for said meeting, and post notices
thereof in three public places in the town of Orwell at
least ten days previous to said meeting.

SEC. 2.   Section three of said act is hereby amended so
as to read as follows:

If at any such meeting, held pursuant to the provisions
of this act, a majority of the pew-owners present shall by
their vote decide to sell or otherwise dispose of said
church, such meeting shall by vote fix the day, which
shall not be less than ten days nor more than twenty days
from the time of said meeting, on which day so fixed upon,
at ten o'clock A. M., three appraisers, who shall be disinterested men, appointed by the selectmen of said town of
Orwell, shall attend at said church, and after hearing the
parties interested who may be present, shall appraise the

pews or parts of pews of all such pew-owners as shall not, in writing, have consented and agreed to such disposition of said house in such way as the resident majority vote may have determined.

Approved, November 24, 1874.

No. 202.—AN ACT TO ENABLE THE PEW-OWNERS AND PROPRIETORS OF THE OLD BRICK CHURCH IN RICHFORD TO DISPOSE OF THE SAME

It is hereby enacted by the General Assembly of the State of Vermont:

SEC. 1. The pew-owners and proprietors of the old brick church situated in the village of Richford, in the county of Franklin, are hereby authorized and empowered to make such disposition of said church as a majority of the pew-owners shall direct, at a meeting warned for that purpose by the pew-owners representing a majority of the pews in said church, who shall sign a call for said meeting, and post notices thereof in three public places in said town of Richford at least ten days prior to said meeting.

SEC. 2. The meeting so called shall be organized by the
election of a chairman, whose duty it shall be to preside
in said meeting, and a secretary who shall keep a true record of all the proceedings of said meeting; and at such
meeting each owner of a pew or pews who shall be present
at such meeting, shall be entitled to one vote for each pew
by him or her owned.

SEC. 3. If at such meeting, held pursuant to the provisions of this act, a majority of the pew-owners, representing a majority of the pews, shall decide to sell or otherwise dispose of such church and site, such meeting shall
by vote fix the day, which shall not be less than twelve nor
more than twenty days from the time of such meeting, on
which day, at ten o'clock in the forenoon, three appraisers,
who shall be disinterested men, appointed by the selectmen of said town of Richford, shall attend at such meeting-
house, and after hearing the parties interested who may
be present, shall appraise the pews or parts of pews of
all such pew-owners as shall not, in writing, have agreed
to the disposition of said meeting-house in such way as the
majority vote may have determined.

SEC. 4. Before selling, or in any way disposing of said
meeting-house, the pew-owners assenting to such disposition shall deposit with the treasurer of said town of Richford the appraised value of all pews, the owners of which
shall not have given their assent, in writing, to such sale
or disposition, by said treasurer to be paid to the parties
thereto, on demand, without interest; and said treasurer
shall be liable for the money so deposited with him to the
several persons entitled thereto.

SEC. 5. If at such meeting, it shall be determined to

sell such church and site, a committee of three persons shall be appointed at said meeting, who shall sell such church and site at private sale or public auction, as such meeting shall direct by vote, and whose deed shall be suffi. cient to convey the same by a good and valid title to the purchaser thereof.

SEC. 6. This act shall take effect from its passage.

Approved, November 23, 1874.

No. 203.—AN ACT TO PAY THE TOWN OF ST. ALBANS THE SUM THEREIN NAMED.

It is hereby enacted by the General Assembly of the State of Vermont:

SEC. 1. The auditor of accounts is hereby authorized and directed to draw his order on the state treasurer, in favor of the town of St. Albans, for the sum of eleven hundred fifty-one and ninety one-hundredths dollars, it being for money paid out and expenses incurred in investigating the circumstances of the murder of Miss Marietta Ball, and in endeavoring to detect and apprehend the murderer.

SEC. 2. This act shall take effect from its passage.

Approved, November 12, 1874.

No. 204.—AN ACT TO PAY THE TOWN OF ST. AL- BANS THE SUM THEREIN NAMED.

It is hereby enacted by the General Assembly of the State of Vermont:

Sec. 1. The auditor of accounts is hereby directed to draw an order on the state treasurer for the sum of two hundred seventy-eight dollars and thirty-seven cents, in favor of the town of St. Albans, it being for money expended by said town of St. Albans in the pursuit and effort to apprehend the murderers of Joseph Menard.

Sec. 2. This act shall take effect from its passage.

Approved, November 17, 1874.

No. 205.—AN ACT TO PAY THE BRADFORD SAV- INGS BANK AND TRUST COMPANY THE SUM THEREIN NAMED.

It is hereby enacted by the General Assembly of the State of Vermont:

Sec. 1. The auditor of accounts is hereby directed to draw an order on the treasurer for the sum of forty-seven dollars and seventeen cents, in favor of L. F. Hale, treasurer of the Bradford Savings Bank and Trust Company, it being for money expended in pursuing and capturing C. P. Wright, a bank defaulter.

Sec. 2. This act shall take effect from its passage.

Approved, November 12, 1874.

No. 206.—AN ACT TO PAY H. S. STREETER AND FRANK ALGER THE SUM THEREIN NAMED.

It is hereby enacted by the General Assembly of the State of Vermont:

SEC. 1. The auditor of accounts is hereby ordered and directed to draw an order on the treasurer of the state, in favor of H. S. Streeter and Frank Alger, for the sum of seventeen and twenty-four one-hundredths dollars, it being for expenses incurred by them in coming from the state of Massachusetts to attend as witnesses before the grand jury at Manchester, in the county of Bennington, in the case of State of Vermont against Norman Gray, charged with the crime of horse stealing.

SEC. 2. This act shall take effect from its passage.

Approved. November 24, 1874.

No. 207.—AN ACT TO PAY MYRON BARTON THE SUM THEREIN NAMED.

It is hereby enacted by the General Assembly of the State of Vermont:

SEC. 1. The auditer of accounts is hereby authorized and directed to draw an order on the treasurer of the state for the sum of thirty-eight and ninety one-hundredths dollars, in favor of Myron Barton of Shaftsbury, it being for time spent and money expended by him in apprehending and bringing to justice in Bennington county, Hazen A Sargeant, charged with the crime of burglary.

SEC. 2. This act shall take effect from its passage.

Approved, November 24, 1874.

No. 208.—AN ACT TO PAY SHELDON BORIGHT THE SUM THEREIN NAMED.

It is hereby enacted by the General Assembly of the State of Vermont:

SEC. 1. The auditor of accounts is hereby directed to draw an order upon the state treasurer for the sum of one hundred and three and thirty one-hundredths dollars, it being for money expended by him in the pursuit and the effort to apprehend the parties who entered the stores of said Sheldon Boright, and Rounds & Carpenter, of Richford, in the county of Franklin, on the night of the first day of October, A. D. 1873, and broke open and robbed the safes therein.

SEC. 2. This act shall take effect from its passage.

Approved, November 5, 1874.

No. 209.—AN ACT TO PAY DANFORD BROWN THE SUM THEREIN NAMED.

It is hereby enacted by the General Assembly of the State of Vermont:

SEC. 1. The auditor of accounts is hereby directed to draw an order on the state treasurer for the sum of eight dollars, in favor of Danford Brown, it being for money expended in trying to procure the arrest of one Darwin Dow, accused of the crime of rape.

SEC. 2. This act shall take effect from its passage.

Approved, November 20, 1874.

No. 210.—AN ACT TO PAY H. Z. AND S. L. CHURCHILL, OF GOSHEN, THE SUM THEREIN NAMED.

It is hereby enacted by the General Assembly of the State of Vermont:

SEC. 1. The auditor of accounts is hereby directed to draw an order upon the treasurer in the sum of nineteen and ninety-three one-hundredths dollars, in favor of H. Z. and S. L. Churchill of Goshen, for money and time expended in recovering a stolen horse, and searching for and arresting the thief, John B. Ferson, who is now in the state prison at Windsor.

SEC. 2. This act shall take effect from its passage.

Approved, November 24, 1874.

No. 211.—AN ACT TO PAY ALBERT CLARKE THE SUM THEREIN NAMED.

It is hereby enacted by the General Assembly of the State of Vermont: .

SEC. 1. The auditor of accounts is hereby directed to draw an order in favor of Albert Clarke of St. Albans, for the sum of three hundred seventy-three and twenty-five one-hundredths dollars, in payment of expenses and damages sustained by him as the official printer of the report of the joint special committee of the legislature of 1872 to investigate certain charges of legislative corruption, and the affairs of the Vermont Central Railroad, by reason of the protracted delay and neglect of the short-hand reporter to write out a part of the testimony and furnish the same for printing.

SEC. 2. This act shall take effect from its passage.

Approved, November 24, 1874.

No. 212.—AN ACT TO PAY GEORGE W. CRAWFORD THE SUM THEREIN NAMED.

It is hereby enacted by the General Assembly of the State of Vermont:

SEC. 1. The auditor of accounts is hereby directed to draw an order on the treasurer of the state for the sum of thirty-seven and sixty-five one-hundredths dollars, in favor of George W. Crawford of Rutland, it being for money paid out by him in the pursuit and arrest of one Loren Perkins, who has been indicted for forgery.

SEC. 2. This act shall take effect from its passage.

Approved, November 17, 1874.

No. 213.—AN ACT TO PAY DAVID CROFUT THE SUM THEREIN NAMED.

It is hereby enacted by the General Assembly of the State of Vermont:

SEC. 1. The auditor of accounts is hereby authorized and directed to draw an order on the treasurer of the state, in favor of David Crofut, sheriff of Bennington county, for the sum of ninety-three and ninety-five one-hundredths dollars, it being for time and money expended by him in searching for J. B. Covey, who escaped from Bennington jail while charged with the crime of murder; and also for time and expense in pursuing, capturing and returning to said Bennington jail, Michael Barrett, an escaped prisoner therefrom.

SEC. 2. This act shall take effect from its passage.

Approved, November 20, 1874.

No. 214.—AN ACT TO PAY H. A. CUTTING THE SUM THEREIN NAMED.

It is hereby enacted by the General Assembly of the State of Vermont:

SEC. 1. The auditor of accounts is hereby directed to draw an order on the state treasurer, in favor of Hiram A. Cutting, for the sum of two hundred and forty-four dollars, being in payment for fifty-eight days service and expenses in collecting specimens for and in care of and arranging the cabinet in the years 1871, 1872 and 1873—other than during the sessions of the legislature.

SEC. 2. This act shall take effect from its passage.

Approved, November 24, 1874.

No. 215.—AN ACT TO PAY LUMAN A. DREW THE SUM THEREIN NAMED.

It is hereby enacted by the General Assembly of the State of Vermont:

SEC. 1. The auditor of accounts is hereby directed to draw an order upon the state treasurer for the sum of two hundred and eighty and ninety-five one-hundredths dollars, in favor of Luman A. Drew, it being for money expended by him in the pursuit of Edward Shioette, charged with the crime of burglary.

SEC. 2. This act shall take effect from its passage.

Approved, November 18, 1874.

No. 216—AN ACT TO PAY D. W. DUDLEY THE SUM THEREIN NAMED.

It is hereby enacted by the General Assembly of the State of Vermont:

SEC. 1.   The auditor of accounts is hereby directed to draw an order on the treasurer of the state for the sum of fifteen dollars, in favor of D. W. Dudley, it being for time and money expended in apprehending and bringing to justice Levi Robinson and W. C. Webster, for the crime of larceny.

SEC. 2.   This act shall take effect from its passage.

Approved, November 24, 1874.

No. 217.—AN ACT TO PAY M. C. EDMUNDS THE SUM THEREIN NAMED.

It is hereby enacted by the General Assembly of the State of Vermont:

SEC. 1.   The auditor of accounts is hereby authorized and directed to draw an order on the treasurer of the state, for the sum of six and fifty one-hundredths dollars, in favor of M. C. Edmunds, it being for time and money expended in procuring the arrest and conviction of Anson Heyward, for arson.

SEC. 2.   This act shall take effect from its passage.

Approved, November 24, 1874.

No. 218.—AN ACT TO PAY MARTIN G. EVERTS THE SUM THEREIN NAMED.

It is hereby enacted by the General Assembly of the State of Vermont:

Sec. 1. The auditor of accounts is hereby directed to draw an order on the state treasurer for the sum of one hundred fifty dollars, in favor of Martin G. Everts, it being for services rendered before the inquest upon the body of Anna Freeze, late of Rutland, deceased, and time spent as counsel in preparation of case for trial, and services upon the trial, of John P. Phair for the murder of the said Anna Freeze.

Sec. 2. This act shall take effect from its passage.

Approved, November 12, 1874.

No. 219.—AN ACT TO PAY JEREMIAH W. FLINN THE SUM THEREIN NAMED.

It is hereby enacted by the General Assembly of the State of Vermont:

Sec. 1. The auditor of accounts is hereby directed to draw an order upon the state treasurer for the sum of fifty dollars, payable to Jeremiah W. Flinn, it being for money expended by him in the pursuit and the effort to apprehend the parties who entered his barn in Milton, Chittenden county, on the night of the 27th day of August, A. D. 1874, and stole a horse and harness therefrom.

Sec. 2. This act shall take effect from its passage.

Approved, November 5, 1874.

No. 220.—AN ACT TO PAY WILLIAM GAY THE SUM THEREIN NAMED.

It is hereby enacted by the General Assembly of the State of Vermont:

SEC. 1.   The auditor of accounts is hereby authorized and directed to draw an order on the treasurer of the state for the sum of fourteen dollars, in favor of William Gay, it being for time and money expended by him in pursuing and apprehending one William Curtis, who stole a watch, horse, harness, money and other property, from the house and premises of said William Gay in Windsor.

SEC. 2.   This act shall take effect from its passage.

Approved, November 24, 1874.

No. 221.—AN ACT TO PAY GEORGE W. GIBSON THE SUM THEREIN NAMED.

It is hereby enacted by the General Assembly of the State of Vermont:

SEC. 1.   The auditor of accounts is hereby directed to draw an order upon the state treasurer for the sum of sixty-seven and fifty-seven one-hundredths dollars, payable to George W. Gibson, it being for money expended by him in the pursuit and apprehension of Charles Miller, charged with committing the crime of burglary in the store of said Gibson, in Richford, in the county of Franklin, in the month of July A. D. 1874.

SEC. 2.   This act shall take effect from its passage.

Approved, November 5, 1874.

No. 222.—AN ACT TO PAY ELIJAH HANSON THE SUM THEREIN NAMED.

It is hereby enacted by the General Assembly of the State of Vermont:

Sec. 1. The auditor of accounts is hereby authorized and directed to draw an order on the treasurer of the state, in favor of Elijah Hanson, of the town of Irasburgh, in the county of Orleans, for the sum of forty-nine and eighty one-hundredths dollars, it being for services rendered and money expended by him in the pursuit and arrest of Frank Kenneston, who has been indicted for horse stealing.

Sec. 2. This act shall take effect from its passage.

Approved, November 5, 1874.

No. 223.—AN ACT TO PAY EDWARD HAWKINS THE SUM THEREIN NAMED.

It is hereby enacted by the General Assembly of the State of Vermont:

Sec. 1. The auditor of accounts is hereby authorized and directed to draw an order on the treasurer of the state in favor of Edward Hawkins, of the town of Salem, in the county of Orleans, in the sum of twenty-three dollars and sixty-three cents, it being for services rendered and money expended by him in apprehending and bringing to justice, in Orleans county, John Green, on the charge of horse stealing, and for time, trouble and expense in recovering his horse which said Green had stolen.

Approved, November 5, 1874.

No. 224.—AN ACT TO PAY EDWIN HORTON THE SUM THEREIN NAMED.

It is hereby enacted by the General Assembly of the State of Vermont :

SEC. 1. The auditor of accounts is hereby directed to draw an order on the state treasurer for the sum of thirty-eight dollars, in favor of Edwin Horton, it being for money expended in pursuing one Darwin Dow, accused of the crime of rape.

SEC. 2. This act shall take effect from its passage.

Approved, November 20, 1874.

No. 225.—AN ACT TO PAY E. O. HUNT THE SUM THEREIN NAMED.

It is hereby enacted by the General Assembly of the State of Vermont:

SEC. 1. The auditor of accounts is hereby directed to to draw an order on the treasurer of the state for the sum of fifteen dollars, in favor of E. O. Hunt, it being money entitled him for bounty on a bear.

SEC. 2. This act shall take effect from its passage.

Approved, November 20, 1874.

No. 226.—AN ACT TO PAY HOMER C. JENNISON THE SUM THEREIN NAMED.

It is hereby enacted by the General Assembly of the State of Vermont:

SEC. 1. The state treasurer is hereby directed to pay Homer C. Jennison the sum of seventy-five dollars, it being for time lost and medical attendance while laid up with a leg fractured while serving in Capt. James P. Place's company of frontier cavalry, in November, 1864.

SEC. 2. This act shall take effect from its passage.

Approved, November 24, 1874.

No. 227.—AN ACT TO PAY CHARLES H. JOYCE THE SUM THEREIN NAMED.

It is hereby enacteq by the General Assembly of the State of Vermont :

SEC. 1. The auditor of accounts is hereby authorized and directed to draw an order on the state treasurer, in favor of Charles H. Joyce of Rutland, in the sum of ninety-five and thirty-five one-hundredths dollars, it being for service rendered and expenses incurred in assisting in the prosecution of Franklin E. Lawrence and Sherrod Farwell, charged with the crime of murder.

SEC. 2. This act shall take effect from its passage.

Approved, November 12, 1874.

No. 228.—AN ACT TO PAY ALLEN KETCHUM THE SUM THEREIN NAMED.

It is hereby enacted by the General Assembly of the State of Vermont:

SEC. 1. The auditor of accounts is hereby directed to draw an order on the treasurer of the state for the sum of twenty-eight dollars and nine cents, in favor of Allen Ketchum of Whiting, it being for money paid out by him in the pursuit and arrest of one James Keefe, who has been convicted of larceny.

SEC. 2. This act shall take effect from its passage.

Approved, November 5, 1874.

No. 229.—AN ACT TO PAY JOHN A. PAGE THE SUM THEREIN NAMED.

It is herey enacted by the General Assembly of the State of Vermont :

SEC. 1.   The auditor of accounts is hereby directed to draw an order on the treasurer of this state, in favor of John A. Page, for the sum of one thousand dollars, it being for services rendered under the requirements of an act approved November 26, 1872, entitled "An act to promote the settlement of soldiers' accounts on the books of the treasurer's office."

SEC. 2.   This act shall take effect from its passage.

Approved, November 9, 1874.

No. 230.—AN ACT TO PAY FRANCIS PHELPS THE SUM THEREIN NAMED.

It is hereby enacted by the General Assembly of the State of Vermont:

SEC. 1.   The auditor of accounts is hereby authorized and directed to draw an order on the treasurer of the state for the sum of thirty-five dollars, in favor of Francis Phelps, it being for money expended and time spent in pursuing Mont Witherell, who was charged with the crime of assault and battery with intent to kill.

SEC. 2.   This act shall take effect from its passage.

Approved, November 12, 1874.

No. 231.—AN ACT TO PAY CHARLES W. PORTER THE SUM THEREIN NAMED.

It is hereby enacted by the General Assembly of the State of Vermont:

SEC. 1. The auditor of accounts is hereby authorized and directed to draw an order on the treasurer of this state, in favor of Charles W. Porter, for the sum of two hundred dollars, the same being for services rendered and expenses incurred as secretary of the state equalizing board, said services having been rendered by the direction of said board at its last session.

SEC. 2. This act shall take effect from its passage.

Approved, November 17, 1874.

No. 232.—AN ACT TO PAY HENRY H. RANKIN AND CASSIUS A. PRATT THE SUM THEREIN NAMED.

It is hereby enacted by the General Assembly of the State of Vermont:

SEC. 1. The treasurer of the state of Vermont is authorized and directed to pay Henry H. Rankin and Cassius A. Pratt the sum of eight dollars and eighty-five cents, it being money spent by them in pursuing and arresting one Edward Shioette, and two accomplices, for the crimes of burglary and larceny.

SEC. 2. This act shall take effect from its passage.

Approved, November 24, 1874.

No. 233.—AN ACT TO PAY CHARLES E. RANSOM THE SUM THEREIN MENTIONED.

It is hereby enacted by the General Assembly of the State of Vermont:

SEC. 1. The auditor of accounts is hereby directed to draw an order on the state treasurer, in favor of Charles E. Ransom, for the sum of thirty dollars, it being for money expended and time spent in pursuing and arresting George Harwood, a horse thief.

SEC. 2. This act shall take effect from its passage.

Approved, November 20, 1874.

No. 234.—AN ACT TO PAY CARLTON H. ROUNDY THE SUM THEREIN NAMED.

It is hereby enacted by the General Assembly of the State of Vermont:

SEC. 1. The auditor of accounts is hereby directed to draw an order on the state treasurer for the sum of twenty-two and twenty-five one-hundredths dollars, in favor of Carlton H. Roundy of Springfield, Vermont, for servic es in enrolling soldiers, subject to draft by order of Adjutant General Washburn, in the year 1862.

SEC. 2. This act shall take effect from its passage.

Approved, November 24, 1874.

No. 235.—AN ACT TO PAY JULIAN SCOTT THE
SUM THEREIN MENTIONED.

*It is hereby enacted by the General Assembly of the State
of Vermont:*

SEC. 1. The auditor of accounts is hereby authorized
and directed to draw his order upon the treasurer of this
state for the sum of four thousand dollars, in favor of
Julian Scott, in payment of extra money and labor expended in completing the historical painting, representing
the action of Vermont troops in the battle of Cedar Creek.

SEC. 2. This act shall take effect from its passage.

Approved, November 24, 1874.

No. 236.—AN ACT TO PAY GEORGE F. SKIFF THE
SUM THEREIN NAMED.

*It is hereby enacted by the General Assembly of the State
of Vermont:*

SEC. 1. The auditor of accounts is hereby authorized
and directed to draw an order on the treasurer of the state
for the sum of twenty-seven dollars and eighty-seven
cents, in favor of George F. Skiff, it being for time and
money spent in procuring the arrest and conviction of
Joseph Bushey, for horse stealing.

SEC. 2. This act shall take effect from its passage.

Approved, November 18, 1874.

No. 237.—AN ACT TO PAY JAMES M. SLADE, Jr., THE SUM THEREIN NAMED.

It is hereby enacted by the General Assembly of the State of Vermont:

SEC. 1. The auditor of accounts is hereby authorized and directed to draw an order on the treasurer of the state for the sum of seventy-five dollars, in favor of James M. Slade, Jr., it being the balance of salary due him for his services as secretary of civil and military affairs from October eighteen hundred and seventy to October eighteen hundred and seventy-two.

SEC. 2. This act shall take effect from its passage.

Approved, November 20, 1874.

No. 238.—AN ACT TO PAY WARREN H. SMITH OF RUTLAND THE SUM THEREIN NAMED.

It is hereby enacted by the General Assembly of the State of Vermont:

SEC. 1. The auditor of accounts is hereby directed to draw an order on the treasurer of this state, in favor of Warren H. Smith of Rutland, in the county of Rutland, for the sum of two hundred dollars, it being for his services and disbursements as solicitor for defendants in the cause of E. Mott Robinson and others against the treasurer of this state and others in the United States Circuit Court.

SEC. 2. This act shall take effect from its passage.

Approved, November 17, 1874.

No. 239.—AN ACT TO PAY A. V. SPALDING THE SUM THEREIN NAMED.

It is hereby enacted by the General Assembly of the State of Vermont:

SEC. 1.   The auditor of accounts is hereby authorized and directed to draw an order on the state treasurer, in favor of A. V. Spalding of Burlington, in the sum of twenty-five dollars, it being for services rendered in the prosecution of Horace Stokes, charged with an assault with intent to kill, at the June term, 1873, of the Addison county court.

SEC. 2.   This act shall take effect from its passage.

Approved, October 28, 1874.

No. 240.—AN ACT TO PAY WILLIAM H. SPAFFORD THE SUM THEREIN MENTIONED.

It is hereby enacted by the General Assembly of the State of Vermont:

SEC. 1.   The auditor of accounts is hereby authorized and directed to draw an order on the state treasurer, in favor of William H. Spafford, for the sum of thirteen dollars and seventy-five cents, the same being for money paid out and expenses incurred in pursuing and arresting one George E. Perkins, charged with the crime of larceny.

SEC. 2.   This act shall take effect from its passage.

Approved, November 17, 1874.

No. 241.—AN ACT TO PAY CHARLES SWAN AND ORSAMUS WILKINS THE SUM THEREIN NAMED.

It is hereby enacted by the General Assembly of the State of Vermont:

SEC. 1. The treasurer of the state of Vermont is authorized and directed to pay Charles Swan and Orsamus Wilkins the sum of thirty-nine and thirty one-hundredths dollars, it being money spent by them pursuing horse theives and searching for stolen property in August and September, 1874.

SEC. 2. This act shall take effect from its passage.

Approved, November 24, 1874.

No. 242.—AN ACT TO PAY CLARK THOMPSON THE SUM THEREIN NAMED.

It is hereby enacted by the General Assembly of the State of Vermont:

SEC. 1. The auditer of accounts is hereby authorized and directed to draw an order on the treasurer of the state for the sum of three hundred dollars, it being for money paid on fine in prosecution, State against said Thompson.

SEC. 2. This act shall take effect from its passage.

Approved, November 24, 1874.

No. 243.—AN ACT TO PAY F. S. THOMPSON OF RUTLAND THE SUM THEREIN NAMED.

It is hereby enacted by the General Assembly of the State of Vermont:

SEC. 1. That the auditor of accounts is hereby authorized and directed to draw an order on the treasurer of the state, in favor of F. S. Thompson, for the sum of eight and seventy-five one-hundredths dollars, the same being in payment of expenses attending the pursuit and arrest of one Patrick McCauley, charged with grand larceny, and who has since been convicted on said charge and is now serving out his term of service therefor in the state prison at Windsor.

SEC. 2. This act shall take effect from its passage.

Approved, November 24, 1874.

No. 244.—AN ACT TO PAY JEREMIAH C. THORNTON THE SUM THEREIN MENTIONED.

It is hereby enacted by the General Assembly of the State of Vermont:

SEC. 1. That the auditor of accounts be authorized and directed to draw an order on the treasurer of the state, in favor of Jeremiah C. Thornton of Rutland, for the sum of two hundred ninety-five and twenty-eight one-hundredths dollars, the same being in payment of expenses incurred in searching for the murderer of one Anna Freeze, and expense of procuring witnesses from without the state to attend and give evidence at the trial before the justice, the coroner, and the Rutland county court.

SEC. 2. This act shall take effect.from its passage.

Approved, November 18, 1874.

No. 245.—AN ACT TO PAY ISAAC M. TRIPP THE SUM THEREIN NAMED.

It is hereby enacted by the General Assembly of the State of Vermont:

SEC. 1. The auditor of accounts is hereby authorized to draw an order on the treasurer of the state for the sum of one hundred and thirteen and twenty-eight one-hundredths dollars, in favor of Isaac M. Tripp, it being for money expended by him in the pursuit of Joseph Wilson, charged with the crime of highway robbery.

SEC. 2. This act shall take effect from its passage.

Approved, November 12, 1874.

No. 246.—AN ACT TO PAY G. M. TUTTLE THE SUM THEREIN NAMED.

It is hereby enacted by the General Assembly of the State of Vermont:

SEC. 1. The auditor of accounts is hereby authorized and directed to draw an order on the treasurer of the state, in favor of G. M. Tuttle, of the town of Newbury, in the county of Orange, for the sum of twenty-four dollars and thirty-seven cents, it being for money expended in pursuing a horce thief, who is now under arrest.

SEC. 2. This act to take effect from its passage.

Approved, November 24, 1874.

No. 247.—AN ACT TO PAY BARNET S. WAIT THE SUM THEREIN NAMED.

It is hereby enacted by the General Assembly of the State of Vermont:

SEC. 1. The auditor of accounts is hereby authorized and directed to draw an order on the treasurer of the state for the sum of one hundred and fifty dollars and twenty-five cents, in favor of Barnet S. Wait, it being for time spent and money expended by him in pursuing and apprehending, upon the requisition of the governor, one Charles R. Brown, an escaped prisoner.

SEC. 2. This act shall take effect from its passage.

Approved, November 5, 1874.

No. 248.—AN ACT TO PAY GARDNER J. WALLACE THE SUM THEREIN NAMED.

It is hereby enacted by the General Assembly of the State of Vermont:

SEC. 1. The auditor of accounts is hereby directed to draw an order on the treasurer of the state for the sum of sixty-five and thirty one-hundredths dollars, in favor of Gardner J. Wallace, for going with and presenting to the governor of New York a requisition from the governor of this state, for P. H. Bowen, charged with obtaining a note for a pretended patent gate by false pretenses.

SEC. 2. This act shall take effect from its passage.

Approved, November 18, 1874.

No. 249.—AN ACT TO PAY EDWIN WHEELER THE SUM THEREIN NAMED.

It is hereby enacted by the General Assembly of the State of Vermont:

SEC. 1. The auditor of accounts is hereby directed to draw an order upon the state treasurer for the sum of nineteen and ninety one-hundredths dollars, payable to Edwin Wheeler of Richford, in the county of Franklin, it being for money expended by him in the pursuit of Hazen E. Sargent, charged with stealing a harness from said Wheeler, and a sleigh and robes from Gilbert L. Goff, on the night of February 18, A. D. 1873.

SEC. 2. This act shall take effect from its passage.

Approved, November 5, 1874.

No. 250.—AN ACT TO PAY CHARLES M. WHITAKER THE SUM THEREIN MENTIONED.

It is hereby enacted by the General Assembly of the State of Vermont:

Sec. 1.   That the auditor of accounts be authorized and directed to draw an order on the treasurer of the state, in favor of Charles M. Whitaker of Brandon, Vermont, for the sum of two hundred dollars, the same being in payment of actual cash expenses of him, the said Whitaker, in an effort to find and arrest certain burglars by whom he was robbed of all his property on the tenth day of July, A. D. 1873.

Sec. 2.   This act shall take effect from its passage.

Approved, November 12, 1874.

No. 251.—AN ACT TO LEGALIZE THE GRAND LIST OF THE TOWN OF BRIDGEWATER FOR THE YEAR 1873.

It is hereby enacted by the General Assembly of the State of Vermont:

Sec. 1.   The grand list of the town of Bridgewater for the year 1873, as made out by the listers of said town, as to all taxes assessed or to be assessed thereon, is hereby declared legal and valid.

Sec. 2.   This act shall take effect from its passage.

Approved, November 20, 1874.

No. 252.—AN ACT TO LEGALIZE THE GRAND LIST OF THE TOWN OF BROOKFIELD FOR THE YEAR 1874.

It is hereby enacted by the General Assembly of the State of Vermont:

SEC. 1. The grand list of the town of Brookfield for the year 1874, as to all taxes assessed thereon, is hereby de-clared legal and valid, the same as if said grand list had been completed within the time prescribed by law.

SEC. 2. This act shall take effect from its passage.

Approved, November 20, 1874.

No. 253.—AN ACT TO LEGALIZE THE GRAND LIST OF THE CITY OF BURLINGTON.

It is hereby enacted by the General Assembly of the State of Vermont:

SEC. 1. The grand list of the city of Burlington for the year 1864, as made out by the assessors of said city, and all taxes assessed thereon, are hereby declared legal and valid, the same as if the assessors had deposited said list in the city clerk's office at the time required by law, and the same as if said grand list had been properly signed and sworn to by the listers of said city of Burlington.

SEC. 2. This act shall take effect from its passage.

Approved, November 21, 1874.

No. 254.—AN ACT TO LEGALIZE THE GRAND LIST OF THE TOWN OF CABOT FOR THE YEARS 1872 AND 1873.

It is hereby enacted by the General Assembly of the State of Vermont:

SEC. 1. The grand list of the town of Cabot for the years 1872 and 1873, as made out by the listers of said town, as ·to all taxes assessed thereon, is hereby declared legal and valid.

SEC. 2. This act shall take effect from its passage.

Approved, November 20, 1874.

No. 255.—AN ACT TO LEGALIZE THE GRAND LIST OF THE TOWN OF DUXBURY FOR THE YEAR 1874.

It is hereby enacted by the General Assembly of the State of Vermont:

SEC. 1. The grand list of the town of Duxbury for the year 1874, as made out by the listers of said town, as to all taxes assessed thereon, is hereby declared legal and valid.

SEC. 2. This act shall take effect from its passage.

Approved, November 20, 1874.

No. 256.—AN ACT TO LEGALIZE THE GRAND LIST OF THE TOWN OF GOSHEN FOR THE YEAR A. D. 1874.

It is hereby enacted by the General Assembly of the State of Vermont:

SEC. 1. The grand list of the town of Goshen for the year A. D. 1874, as to all taxes which have been raised or may hereafter be raised upon said grand list, is hereby declared legal and valid.

Approved, November 17, 1874.

No. 257.—AN ACT TO LEGALIZE THE GRAND LISTS OF THE TOWN OF GRAFTON FOR THE YEARS 1872, 1873 AND 1874.

It is hereby enacted by the General Assembly of the State of Vermont:

SEC. 1. The grand lists of the town of Grafton for the years 1872, 1873 and 1874, including the quadrennial valuation and appraisal of the real estate for 1874, as to all taxes assessed and to be assessed on said lists, are hereby declared legal and valid.

SEC. 2. This act shall take effect from its passage.

Approved, November 5, 1874.

No. 258.—AN ACT TO LEGALIZE THE GRAND LIST OF THE TOWN OF HARDWICK FOR THE YEAR 1874.

It is hereby enacted by the General Assembly of the State of Vermont:

SEC. 1.	The grand list of the town of Hardwick for the year 1874 is hereby declared legal and valid, as to all taxes assessed or to be assessed thereon.

SEC. 2.	This act shall take effect from its passage.

Approved, November 21, 1874.

No. 259.—AN ACT LEGALIZING THE GRAND LIST OF THE TOWN OF JAY FOR THE YEAR OF 1874.

It is hereby enacted by the General Assembly of the State of Vermont:

SEC. 1.	The grand list of the town of Jay for the year of 1874, as made out by the listers of said town, as to all taxes assessed thereon, is hereby declared legal and valid, the same as if it had been placed in the grand list book designed for that purpose, and the proper oath subscribed to by said listers.

SEC. 2.	This act shall take effect from its passage.

Approved, November 12, 1874.

No. 260.—AN ACT TO LEGALIZE THE GRAND LIST OF THE TOWN OF LEICESTER.

It is hereby enacted by the General Assembly of the State of Vermont:

SEC. 1. The grand list of the town of Leicester for the year 1874, as to all taxes assessed and to be assessed on said list, is hereby made legal and valid.

SEC. 2. This act shall take effect from its passage.

Approved. November 24, 1874.

No. 261.—AN ACT TO LEGALIZE THE GRAND LISTS OF THE TOWN OF LEMINGTON FOR THE YEARS 1873 AND 1874.

It is hereby enacted by the General Assembly of the State of Vermont:

SEC. 1. The grand lists of the town of Lemington for the years 1873 and 1874, including the quadrennial appraisal of the real estate for 1874, as to all taxes assessed and to be assessed thereon, are hereby declared legal and valid.

SEC. 2. This act shall take effect from its passage.

Approved, November 5, 1874.

No. 262.—AN ACT TO LEGALIZE THE GRAND LIST OF FIRE DISTRICT NUMBER ONE IN THE TOWN OF LONDONDERRY FOR THE YEAR 1874.

It is hereby enacted by the General Assembly of the State of Vermont :

SEC. 1. The grand list which was designated, set apart and established as the grand list of fire district number one in the town of Londonderry, in the county of Windham, on the eighth day of August, A.D. 1874, by the selectmen of said town of Londonderry, as to all taxes which heretofore have been or which hereafter may be assessed thereon by said district, for and during the time said grand list shall remain in force, are hereby made and declared legal and valid.

SEC. 2. This act shall take effect from its passage.

Approved, November 20, 1874.

No. 263.—AN ACT TO LEGALIZE THE GRAND LIST OF THE TOWN OF MILTON FOR THE YEAR 1874.

It is hereby enacted by the General Assembly of the State of Vermont:

SEC. 1. The grand list of the town of Milton for the year 1874, as made out by the listers of said town, as to all taxes assessed or to be assessed thereon, is hereby declared legal and valid.

SEC. 2. This act shall take effect from its passage.

Approved, November 24, 1874.

No. 264.—AN ACT TO LEGALIZE THE GRAND LIST OF THE TOWN OF NORWICH FOR THE YEAR 1874.

It is hereby enacted by the General Assembly of the State of Vermont :

Sec. 1. The grand list of the town of Norwich, including the valuation and appraisal of the real estate of said town for the year 1874, as made out by the listers of said town, as to all taxes assessed or to be assessed thereon, is hereby declared legal and valid.

Sec. 2. This act shall take effect from its passage.

Approved, November 20, 1874.

No. 265.—AN ACT TO LEGALIZE THE QUINQUEN-NIAL VALUATION OF REAL ESTATE AND THE GRAND LISTS OF THE TOWN OF PLYMOUTH.

It is hereby enacted by the General Assembly of the State of Vermont :

Sec. 1. The grand list of the town of Plymouth, including the valuation and appraisal of the real estate of said town for the year 1870, and the several grand lists of said town for the years 1871, 1872, 1873 and 1874, as to all taxes assessed and to be assessed on said lists, are hereby declared legal and valid.

Sec. 2. This act shall take effect from its passage.

Approved, November 17, 1874.

No. 266.—AN ACT TO LEGALIZE THE GRAND LIST OF THE TOWN OF RUPERT.

It is hereby enacted by the General Assembly of the State of Vermont:

SEC. 1. The grand list of the town of Rupert for the year 1874, as made out by the listers of said town, as to all taxes assessed thereon, is hereby declared legal and valid, the same as if said list had been signed and sworn to, and deposited in the town clerk's office within the time required by law.

SEC. 2. This act shall take effect from its passage.

Approved, November 17, 1874.

No. 267.—AN ACT TO LEGALIZE THE GRAND LIST OF THE TOWN OF STANNARD FOR THE YEARS 1872, 1873 AND 1874.

It is hereby enacted by the General Assembly of the State of Vermont:

SEC. 1. The grand list of the town of Stannard for the years 1872, 1873 and 1874, as made out by the listers of said town, as to all taxes assessed thereon, is hereby declared legal and valid.

SEC. 2. This act shall take effect from its passage.

Approved, November 20, 1874.

No. 268.—AN ACT TO LEGALIZE THE GRAND LIST OF THE TOWN OF TUNBRIDGE FOR 1872 AND 1873.

It is hereby enacted by the General Assembly of the State of Vermont:

SEC. 1. The grand list of the town of Tunbridge for the years of 1872 and 1873, as to all taxes assessed thereon and to be assessed on said lists, is hereby declared legal and valid.

SEC. 2. This act shall take effect from its passage.

Approved, November 24, 1874.

No. 269.—AN ACT TO LEGALIZE THE GRAND LIST OF THE TOWN OF WESTFORD.

It is hereby enacted by the General Assembly of the State of Vermont:

SEC. 1. The grand list of the town of Westford for the years 1871 and 1872, as to all taxes assessed thereon, is hereby declared legal and valid, the same as if said grand list had been properly signed and sworn to by the listers of said Westford.

SEC. 2. This act shall take effect from its passage.

Approved, November 20, 1874.

No. 270.—AN ACT TO LEGALIZE THE GRAND LIST OF THE TOWN OF WOODFORD FOR THE YEARS 1873 AND 1874.

It is hereby enacted by the General Assembly of the State of Vermont:

SEC. 1. The grand list of the town of Woodford for the years 1873 and 1874, as made out by the listers of said town, as to all taxes assessed thereon, is hereby declared legal and valid.

SEC. 2. This act shall take effect from its passage.

Approved, November 24, 1874.

No. 271.—AN ACT TO CHANGE THE NAME OF ELLSWORTH BIGELOW ABBOTT TO ELLSWORTH BIGELOW.

It is hereby enacted by the General Assembly of the State of Vermont:

SEC. 1. Ellsworth Bigelow Abbott of Chelsea, in the county of Orange, shall hereafter be known and called by the name of Ellsworth Bigelow.

SEC. 2. This act shall take effect from its passage.

Approved, November 24, 1874.

No. 272.—AN ACT TO CHANGE THE NAME OF HARRY C. BURBANK.

It is hereby enacted by the General Assembly of the State of Vermont:

SEC. 1. Harry C. Burbank of Peacham, in the county of Caledonia, shall hereafter be called and known as Harry C. Moulton ; and he is hereby constituted heir-at-law of Van Ness D. Moulton and Addie E. Moulton of said Peacham.

SEC. 2. This act shall not take effect until said Van Ness D. Moulton and Addie E. Moulton shall give their assent thereto, in writing, under their hands and seals, in the presence of two witnesses, and cause the same to be recorded in the town clerk's office in said Peacham.

Approved, November 13, 1874.

No. 273.—AN ACT TO MAKE LEGITIMATE THE CHILDREN OF EDWIN E. WORDEN AND BRIDGET WORDEN OF BRANDON, VERMONT; AND TO CONSTITUTE SAID CHILDREN HEIRS-AT-LAW OF THE SAID EDWIN E. WORDEN AND BRIDGET WORDEN.

It is hereby enacted by the General Assembly of the State of Vermont:

SEC. 1. That the births of Mary Carlisle Worden,

Ellen Grant Worden, John Otis Worden and Frederick Allston Worden, children of Edwin E. Worden and Bridget Worden of Brandon, Rutland county, Vermont, are hereby made legitimate; and they, the said above named children, are hereby made and constituted the heirs-at-law of the said Edwin E. Worden and Bridget Worden, as fully and completely, and for all intents and purposes, as though they had been born in lawful wedlock.

Sec. 2. This act shall take effect from its passage.

Approved, November 20, 1874.

STATE OF VERMONT.

Office of Secretary of State, {
Montpelier, Jan. 1, 1875. }

I hereby certify that the foregoing two hundred and seventy-three numbers are true copies of the Acts and Resolves passed by the General Assembly at its Biennial Session A. D. 1874, as appears from the files and records of this office.

GEORGE NICHOLS, *Secretary of State.*

ADOPTIONS

AND

CHANGE OF NAMES.

Returned to the Office of the Secretary of State, in pursuance of Section Eleven of Chapter Fifty-Six of the General Statutes.

Jennie Branch, adopted by and made heir-at-law of Nelson Branch of Whiting, and to be known by the name of Jennie Branch.

Louisa Tredo, adopted by and made heir-at-law of Fred Marsal of Middlebury, and name changed to Louisa Marsal.

Sarah Marcy, a minor, adopted by William T. Britton, and Melinda C. Britton, his wife, of Windsor, constituted their heir-at-law, and name changed to Amelia Britton.

Minnie A. Williams, a minor, adopted by William H. H. Perkins and Candace M. Perkins, his wife, of Windsor, constituted their heir-at-law, and name changed to Minnie A. Perkins.

CIVIL GOVERNMENT—1874-75.

FEDERAL OFFICERS.

DAVID A. SMALLEY........Burlington.....District Judge.
BENJAMIN F. FIFIELD.....Montpelier ....District Attorney.
GEORGE P. FOSTER........Burlington ....Marshal.
BRADLEY B. SMALLEY.....Burlington... .Clerk.
WILLIAM WELLS. ... .Burlington ....Collector.
JOHN L. MASON............Richmond......Collector Int. Rev.

CONGRESSIONAL DELEGATION.

JUSTIN S MORRILL.......Strafford.......Senator.
GEORGE F. EDMUNDS,.....Burlington ....Senator.
*CHARLES W. WILLARD...Montpelier.....Representative.
CHARLES H JOYCE........Rutland ....Representative.
*LUKE P. POLAND.. .....St. Johnsbury..Representative.
DUDLEY C. DENISON......Royalton.... ..Representative.
GEORGE W. HENDEE .....Morristown ...Representative.
     *Term expires March 3d, 1875.

SUPREME COURT.

JOHN PIERPOINT ....Vergennes......Chief Justice.
JAMES BARRETT. ... .Woodstock.....Assistant Justice.
HOYT H. WHEELER........Jamaica.......Assistant Justice.
HOMER E. ROYCE ....St. Albans......Assistant Justice.
TIMOTHY P. REDFIELD....Montpelier.....Assistant Justice.
JONATHAN ROSS..........St. Johnsbury..Assistant Justice.
H. HENRY POWERS........Morristown ....Assistant Justice.
JOHN W. ROWELL... .....Randolph......Reporter.

EXECUTIVE DEPARTMENT.

ASAHEL PECK.............Jericho.........Governor.

LYMAN G. HINCKLEY......Chelsea.........Lieut. Governor.

WILLIAM P. DILLINGHAM.Waterbury......Sec. Civ. & Mil. Aff.

FRANK TUTTLE ....Montpelier......Messenger.

HENRY SMITH....,........Montpelier.....Page.

JOHN A. PAGE... ....Montpelier.....Treasurer.

JOHN W. PAGE............Montpelier.....Clerk.

JOHN PIERCE.............Montpelier.....Messenger.

CHARLES MORGAN.........Rochester.......Inspector of Finance.

GEORGE NICHOLS.. ......Northfield......Secretary of State.

CHARLES W. PORTER......Montpelier.....Deputy Sec. of State.

GEORGE R. CHAPMAN . ...Vergennes......Chief Clerk.

JOHN H. MERRIFIELD ....Newfane.......Engrossing Clerk.

JOHN K. STEARNS ....Woodstock.....Messenger.

WHITMAN G. FERRIN......Montpelier.....Auditor of Accounts.

ALBERT W. FERRIN.......Montpelier.....Clerk.

GEORGE F. PEASE.........Rutland........Messenger.

TRUMAN C. PHINNEY......Montpelier.....Sergeant-at-Arms.

ERASTUS S. CAMP.........Montpelier.....First Clerk.

JOSEPH W. SAULT..... ...Montpelier.....Second Clerk.

EDWARD S. EASTMAN.....Montpelier.....Messenger.

CHARLES NEWCOMB......Montpelier.....Messenger.

CHARLES L. ROBINSON....Reading...,....Messenger.

MYRON O. CLARK.........W. Charleston .Messenger.

EDWARD CONANT.........Randolph...... { State Sup't of Education.

MYRON W. BAILEY........St. Albans......R. R. Comm'r.

HIRAM H. ATWATER.......Burlington.....Comm'r of Insane.

CHARLES E. HOUGHTON...No. Bennington.
MARCUS D. GILMAN.......Montpelier..... } Directors of State Prison.
ELON D. PETTIGREW.......Ludlow........

JOHN F. BAILEY............Windsor.......Supt. State Prison.

PAUL DILLINGHAM.........Waterbury ....⎤ Trustees of the
VICTOR ATWOOD..........St. Albans......⎬Vermont Reform
CHARLES ROGERS, Jr......Wheelock......⎦   School.

WILLIAM G. FAIRBANK....Waterbury.....Supt. Reform School.

HIRAM A. HUSE.............Montpelier... .Librarian.
JAMES W. FARGO..........Randolph......Assistant Librarian.
MISS LETTIE E. DURANT..Montpelier.....Assistant Librarian.
FRANK A. LEAVENWORTH.New Haven....Messenger.

HIRAM A. CUTTING........Lunenburgh.... ⎰ Curator of Cabinet
                                        ⎱ & State Geologist
ROLLIN C. BROMLEY.......Huntington ....Messenger.

MILITARY DEPARTMENT.

ASAHEL PECK..............Jericho........Gov.& Com.-in-Ch'f.
JAMES S. PECK............Montpelier.....Adj't & Ins. Gener'l.
LEVI G. KINGSLEY... .....Rutland........Q. M. General.
JOEL H. LUCIA............Vergennes.....Judge Adv. General.

GOVERNOR'S STAFF.

DAN P. WEBSTER..........Putney ....Surgeon General.

JONATHAN M. HOYT..... .New Haven....⎤
WILLIAM BRINSMAID.... .Burlington.....⎥ Aides-de Camp
HENRY C. TENNANT......Bethel......... ⎢ with rank of Col.
HENRY C. HASTINGS.......St. Johnsbury..⎦

THE SENATE.

LYMAN G. HINCKLEY ......Chelsea........President.

FREDERIC W. BALDWIN....Barton.........Secretary.
CHA'CY W. BROWNELL, Jr.,Burlington......Assistant Secretary.
N. NEWTON GLAZIER......Montpelier.....Chaplain.
ROBERT ROBERTS.........Burlington .....Reporter.
WILLIAM A. LORD.........Montpelier.....Reporter,

Addison County......ALEXIS T. SMITH..........New Haven.

THURMAN BROOKINS......Shoreham.

Bennington County..MASON S. COLBURN........Manchester.

CHARLES E. HOUGHTON..N. Bennington.

Caledonia County ...CHARLES ROGERS, JR......Wheelock.

PLINY N. GRANGER.......Peacham.

Chittenden County...WILLIAM W. HENRY.....Burlington.

CHARLES I. LADD........Milton.

ALWIN H. CHESSMORE....Huntington

Essex County........CHARLES E. BENTON......Guildhall.

Franklin County.....ALBERT CLARKE..........St. Albans.

WILLIAM C. ROBIE........Franklin.

VICTOR ATWOOD.........St. Albans.

Grand Isle County...ASA REYNOLDS...........Alburgh.

Lamoille County.....CARROLL S. PAGE........Hyde Park.

Orange County......JOHN W. ROWELL........Randolph.

WILLIAM T. GEORGE......Topsham.

Orleans County......HENDERSON C. WILSON...North Troy.

HENRY S. TOLMAN........Greensboro.

Rutland County......REDFIELD PROCTOR......Rutland.

SIMEON ALLEN...........Fair Haven.

LUTHER P. HOWE........Mt. Tabor.

FAYETTE HOLMES........Sudbury.

Washington County..CLARK KING..............E. Montpelier.

ELIAKIM P. WALTON.....Montpelier.

Windham County....GEORGE HOWE...........Brattleboro.

ANDREW A. WYMAN.......Athens.

Windsor County.....JAMES J. WILSON........Bethel.

JOSEPH C. PARKER........Hartford.

MERRITT C. EDMUNDS....Weston,

CHESTER B. DOW...........Strafford.......Doorkeeper.

CARTER L. BEERS..........Monkton.......Ass't Doorkeeper.

GEORGE M. POWERS........Morristown....Page.

EDWIN H. JOHNSON........Burlington.....Page.

THE HOUSE.

JOSIAH GROUT..............Newport........Speaker.
DAVID M. CAMP.............Newport.......Clerk.
W. H. H. KENFIELD.........Hyde Park......1st Assistant Clerk
MILO S. BUCK..............Cavendish.......2d Assistant Clerk.
HAZLETON A. SPENCER....Montpelier.....Chaplain.
AND EW C. BROWN........Montpelier .. .Reporter.
ORVILLE S. BLISS..........Georgia........Reporter.

ADDISON COUNTY.

Addison.......................RUFUS SMITH.
Bridport......................WILLIAM R. BRAISTED.
Bristol. ....EDWIN D. BARNES.
Cornwall......................EDWARD S. DANA.
Ferrisburgh...................HARVEY F. CRAM.
Goshen........................HARVEY Z. CHURCHILL.
Granville.................HOMER P. HAYES.
Hancock.......................TITUS HUTCHINSON.
Leicester..................ALBERT E. STANLEY.
Lincoln....................ALMER A. HIER.
Middlebury....................JAMES M. SLADE, Jr.
Monkton ... .HARRY J. FINNEY.
New Haven.....................JOSEPH R. NASH.
Orwell........................ETHAN M. WRIGHT.
Panton........................ENOCH J. KENT.
Ripton ....CORNELIUS BILLINGS.
Salisbury.....................JAMES FITTS.
Shoreham ....EDSON A. BIRCHARD.
Starksboro....................BURRITT J. GRINNELL.
Vergennes.....................WALTER G. SPRAGUE.
Waltham.......................WILLIAM S. WRIGHT.
Weybridge ....ELIPHALET SAMSON.
Whiting.......................EDWARD A. CASEY.

BENNINGTON COUNTY.

Arlington.....................JAMES K. BATCHELDER.
Bennington....................LUMAN P. NORTON.

Dorset....................DUANE L. KENT.
Glastonbury ....TRUMAN T. ELWELL.
Landgrove..................HORACE II. HARLOW.
Manchester..................LOVELAND MUNSON.
Peru.........................CHARLES BATCHELDER.
Pownal......................ICHABOD F. PADDOCK.
Readsboro..................MERRITT M. HOUGTHON.
Rupert......................J. HENRY GUILD.
Sandgate....................WILLIS S. BENTLEY.
Searsburgh...................WILLIAM O'BRIEN
Shaftsbury...................HORACE B. BOTTUM.
Stamford,....................ALBERT W. WILLMARTH.
Sunderland..................EDWARD G. BACON.
Winhall....................ELIAKIM AMEDEN.
Woodford ....GEORGE W. BICKFORD.

CALEDONIA COUNTY.

Barnet....................CLAUDE HARVEY.
Burke.........................CHARLES A. IIARRIS
Danville....................GEORGE B. DAVIS.
Groton.......................THOMAS B. HALL.
Hardwick.....................CHARLES G. MONTGOMERY.
Kirby ....PRESTON H. GRAVES.
Lyndon......................STEPHEN R McGAFFEY.
Newark ....CHARLES C. LEE.
Peacham....................ASHBEL MARTIN.
Ryegate......................EDWARD MILLER.
Sheffield...................SPENCER DRAKE.
St. Johnsbury.................ELIJAH D. BLODGETT.
Stannard ....ZACHARIAH L. PIERCE.
Sutton.....................REUBEN ELLIS,
Walden.....................WILLIAM G. PERKINS.
Waterford...................WILLARD KINNE.
Wheelock....................SANFORD G. GRAY.

CHITTENDEN COUNTY.

Bolton.......................SMITH N. PEASE.
Burlington,..................BRADLEY B. SMALLEY.

Charlotte...............JOSEPH S. SHAW.
Colchester.....................CHARLES LAFOUNTAIN.
Essex ....ERASTUS F. WHITCOMB.
Hinesburgh.....................ANDREW CURRY.
Huntington.....................GEORGE W. SAYLES.
Jericho.........................GORDON SMITH.
Milton.......................LUCIUS J. DIXON.
Richmond ....HENRY GILLETT.
Shelburne.....................HENRY N. NEWELL.
South Burlington...............HIRAM S. LANDON.
St. George...... ....HARRY SUTTON.
Underhill.....................FRANCIS BARRETT.
Westford ....ASHER C. ROBINSON.
Williston......... .... HIRAM WALSTON.

ESSEX COUNTY.

Bloomfield...... ....JOHN C. PATTEE.
Brighton.....................DAVID S. STORRS.
Brunswick.....................JAMES H. BEATTIE.
Canaan......... ... .SIDNEY MORRISON.
Concord........... ....DAVID W. HIBBARD.
East Haven.....................DAVID H. HUDSON.
Granby.........................LOOMIS WELLS.
Guildhall................. .....No election.
Lemington.....................ARTHUR T. HOLBROOK.
Lunenburgh.....................CHARLES W. KING.
Maidstone.................. ...HORACE ADAMS.
Victory.......................ISAAC R. HOUSTON.

FRANKLIN COUNTY.

Bakersfield......... ....GEORGE B. CUTLER.
Berkshire.....................HENRY COMINGS.
Enosburgh..................... SILAS HOPKINS.
Fairfax.......................CURTIS F. HAWLEY.
Fairfield.....................THOMAS B. KENNEDY.
Fletcher............. ....CHARLES B. PARSONS,
Franklin.....................JOHN WEBSTER.
Georgia ....MOSES WIGHTMAN.

Highgate......................HORACE L. CUTLER.
Montgomery...................OTIS N. KELTON.
Richford......................E. HENRY POWELL.
Sheldon.......................JOHN F. DRAPER.
St. Albans....................PARK DAVIS.
Swanton...................... JAMES A BARNEY.

GRAND ISLE COUNTY.

Alburgh.......................JED P. LADD.
Grand Isle...... ....MATTHIAS LEFEVRE.
Isle La Motte...................NATHAN G. HILL.
North Hero...... ....JEROME HUTCHINS.
South Hero....................HENRY W. CONRO.

LAMOILLE COUNTY.

Belvidere.....................CHARLES B. WESTON.
Cambridge.....................GEO. W. POWELL.
Elen...........................JONAS T. STEVENS.
Elmore.............. ....WILLIAM J. CHURCHILL.
Hyde Park....................NATHAN McFARLAND.
Johnson ....,........LUCIUS H. WHEELER.
Morristown.......... ..,.. ....Vacancy.*
Stowe..... ....No election.
Waterville....................GEORGE W. HULBURD.
Wolcott ....ERASTUS P. FAIRMAN.

* H. HENRY POWERS, elected Assistant Justice of Supreme Court.

ORANGE COUNTY.

Bradford...........................JOSEPH W. BLISS.
Braintree......................H. SHERMAN HARWOOD.
Brookfield................. ...MARSHAL L. GREEN
Chelsea.......................ASA A. GOODWIN.
Corinth....... ....GEORGE C. COOKE.
Fairlee......................:ALEXANDER N. RENFREW.
Newbury......... ....,......EBENEZER C. STOCKER.
Orange........................AARON S. MARTYN.
Randolph ....BAILEY F. ADAMS.
Strafford.....................HARVEY C. BROWN.

Thetford... ... .HEMAN II. GILLETT.
Topsham........ ....No election.
Tunbridge....................SYLVESTER G. GOODWIN.
Vershire......................SILAS TITUS.
Washington..... ....JOHN A. STANLEY.
West Fairlee..... ....JOHN G. EASTMAN.
Williamstown..................JOHN M. PALMER.

ORLEANS COUNTY.

Albany................... ....JOHN F. TENNEY.
Barton..................... ...WILLIAM W. GROUT.
Brownington.. ....ELISHA FOSTER.
Charleston ... . .ROSWELL P. STEVENS.
Coventry.....................WARREN MITCHELL.
Craftsbury............. .. ...JOSEPH SCOTT.
Derby......... ....MOSES M. KELSEY.
Glover......... ....ANDREW C. ATHERTON.
Greensboro..... ... ...HARVEY S. CALDERWOOD
Holland ....STEPHEN M. DAVIS.
Irasburgh... ....WILLIAM D. TYLER.
Jay..... ....HENRY D. CHAMBERLIN.
Lowell ....JAMES BROWN.
Morgan ....WILLIAM A. BARTLETT.
Newport......... ... .JOSIAH GROUT.
Salem.......... ....HORACE RUITER
Troy............. ... .JOHN W. CURRIER.
Westfield.. ... .MEDAD C. HITCHCOCK.
Westmore......... ... . ORANGE C. SPENCER.

RUTLAND COUNTY.

Benson.... ... .ALVAH S. BARTHOLOMEW.
Brandon ... .STEPHEN L. GOODELL.
Castleton........ ... ...PITT W. HYDE.
Chittenden.. ....RILEY V. ALLEN,
Clarendon ....ELI L. HOLDEN.
Danby .. ..ANTHONY S. NICHOLS.
Fair Haven....................SAMUEL W. BAILEY.
Hubbardton. ... . .HENRY WILSON.

Ira............................SIMON L. PECK.
Mendon ....OREL COOK.
Middletown....................ROSWELL BUEL.
Mount Holly ....WILLIAM LORD.
Mount Tabor...................JOHN MINETT.
Pawlet ....CURTIS E. REED.
Pittsfield.....................JOSIAH BABCOCK.
Pittsford.....................WILLIAM B. SHAW.
Poultney......................HARVEY ROWE.
Rutland......................NATHANIEL F. PAGE.
Sherburne ....EDWIN S. COLTON.
Shrewsbury...................JOHN C. FIFIELD.
Sudbury....................DIGHTON C. KETCHAM.
Tinmouth.....................HENRY D. NOBLE.
Wallingford...................JOSEPH DOTY.
Wells ....HENRY McFADDEN.
West Haven...................RODNEY C. ABELL.

WASHINGTON COUNTY.

Barre........................ELI HOLDEN.
Berlin ....J. NEWTON PERRIN
Cabot.. ....NATHANIEL K. ABBOTT.
Calais.......................JAMES K. TOBEY.
Duxbury.....................HARRY BULKLEY.
East Montpelier..............HENRY D. FOSTER.
Fayston ....MATTHEW S. STRONG.
Marshfield...................GEORGE A. PUTNAM.
Middlesex ....SYLVANUS DANIELS.
Montpelier...................MARCUS D. GILMAN.
Moretown ....GOIN B. EVANS.
Northfield...................ELBRIDGE G. PIERCE.
Plainfield. ....STEPHEN C. SHURTLEFF.
Roxbury.....................ENOS K. YOUNG.
Waitsfield ....MOSES E. HADLEY.
Warren......................GEORGE W. CARDELL.
Waterbury...................JOHN B. PARKER.
Woodbury ....SYLVANUS K. CAMERON.
Worcester ....No election.

WINDHAM COUNTY.

Athens...........................ALVAN PARKHURST.
Brattleboro......................JOHN S. CUTTING.
Brookline........................WILLIAM P. STEBBINS.
Dover............................J. ARNOLD NEWELL.
Dummerston.......................SAMUEL N. BEMIS.
Grafton..........................ALBERT H. BURGESS.
Guilford.........................WILLIAM W. BARNEY.
Halifax..........................ALPHEUS H. STONE.
Jamaica..........................JONATHAN G. EDDY.
Londonderry......................JAMES L. MARTIN.
Marlboro.........................WILLIAM W. LYNDE.
Newfane..........................ALVIN B. FRANKLIN.
Putney...........................DAN P. WEBSTER.
Rockingham.......................CARLTON E. WEBB.
Somerset.........................No election.
Stratton.........................MOSES PIKE.
Townshend........................JOHN S. FULLERTON.
Vernon...........................ADDISON WHITHED.
Wardsboro........................OSMER C. FITTS.
Westminster......................ALEXANDER ATCHESON.
Whitingham.......................WELLS P. JONES.
Wilmington.......................STEPHEN T. DAVENPORT.
Windham..........................LEWIS E. WOODWARD.

WINDSOR COUNTY.

Andover..........................HENRY J. PARKER.
Baltimore........................SYLVESTER ELLISON.
Barnard..........................WILLIAM C. DANFORTH.
Bethel...........................NATHANIEL F. CLARK.
Bridgewater......................PETER KING.
Cavendish........................ALVIN S. BURBANK.
Chester..........................HUGH HENRY.
Hartford.........................EDWIN C. WATSON.
Hartland.........................ELAM M. GOODWIN.
Ludlow...........................ELON G. PETTIGREW.
Norwich..........................JOHN DUTTON.

Plymouth......................JOHN C. COOLIDGE
Pomfret........ ....HOMER W. VAIL.
Reading......................GILBERT A. DAVIS.
Rochester... ....PHILANDER BAKER
Royalton......................EBENEZER WINSLOW.
Sharon.......................MARIOT G. HOWE
Springfield........ ....C. HORACE HUBBARD
Stockbridge................... GEORGE N. CULVER.
Weathersfield................JUSTUS DARTT
Weston............. ....SIMEON D. SPAULDING.
West Windsor... ....EUGENE H. SPAULDING.
Windsor................... .. JOHN F. BAILEY.
Woodstock.. ....HENRY BOYNTON.

FRANCIS PHELPS....... ...Grafton........Doorkeeper.
TRACY B. WILLEY...........St. Johnsbury..Ass't Doorkeeper.
ROMEO G. BROWN..........Montpelier.....Page.
CLAUDE M. SEVERANCE...Orwell.........Page.
JOHN S. HARD..............Arlington......Page.
JAMES C. FLANDERS.......Chester........Page.

GRAND LIST FOR 1873

AS REPORTED BY THE GRAND LIST COMMITTEE.

ADDISON COUNTY.

TOWNS.	Polls.	Dogs.	Real Estate.		Personal Property.	1 per cent.	Deductions.	List for State Taxe
	dolls.	dolls.	acres.	dolls.	dolls.	dolls. cts.	dolls.	dolls.cts.
Addison,	380	95	24672	464456	68799	5332 55		5807 55
Bridport,	350	70	25337	493546	70546	5640 92		6060 92
Bristol,	386	76	18420	240796	76303	3170 99		3932 99
Cornwall,	396	87	16816	360983	89263	4502 46		4985 46
Ferrisburgh,	578	118	26417	628685	77668	7003 53		7759 53
Goshen,	144	20	10740	52906	729	536 35		700 35
Granville,	380	57	28326	88258	14089	1023 47		1460 47
Hancock,	191	28	21292	62798	14508	773 06		995 06
Leicester,	150	30	11927	169210	22755	1919 65		2099 65
Lincoln,	562	95	22455	142751	22652	1654 03		2311 03
Middlebury,	980	99	22083	664207	201267	8654 74	64,	9669 74
Monkton,	426	88	20492	294247	32398	3266 45		3780 45
New Haven,	502	90	23269	463816	70777	5345 93		5937 93
Orwell,	524	112	24983	528218	150103	6783 21		7419 21
Panton,	150	33	9149	176636	30220	2068 56		2251 56
Ripton,	256	55	26941	83114	3413	865 29		1176 29
Salisbury,	354	60	16713	242418	72063	3144 81		3558 81
Shoreham,	432	86	29353	517561	141976	6295 37		7113 37
Starksboro',	532	86	22037	175627	28231	2032 58		2650 58
Vergennes,	746	69	1200	309265	107500	4167 65	50,	4932 65
Waltham,	88	23	5403	107542	15435	1229 77		1342 77
Weybridge,	258	52	10038	195063	28143	2232 06		2542 06
Whiting,	194	26	7851	146599	32398	1789 97		2009 97
Totals,	9262	1557	420714	6608102	1371238	79793 40	114,	90498 40

BENNINGTON COUNTY.

TOWNS.	Polls. dolls.	Dogs. dolls.	Real Estate. acres.	dolls.	Personal Property. dolls.	1 per cent. dolls. cts.	Deductions. dolls.	List for State Taxes. dolls.cts.
Arlington,	706	74	22300	308170	118045	4868 15		5648 15
Bennington,	2360	219	24256	1327160	334358	16615 18		19194 18
Dorset,	750	157	25482	410625	64960	4756 14		5663 14
Glastenbury,	38	7	26702	25734	0000	257 34		302 34
Landgrove,	118	25	5664	46219	7750	539 69		682 69
Manchester,	816	124	22162	590635	109762	7003 97		7943 97
Peru,	216	36	18944	104578	9877	1144 55		1396 55
Pownal,	800	107	26626	480144	51932	5350 76		6257 76
Readsboro',	476	66	21549	111189	6840	1180 29		1722 29
Rupert,	472	84	23432	309400	49952	3593 52		4149 52
Sandgate,	266	64	22086	135149	7919	1430 68		1760 68
Searsburgh,	120	10	16037	27792	2000	297 92		427 92
Shaftsbury,	700	131	23640	453608	42599	4002 07		5793 07
Stamford,	304	60	24470	139600	21580	1611 80		1975 80
Sunderland,	304	49	20850	112775	22246	1350 21		1703 21
Winhall,	310	40	25853	122482	14433	1369 15		1749 15
Woodford,	150	20	27044	60574	4000	645 74		815 74
Totals,	8936	1273	371457	4825834	871882	56977 16		67186 16

CALEDONIA COUNTY.

TOWNS.	Polls.	Dogs.	Real Estate. acres.	dolls.	Personal Property.	1 per cent.	Deductions.	List for State Taxes.
Barnet,	820	69	25168	519521	173547	6930 68		7819 68
Burke,	610	39	19808	280732	110066	3913 98		4562 98
Danville,	860	93	34027	575229	136135	7113 64		8006 64
Groton,	366	49	25212	179060	14026	1939 86		2354 86
Hardwick,	700	46	22293	363968	64131	4230 99		5026 99
Kirby,	190	36	15013	131442	11961	1431 03		1660 03
Lyndon,	1190	79	23336	635890	183123	8390 03		9659 03
Newark,	304	45	21045	112125	10712	1231 57		1580 57
Peacham,	488	46	21470	279191	1151	3943 14		4177 14
Ryegate,	380	48	21224	266668	8852	3551 88		3979 88
Sheffield,	376	43	17796	149194	19821	1690 15		2109 15
St. Johnsbury,	2674	119	20614	1750657	846256	23969 13	300,	26462 13
Stannard,	120	13	6779	35380	553	361 35		494 35
Sutton,	450	29	21965	190837	44054	2357 91		2836 91
Walden,	392	33	21671	191249	18024	2092 73		2517 73
Waterford,	346	61	23849	314648	71742	3863 90		4270 90
Wheelock,	340	35	ex'pt		25024	259 24		634 24
Totals,	10606	883	343570	6797181	1935240	77324 21	300,	88513 21

CHITTENDEN COUNTY.

TOWNS.	Polls.	Dogs.	Real Estate.		Personal Property.	1 per cent.	Deductions.	List for State Taxes.
	dolls.	dolls.	acres.	dolls.	dolls.	dolls. cts.	dolls.	dolls.cts.
Bolton,	304	48	23431	149179	4317	1537 96		1880 96
Burlington,	3836	248	5615	3121662	1074219	41956 82	366,	45676 82
Charlotte,	488	103	23700	718493	95903	8143 96		8734 96
Colchester,	1612	189	23449	701960	111227	8131 87		9032 87
Essex,	650	75	22582	663022	10810	6738 32		7463 32
Hinesburgh,	550	90	20817	539082	85575	6247 57		6887 57
Huntington,	382	65	20135	252400	31390	2837 90		3384 90
Jericho,	718	101	20361	579620	109686	6893 06		7712 06
Milton,	720	201	28315	691453	138192	8296 45		9217 45
Richmond,	534	87	18070	508026	43928	5519 54		6160 54
Shelburne,	416	86	14126	415233	46004	4612 37		5114 37
So. Burlington,	270	61	9091	263130	57060	3201 90		3532 90
St. George,	34	6	2263	49012	4726	537 38		577 38
Underhill,	556	115	28507	416524	38058	4545 82		5216 82
Westford,	390	41	22354	415305	10000	4253 05		4684 05
Williston,	358	113	18582	532209	38831	5710 40		6181 40
Totals,	11838	1629	299398	10016611	1900026	119166 37	366,	132267 37

ESSEX COUNTY.

Bloomfield,	214	9	21480	82628	6047	886 75	1109 75
Brighton,	682	76	28572	177312	12650	1899 62	2657 62
Brunswick,	54	6	12145	65155	4575	697 30	757 30
Canaan,	210	30	16503	116329	24125	1404 54	1644 54
Concord,	716	68	28150	399384	83811	4832 25	5616 25
East Haven,	86	20	20280	49212	2620	518 41	624 41
Granby,	92	9	21800	29355	1137	395 22	406 22
Guildhall,	242	37	18835	120337	19318	1396 55	1675 55
Lemington,	86	5	2047	55320	8247	585 67	676 67
Lunenburgh,	424	46	25136	223979	27242	2512 21	2982 21
Maidstone,	102	11	16384	90877	5700	935 77	1078 77
Victory,	130	10	22800	58289	1187	597 76	737 76
Totals,	3038	327	235240	1168207	191998	16602 05	19967 05

FRANKLIN COUNTY.

TOWNS.	Polls.	Dogs.	Real Estate.		Personal Property.	1 per cent.	Deductions.	List for State Taxes.
	dolls.	dolls.	acres.	dolls.	dolls.	dolls. cts.	dolls.	dolls.cts
Bakersfield,	474	101	21030	298240	56898	3551 47		4128 47
Berkshire,	518	112	23880	437445	41006	4784 51		5114 51
Enosburgh,	760	90	26204	495231	67691	5329 22		6479 22
Fairfax,	700	125	22503	450231	41968	4921 99		5743 99
Fairfield,	713	194	38181	682977	61150	7440 27		8346 27
Fletcher,	356	81	20360	253185	20424	2876 09		3313 09
Franklin,	512	103	21833	449498	47114	4969 12		5584 12
Georgia,	550	110	23065	506935	78156	5791 21		6451 21
Highgate,	840	155	29071	589873	80892	6766 75		7761 75
Montgomery,	574	102	28325	219919	20945	2798 64		3474 64
Richford,	494	92	21383	282770	17019	2097 89		3583 89
Sheldon,	602	123	22635	507965	43976	5539 41		6264 41
St. Albans,	3036	211	22579	1754984	491686	21586 70	260,	24583 70
Swanton,	828	107	24833	650148	105392	7650 40		8595 40
Totals,	10955	1733	318013	7617340	1111027	87233 67	260,	91715 67

GRAND ISLE COUNTY.

Albuigh,	564	87	17226	332919	63651	3959 70		4610 70
Grand Isle,	278	57	9733	195031	40411	2354 47		2689 47
Isle La Motte,	210	21	4324	72283	6003	782 86		1013 86
North Hero,	210	38	8000	144377,	10727	1531 01		1799 01
South Hero,	238	61	8727	173452	51965	2251 17		2553 17
Totals,	1500	264	48010	918062	172162	10902 24		12666 24

LAMOILLE COUNTY.

Belvidere,	156	29	17783	60740	2175	629 15		814 15
Cambridge,	672	112	27741	470627	108919	5795 76		6579 76
Eden,	356	47	31302	152923	4797	1577 20		1980 20
Elmore,	301	37	20014	103185	12305	1204 90		1545 91
Hyde Park,	830	89	22151	328262	43834	3720 93		4659 96
Johnson,	740	97	24906	291907	50368	3422 75		4259 75
Morristown,	1020	83	27473	451098	76092	5271 90		6380 90
Stowe,	854	87	37475	507754	59699	5664 53		6605 53
Waterville,	249	31	9907	108475	11109	1195 81		1472 81
Wolcott,	604	51	19436	192383	10347	2027 30		2682 30
Totals,	5802	669	238531	2672354	378373	30519 29		35981 29

ORANGE COUNTY.

TOWNS.	Polls.	Fogs.	Real Estate.		Personal Property.	1 per cent.	Deductions.	List for State Taxes.
	dolls.	dolls.	acres.	dolls.	dolls.	dolls. cts.	dolls.	dolls cts.
Bradford,	804	97	18363	401475	120697	5221 72	80,	6042 72
Braintree,	502	75	21557	223924	46253	2701 77		3278 77
Brookfield,	628	85	24391	314697	67736	3824 33		4537 33
Chelsea,	700	87	23338	327713	76506	4042 19		4829 19
Corinth,	700	93	28421	344628	76541	4211 69		5004 69
Fahlee,	192	27	11351	145735	25192	1709 27		1928 27
Newbury,	1016	141	37029	588553	308055	8966 08		10123 08
Orange,	308	39	20130	144838	12081	1575 19		1922 19
Randolph,	1280	180	28482	778353	108200	9465 53		10925 53
Strafford,	562	92	24407	304826	65130	3699 56		4353 56
Thetford,	668	53	24027	388009	58055	4460 64		5181 64
Topsham,	610	65	28314	244529	41153	2856 82		3531 82
Tunbridge,	606	120	23675	325811	36080	3624 91		4350 91
Vershire,	480	50	21212	201708	28121	2298 29		2828 29
Washington,	494	62	21375	206864	128308	3291 72		3847 72
West Fairlee,	374	40	12258	127483	8040	1364 23		1778 23
Williamstown,	510	88	23584	280394	59584	3399 78		3997 78
Totals,	10434	1394	391914	5349549	1327832	66713 72	80,	78461 72

ORLEANS COUNTY.

Albany,	462	78	16008	275866	26524	3023 90		3563 90
Barton,	856	62	24077	436526	56072	4925 98		5843 98
Brownington,	360	27	16382	167987	11478	1794 65		2181 65
Charleston,	530	34	19551	243145	24403	2675 48		3239 48
Coventry,	454	59	17386	300562	101823	4023 85		4536 85
Craftsbury,	560	66	22054	357397	73100	4304 97		4930 97
Derby,	800	108	20000	506796	222725	7295 21		8203 21
Glover,	536	58	21421	306677	57779	3644 56		4238 56
Greensboro',	504	67	21263	213139	18546	2316 85		2887 85
Holland,	308	50	20332	174270	12843	1871 13		2229 13
Irasburgh,	486	78	24234	315293	60529	3758 22		4322 22
Jay,	220	45	13075	61702	8614	703 16		968 16
Lowell,	414	55	33138	172617	15265	1870 02		2348 02
Morgan,	244	34	17850	97525	11192	1087 17		1365 17
Newport,	810	102	24484	423640	43855	4674 95		5556 95
Salem,	220	34	9176	91230	6253	974 83		1228 83
Troy,	538	76	22560	258799	31861	2906 60		3520 60
Westfield,	288	34	22021	123884	13165	1370 49		1692 49
Westmore,	154	8	19501	56433	996	574 29		736 29
Totals,	8744	1075	383503	4583488	797043	58805 31		63624 31

RUTLAND COUNTY.

TOWNS.	Polls.	Dogs	Real Estate (acres)	Real Estate (dolls)	Personal Property.	1 per cent.	Deductions.	List for State Taxes.
	dolls.	dolls.	acres.	dolls.	dolls.	dolls. cts.	dolls.	dolls. cts.
Benson,	500	98	24634	373621	75172	4490 93		5088 93
Brandon,	1400	135	22138	817465	530238	13777 03		15312 03
Castleton,	1218	180	22132	596816	122279	7190 95	100,	8488 15
Chittenden,	334	65	36948	171118	15585	1867 03		2236 03
Clarendon,	414	92	19100	425438	74849	5002 87		5508 87
Danby,	483	64	24449	331410	91283	4226 93		4773 93
Fair Haven,	1012	132	9692	416245	141182	6574 27		6718 27
Hubbardton,	242	49	15933	153486	82573	2360 59		2651 59
Ira,	160	46	11152	120532	38078	1587 10		1793 10
Mendon,	300	55	22185	120535	5249	1257 84		1612 84
Middletown,	336	65	12089	181781	35488	2372 69		2773 69
Mount Holly,	620	123	26577	248348	37325	2856 73		3599 73
Mount Tabor,	122	31	24338	105037	3559	1085 96		1233 96
Pawlet,	570	118	22350	439692	26174	4658 66		5346 66
Pittsfield,	230	32	10700	81670	15667	973 37		1235 37
Pittsford,	770	95	26560	653666	211346	8650 12		9515 12
Poultney,	1378	185	24356	617386	194513	8118 99		9081 99
Rutland,	3822	425	28010	2656130	1051933	37080 63	346,	40931 63
Sherburne,	220	29	24341	88621	6833	954 54		1203 54
Shrewsbury,	478	88	26817	285323	90559	3758 82		4321 82
Sudbury,	252	37	22440	171015	23582	1945 97		2234 97
Tinmouth,	224	70	16042	176697	19872	1905 69		2259 69
Wallingford,	832	116	22818	469140	160068	6292 08		7240 08
Wells,	296	64	12209	197237	20151	2173 91		2533 91
West Haven,	180	59	15003	167049	45549	2195 98		2364 98
Totals,	16396	2153	523014	10005558	3139410	132349 68	446,	150752 68

WASHINGTON COUNTY.

TOWNS.	Polls.	Dogs	Real Estate (acres)	Real Estate (dolls)	Personal Property.	1 per cent.	Deductions.	List for State Taxes.
Barre,	960	82	20281	620094	166768	7868 62	98,	8812 62
Berlin,	602	92	21593	426925	55800	4827 25	20,	5501 25
Cabot,	648	72	21452	317823	85233	4030 56	60,	4690 56
Calais,	602	77	21423	374573	65591	4401 64		5080 64
Duxbury,	408	53	24187	166025	12954	1789 79		2249 79
E. Montpelier,	496	64	17499	402275	118314	5205 89		5705 89
Fayston,	262	58	20820	104851	4781	1096 32		1416 32
Marshfield,	472	64	23965	233237	29242	2624 79	•	3150 79
Middlesex,	568	57	20707	249587	52113	3017 00		3642 00
Montpelier,	1508	107	4419	815720	412973	12286 93	390,	13511 93
Moretown,	520	80	23168	246703	20967	2676 70		3276 70
Northfield,	1400	161	24239	676684	104412	7810 96	222,	9149 96
Plainfield,	280	31	9324	163615	30976	1945 91		2256 91
Roxbury,	438	45	21898	194135	14334	2084 69		2567 69
Waitsfield,	380	50	15241	246463	67873	3143 36		3573 36
Warren,	502	59	22366	177725	39564	2172 89		2733 89
Waterbury,	956	125	27796	673550	151330	8248 80	60,	9269 80
Woodbury,	414	43	20901	150099	17812	1679 11	,	2133 11
Worcester,	340	52	22401	140234	4256	1504 90		1896 90
Totals,	11756	1371	383653	6386318	1455293	78416 11	850,	90693 11

WINDHAM COUNTY.

TOWNS.	Polls.	Dogs.	Real Estate		Personal Property.	1 per cent.	Deductions.	List for State Taxes.
	dolls.	dolls.	acres.	dolls.	dolls.	dolls. cts.	dolls.	dolls. cts.
Athens,	124	24	8218	65136	0000	651 36		799 36
Brattleboro',	2660	258	19195	1548574	495797	42043 71	638,	22723 71
Brookline,	96	19	6541	60351	13655	740 09		855 09
Dover,	284	39	21409	18420	64456	2493 76		2816 76
Dummerston,	448	64	18481	276167	57051	3333 18		3844 18
Grafton,	474	75	23050	266609	45799	3124 08		3673 08
Guilford,	520	88	21599	258858	49139	3079 97		3687 97
Halifax,	488	103	23036	195739	38159	2341 98		2982 98
Jamaica,	608	89	27328	279092	90693	3703 85		4400 85
Londonderry,	596	89	18433	213048	41229	2542 77		3227 77
Marlboro,	302	52	22890	169460	33296	2017 53		2371 56
Newfane,	486	63	22930	313959	101768	4157 27		4706 27
Putney,	578	58	16123	297049	108830	4058 79		4694 79
Rockingham,	1518	202	25472	875039	319719	11947 58		13067 58
Somerset,	46	6	14331	21457	608	220 65		272 65
Stratton,	130	32	26821	61943	5839	677 82		839 82
Townshend,	542	85	26082	316487	94110	4105 97		4732 97
Vernon,	376	48	11589	209216	47604	2568 20		2992 20
Wardsboro',	382	42	17082	184072	54983	2390 55		2814 55
Westminster,	590	111	24995	397831	81081	4789 12		5450 12
Whitingham,	614	75	23801	242858	59885	3027 43		3716 43
Wilmington,	588	71	24427	332494	91854	4243 48		4902 48
Windham,	250	50	25225	125950	48916	1748 66		2048 66
Totals,	12700	1743	459808	6896912	1943771	88406 83	638,	102211 83

WINDSOR COUNTY.

TOWNS.	Polls.	Dogs.	Real Estate		Personal Property.	1 per cent.	Deductions.	List for State Taxes.
Andover,	256	28	15083	111508	20463	1319 71		1613 71
Baltimore,	46	8	2860	33037	2563	362 00		416 00
Barnard,	584	87	23050	256130	61624	3177 54		3848 54
Bethel,	878	83	25154	376132	82792	4589 24		5550 24
Bridgewater,	544	72	28333	241561	70117	3116 78		3732 78
Cavendish,	680	88	24017	435224	132964	5681 88		6449 86
Chester,	1012	152	33856	658810	262304	9211 14		10375 14
Hartford,	1236	150	25056	642244	178926	8211 70		9597 70
Hartland,	730	135	27095	485650	119162	6048 12		6913 12
Ludlow,	842	113	18308	424088	18559	5226 47	70,	6111 47
Norwich,	674	63	23223	372610	77408	4500 18		5237 18
Plymouth,	464	74	25942	233548	25650	2504 98		3132 98
Pomfret,	512	90	22459	297815	81849	3796 64		4398 64
Reading,	484	74	25162	258185	74038	3322 18		3879 18
Rochester,	630	90	28801	296648	63203	3598 51		4318 51
Royalton,	766	73	23584	403484	83518	4870 02		5709 02
Sharon,	442	79	22565	282666	31889	3145 55		3666 55
Springfield,	1424	145	29412	974877	483916	14587 93		16156 93
Stockbridge,	522	50	24090	255876	32352	2882 28		3454 28
Weathersfield,	642	99	25217	466812	91892	5587 04		6328 04
Weston,	412	60	19387	178871	58521	2873 92		2845 92
West Windsor,	316	39	14006	265640	66517	3321 57		3676 55
Windsor,	728	79	11062	487790	181095	6668 85	66,	7429 87
Woodstock,	1314	116	26327	1154266	428907	15931 73	166,	17095 73
Totals,	16138	2056	548149	9594072	2810524	121045 96	302,	141937 96

GORES AND UNORGANIZED TOWNS.

TOWNS.	Polls.	Dogs.	Real Estate.		Personal Property.	1 per cent.	Deductions.	List for State Taxes.
	dolls.	dolls.	acres	dolls.	dolls.	dolls. cts.	dolls.	dolls. cts.
Averill,			20468	11375		113 75		113 75
*Avery's Gore,		See Buel's Gore.						
†Avery's Gore,			10625	3000		30 00		30 00
‡Avery's Gore,	8		7450	8850		88 50		96 50
Buel's Gore,	12	2	3600	12020		120 20		134 20
Ferdinand,			27264	24765		247 65		247 65
Goshen Gore,		See Harris' Gore.						
Harris' Gore,	24		9918	16080		160 80		184 80
Lewis,			21384	16150		161 50		161 50
Norton,	164		20520	18915	17850	367 65		531 65
Warner's Grant,			2000	1500		15 00		15 00
Warren's Gore,			5296	6095		60 95		60 95
Totals,	208	2	129834	118750	17850	1346 00		1576 00

*Chittenden County. †Essex County. ‡Franklin County.

GRAND LIST, 1873—AGGREGATE.

Addison,	9262	1557	420714	6608102	1371238	79793 40	114,	90498 40
Bennington,	8936	1273	371457	4825834	871882	56977 16		67186 16
Caledonia,	10606	883	343570	5797181	1935240	77324 21	300,	88513 21
Chittenden,	11838	1620	299398	10016611	1900026	119166 37	366,	132167 37
Essex,	3038	327	235240	1468207	191998	16603 05		19967 05
Franklin,	10956	1736	348948	7617340	1111027	87283 67	260,	99715 67
Grand Isle,	1500	264	48010	918062	172162	10902 24		12686 24
Lamoille,	5802	669	238551	2672354	378675	36510 29		36981 29
Orange,	10434	1394	391914	5343540	1327832	66713.72	80,	78461 72
Orleans,	8744	1075	383503	4583488	797043	53805 31		63624 31
Rutland,	16396	2453	523014	10095358	3139410	132349 68	446,	150752 68
Washington,	11756	1371	383653	6386318	1455293	78416 11	850,	90693 11
Windham,	12700	1743	459808	6896912	1943771	88406 83	638,	102211 83
Windsor,	16138	2056	548149	9594072	2810524	124045 96	302,	141937 96
Gores, &c.,	208	2	129834	118750	17850	1346 00		1576 00
Totals,	138314	18432	5125663	82942329	19423971	1023663 00	3356,	1177063 00

STATE OF VERMONT.

OFFICE OF SECRETARY OF STATE, }
Northfield, October 23d, 1873. }

I hereby certify that the foregoing is a true list of the polls and ratable estate of the State of Vermont, as appears from the abstract of the grand list for 1873, on file in this office.

GEORGE NICHOLS, *Secretary of State.*

GRAND LIST FOR 1874

AS REPORTED BY THE GRAND LIST COMMITTEE.

ADDISON COUNTY.

TOWNS.	Polls.	Dogs.	Real Estate.		Personal Property.	1 per cent.	Deductions.	List for State Taxes
	dolls.	dolls.	acres.	dolls.	dolls.	dolls. cts.	dolls.	dolls cts.
Addison,	372	85	21376	435020	59376	4954 05		5411 05
Bridport,	354	67	25361	477575	76272	5538 47		5959 47
Bristol,	680	89	18420	245208	75236	3205 24		3974 24
Cornwall,	412	78	17240	353530	80747	4342 77		4832 77
Ferrisburgh,	586	123	26171	631549	90512	7230 91		7934 91
Goshen,	170	21	10755	51894	4319	552 13		743 13
Granville,	336	53	28437	87032	11076	1020 68		1444 68
Hancock,	181	23	20905	66532	11007	806 59		1018 59
Leicester,	170	30	10722	135950	20273	1762 32		1962 82
Lincoln,	530	110	22771	145005	28308	1752 13		2453 13
Middlebury,	1033	125	22185	685193	197134	8839 30	64,	9936 30
Monkton,	411	80	21511	309333	27857	3371 89		3865 89
New Haven,	510	88	21375	446317	70920	5373 46		5973 46
Orwell,	506	89	25008	511425	158035	6724 90		7310 90
Panton,	153	42	9163	163367	21285	1929 52		2127 52
Ripton,	280	50	27315	80714	3553	842 66		1181 66
Salisbury,	330	50	15813	251452	51342	3052 84		3471 84
Shoreham,	430	85	21317	495318	136349	6331 67		7176 67
Starksboro',	553	115	24110	175551	30313	2061 96		2724 93
Vergennes,	774	96	1145	359231	112100	4313 51	74,	5009 51
Waltham,	84	25	5333	108019	1023	1234 77		1393 77
Weybridge,	234	53	11133	195332	28373	2227 24		2347 24
Whiting,	193	18	7879	151525	28033	1344 58		2018 08
Totals,	9472	1521	422932	6571115	1384414	79525 59	133,	90480 59

30

BENNINGTON COUNTY.

TOWNS.	Polls.	Dogs.	Real Estate.		Personal Property.	1 per cent.	Deductions.	List for State Taxes.
	dolls.	dolls.	acres.	dolls.	dolls.	dolls. cts.	dolls.	dolls. cts.
Arlington,	768	101	21722	343836	113819	4927 35		5496 35
Bennington,	2100	196	24711	1311084	333897	16455 81		19051 81
Dorset,	740	115	24927	375314	53847	4281 61		5139 61
Glastonbury,	120	13	24961	35201	2022	372 23		505 23
Landgrove,	110	26	5357	41211	7833	497 74		626 74
Manchester,	876	151	23305	569758	139029	6787 87		7814 87
Peru,	256	38	19817	97156	9815	1069 71		1363 71
Pownal,	710	80	29626	483386	40290	5243 76		6033 76
Readsboro',	444	61	21005	115309	9333	1243 42		1750 42
Rupert,	441	91	24006	323783	57413	3882 01		4397 01
Sandgate,	250	50	22111	123333	17956	1115 89		1715 89
Searsburgh,	112	18	10974	27610	3050	306 60		436 60
Shaftsbury,	694	130	24444	407690	34785	4424 75		5248 75
Stamford,	336	61	24924	139781	16935	1477 36		1874 36
Sunderland,	280	42	20347	112513	23225	1357 38		1679 38
Winhall,	300	44	25817	115753	12197	1379 50		1623 50
Woodford,	166	29	16342	57100	2700	598 00		798 00
Totals,	9008	1246	363966	4677373	852226	55295 99		65549 99

CALEDONIA COUNTY.

Barnet,	819	75	28033	450616	167692	6182 93		7075 93
Burke,	608	43	20111	270613	102861	3735 04		4391 04
Danville,	860	104	34175	525913	141181	6663 14		7629 14
Groton,	400	50	24306	210317	20635	2500 32		2957 32
Hardwick,	600	46	22337	362836	61878	4267 14		5003 14
Kirby,	182	33	15242	122429	13394	1354 23		1573 23
Lyndon,	1100	88	24465	537509	197133	7316 42		8534 42
Newark,	284	42	21663	104026	9280	1133 06		1459 06
Peacham,	474	60	26812	253381	93678	3570 59		4104 59
Ryegate,	278	42	21303	253317	96881	3471 98		3891 98
Sheffield,	380	58	18496	144603	22340	1669 43		2107 43
St. Johnsbury,	2350	121	21254	2163321	840870	30046 91	300,	32417 91
Stannard,	108	14	7060	40077	840	409 17		529 17
Sutton,	454	29	20027	173237	41437	2146 74		2629 74
Walden,	410	83	21522	173458	19144	1926 00		2363 00
Waterford,	370	60	24659	270332	73385	3159 67		3829 67
Wheelock,	350	80	24530	ex'pt	45284	472 84		832 84
Totals,	10116	931	374580	6067913	1906253	80841 66	300,	91338 66

CHITTENDEN COUNTY.

TOWNS.	Polls.	Dogs.	Real Estate.		Personal Property.	1 per cent.	Deductions.	List for State Taxes.
	dolls.	dolls.	acres.	dolls	dolls.	dolls. cts.	dolls.	dolls.cts.
Bolton,	288	41	23271	101671	4235	1059 06		1388 06
Burlington,	3912	223	5495	2715742	804222	35199 61	354,	38080 61
Charlotte,	462	121	23700	548639	88257	6368 86		6851 86
Colchester,	1560	190	21380	827393	91404	9487 99		10917 99
Essex,	678	85	22532	521618	11771	5363 97		6126 97
Hinesburgh,	548	92	21416	460375	81685	5120 60		6069 60
Huntington,	388	74	20566	241003	31562	2726 55		3188 55
Jericho,	714	104	20353	445274	103045	5483 19		6301 19
Milton,	702	170	29180	651513	237011	8885 24		9757 24
Richmond,	532	78	18054	416048	39750	4157 98		5087 98
Shelburne,	452	85	13706	331797	50232	3830 29		4357 29
So. Burlington,	296	63	9231	224000	45035	2630 85		3048 35
St. George,	46	5	2280	41405	5141	465 46		516 46
Underhill,	570	120	28324	343802	40611	3874 13		4564 13
Westford,	408	53	22263	325947	8000	3339 47		3803 47
Williston,	400	80	16280	421405	38133	4628 58		5106 58
Totals,	11956	1586	300235	8616812	1680124	102960 86	354,	116157 36

ESSEX COUNTY.

Bloomfield,	223	11	21131	80350	9388	906 47		1235 47
Brighton,	733	83	28662	230343	10540	2306 83		3128 83
Brunswick,	56	6	13073	61392	2393	636 84		718 84
Canaan,	196	29	16749	120618	24150	1448 48		1673 48
Concord,	638	73	27343	380960	319436	7033 96		7765 96
East Haven,	84	26	21208	49563	2008	521 70		634 70
Granby,	86	9	21921	32252	883	331 40		426 40
Guildhall,	234	36	18815	130531	17833	1433 54		1753 54
Lemington,	88	9	20101	53504	2303	558 96		635 96
Lunenburgh,	426	43	28230	204138	26789	2309 25		2780 25
Maidstone,	96	21	17283	83094	6333	950 27		1067 27
Victory,	138	17	22293	81016	1100	821 16		976 16
Totals,	3058	363	255739	1511440	421943	19393 86		22814 56

FRANKLIN COUNTY.

TOWNS.	Polls.	Dogs.	Real Estate.		Personal Property.	1 per cent.	Deductions.	List for State Taxes.
	dolls.	dolls.	acres.	dolls.	dolls.	dolls. cts.	dolls.	dolls. cts.
Bakersfield,	453	106	24053	283425	30972	3143 97		3701 97
Berkshire,	513	113	23947	411831	44156	4554 87		5199 87
Enosburgh,	830	103	20638	453290	63306	5165 06		6088 06
Fairfax,	673	125	22421	385121	37510	4226 31		5029 31
Fairfield,	702	108	38664	584921	61111	6163 32		7363 32
Fletcher,	346	82	19953	225363	33024	2543 86		3011 86
Franklin,	508	101	21901	388570	45957	4345 27		4957 27
Georgia,	534	127	23143	401085	77984	4819 79		5483 79
Highgate,	894	130	28975	527239	53035	5853 74		6786 74
Montgomery,	531	190	29205	217837	34017	2513 51		3183 51
Richford,	519	95	21912	279649	20737	3003 86		3608 86
Sheldon,	513	103	23581	434051	43316	4770 99		5115 99
St. Albans,	3243	275	22553	1163539	323006	17015 75	312,	21120 75
Swanton,	838	96	23582	626185	107339	7338 24		8272 24
Totals,	11072	1757	351340	6680347	980410	76702 57	312,	89219 57

GRAND ISLE COUNTY.

Alburgh,	543	91	17058	362393	58353	4207 46		4843 46
Grand Isle,	280	56	9810	195134	48229	2433 63		2769 63
Isle La Motte,	208	24	4329	74230	5898	801 28		1033 28
North Hero,	208	34	7973	138147	8989	1471 36		1713 36
South Hero,	243	54	8673	174322	49708	2240 30		2534 30
Totals,	1478	262	47813	944226	171177	11154 03		12894 03

LAMOILLE COUNTY.

Belvidere,	144	33	17043	53261	2143	553 04		710 04
Cambridge,	700	101	80553	433579	101513	5350 04		6101 94
Eden,	328	43	83768	155205	4995	1692 00		1998 00
Elmore,	293	41	20150	103770	11430	1152 00		1491 00
Hyde Park,	790	78	23184	322435	36842	3502 77		4460 77
Johnson,	736	47	26700	206170	42538	3389 08		4222 08
Morristown,	1070	49	27951	462297	75796	5380 93		6549 93
Stowe,	913	113	39071	520588	66305	5874 83		6899 83
Waterville,	250	30	4804	90485	9587	1000 73		1280 73
Wolcott,	614	66	19142	201935	23023	2233 17		2441 17
Totals,	5842	705	246351	2636335	374561	30115 43		36663 43

ORANGE COUNTY.

TOWNS.	Polls.	Dogs.	Real Estate.		Personal Property.	1 per cent.	Deductions.	List for State Taxes.
	dolls.	dolls.	acres.	dolls.	dolls.	dolls. cts.	dolls.	dolls. cts.
Bradford,	786	83	18336	398321	123027	5263 48	80,	6351 48
Braintree,	496	73	21683	223695	47634	2683 19	.	3232 19
Brookfield,	622	88	24365	319072	67881	3878 53		4688 53
Chelsea,	678	96	22963	321737	85098	4068 35		4842 35
Corinth,	630	91	28441	344632	78425	4230 57		4981 57
Fairlee,	184	25	11351	145157	24029	1691 86		1900 86
Newbury,	990	136	37780	582892	355000	9378 92		10304 92
Orange,	292	50	20060	131805	8449	1402 54		1744 54
Randolph,	1320	190	28419	767502	167700	9352 02		10562 02
Strafford,	560	132	24427	292889	65210	3580 19		4242 19
Thetford,	654	68	23405	361634	61732	4433 86		5155 86
Topsham,	620	65	28606	230613	52087	2827 20		3512 20
Tunbridge,	593	134	23000	325245	35617	3608 62		4334 62
Vershire,	612	76	20987	207609	31063	2386 78		3074 78
Washington,	404	59	21398	199077	22275	2222 52		2745 52
West Fairlee,	380	50	12133	127783	8939	1367 22		1797 22
Williamstown,	526	86	23323	276389	58082	3346 71		3958 71
Totals,	10496	1471	383894	5275392	1137244	63723 36	80,	77550 36

ORLEANS COUNTY.

Albany,	516	87	17409	273015	27193	3002 08		3605 08
Barton	876	67	24374	431778	61803	4935 81		5878 81
Brownington,	360	32	16230	170954	11874	1828 28		2220 28
Charleston,	560	34	20769	245554	33317	2828 71		3424 71
Coventry,	436	53	18244	265650	139793	4054 43		4512 43
Craftsbury,	540	73	22523	361914	72278	4341 92		4957 92
Derby,	844	106	27221	519053	212753	7318 11		8268 11
Glover,	550	58	21431	313240	55389	3659 29		4297 29
Greensboro',	480	65	21248	223308	28367	2518 75		3061 75
Holland,	316	50	20561	171740	15406	1871 46		2237 46
Irasburgh,	466	71	21146	309044	58135	3671 79		4208 79
Jay,	210	20	13887	63448	4520	679 38		918 38
Lowell,	389	53	32763	177025	15508	1923 33		2371 33
Morgan,	288	36	17819	105526	10501	1160 27		1481 27
Newport,	843	107	23093	427722	37523	4652 45		5601 45
Salem,	214	35	9680	97916	5338	1032 54		1284 54
Troy,	500	73	24454	267538	98174	3660 12		4232 12
Westfield,	292	38	20702	130318	14310	1451 28		1781 28
Westmore,	184	6	17144	53770	3914	626 84		816 84
Totals,	8860	1085	379734	4615186	909698	55948 84		65193 84

RUTLAND COUNTY.

TOWNS.	Polls.	Dogs.	Real Estate.		Personal Property.	½ per cent.	Deductions.	List for the Taxes.
	dolls.	dolls.	acres.	dolls.	dolls.	dolls. cts.	dolls.	dolls cts.
Benson,	484	94	24311	413605	74904	4885 09		5163 09
Brandon,	1540	150	24161	879831	505809	13856 40	42,	15504 40
Castleton,	1154	179	22612	583077	198589	7816 66	64,	9085 66
Chittenden,	322	65	37987	185134	23013	2081 46		2468 46
Clarendon,	436	85	19174	436512	70536	5070 48		5542 48
Danby,	492	86	24417	355957	111975	4679 32		5257 32
Fair Haven,	992	110	9693	311940	131503	4434 43		5566 43
Hubbardton,	264	41	15988	154932	78723	2327 55		2632 55
Ira, •	152	43	11100	124103	39833	1039 35		1839 35
Mendon,	310	54	23069	106350	4778	1110 38		1474 38
Middletown,	334	67	13602	181182	56976	2361 58		2782 58
Mount Holly,	638	96	26570	242597	38717	2813 14		3517 14
Mount Tabor,	160	33	24851	106766	6013	1127 79		1317 79
Pawlet,	600	116	23200	446117	44584	4907 01		5623 01
Pittsfield,	200	23	11231	79330	14314	936 74		1164 74
Pittsford,	896	123	26826	684964	254942	9399 06		10418 06
Poultney,	1392	203	23215	665635	200701	8623 36		10221 36
Rutland,	4036	592	28328	2506047	1014663	35207 10	334,	39501 10
Sherburne,	203	30	24993	103012	7603	1106 45		1342 45
Shrewsbury,	538	91	27159	277931	113143	3910 73		4539 73
Sudbury,	274	36	13440	171903	26140	1980 45		2390 45
Tinmouth,	242	68	16173	173383	11279	1896 02		2196 02
Wallingford,	778	145	23989	473365	180766	6541 31		7464 31
Wells,	293	63	12320	184053	16650	2007 13		2373 13
West Haven,	106	48	15003	174573	33753	2083 26		2297 26
Totals.	16894	2687	522574	10013350	3468935	132622 85	440,	151963 65

WASHINGTON COUNTY.

Barre,	946	89	20242	567519	169762	7373 11	92,	8318 11
Berlin,	622	102	21933	361472	58600	4400 72	26,	5068 72
Cabot,	612	78	21375	301601	86805	3884 06	62,	4542 06
Calais,	598	74	21335	337716	60571	3983 87		4654 87
Duxbury,	414	48	23947	178548	13362	1919 10		2381 10
E. Montpelier,	488	65	17616	343421	120529	4639 50		5193 50
Fayston,	230	56	21737	101772	4164	1062 36		1378 36
Marshfield,	500	81	23330	261887	32590	2974 77		3555 77
Middlesex,	556	67	20326	280541	50064	3306 05		3929 05
Montpelier,	1420	90	4243	750304	410127	11604 31	428,	12686 31
Moretown,	548	91	23180	267112	21162	2882 74		3531 74
Northfield,	1402	150	23983	603074	96630	7017 04	236,	8333 04
Plainfield,	290	29	9251	166238	31893	1981 31		2300 31
Roxbury,	418	51	22309	184319	13210	1975 38		2444 38
Waitsfield,	403	58	15052	265815	62605	3284 20		3750 20
Warren,	484	74	21617	181904	79680	2211 84		2772 84
Waterbury,	836	135	27744	615900	153345	7692 55		8713 55
Woodbury,	413	46	20936	150740	19320	1700 00		2138 60
Worcester,	330	60	23196	135740	3272	1391 12		1781 12
Totals.	11036	1444	383511	6078563	1450140	75206 63	844,	87512 63

WINDHAM COUNTY.

TOWNS.	Polls.	Dogs.	Real Estate.		Personal Property.	1 per cent.	Deductions.	List for State Taxes.
	dolls.	dolls.	acres.	dolls.	dolls.	dolls. cts.	dolls.	dolls cts.
Athens,	128	24	8320	5.250	0000	59 50		744 50
Brattleboro',	28 8	265	19271	1576173	446673	20230 46	654,	22659 46
Brookline,	94	22	6524	51756	8771	605 27		721 27
Dover,	290	35	21694	163219	588 9	2221 38		2516 88
Dummerston,	430	62	18181	218215	59573	3085 88		3577 88
Grafton,	466	68	23064	273246	45994	3192 40		3726 40
Guilford,	520	88	21590	233550	40507	2740 57		3348 57
Halifax,	474	94	23040	109176	43234	2126 98		2694 98
Jamaica,	563	86	26769	215120	49071	2944 91	.	3598 91
Londonderry,	612	71	18660	194655	36680	2313 35		2996 35
Marlboro,	320	48	21374	139931	29646	1695 79		2063 79
Newfane,	490	54	23002	242814	99126	3419 40		3963 40
Putney,	534	63	16228	280543	108070	3886 13		4503 31
Rockingham,	1548	200	25381	958199	337391	12955 20	.	14703 20
Somerset,	36	6	14330	20553	537	210 90		253 90
Stratton,	140	27	25359	49023	4895	548 23		715 23
Townshend,	498	82	25913	277683	79899	3575 82		4155 82
Vernon,	356	65	11563	190467	46437	2359 04		2780 04
Wardsboro',	396	49	17915	155381	53890	2092 71		2537 71
Westminster,	540	96	25750	342971	80000	4229 71		4865 71
Whitingham,	588	105	23738	246137	73434	3193 71		3886 71
Wilmington,	576	62	23040	324824	89387	4142 11	60,	4720 11
Windham,	254	52	15281	109593	42181	1520 74		1826 74
Totals,	13596	1724	456489	6555007	1833312	83883 19	714,	97585 19

WINDSOR COUNTY.

TOWNS.	Polls.	Dogs.	Real Estate.		Personal Property.	1 per cent.	Deductions.	List for State Taxes.
Andover,	242	35	16114	97870	23251	1211 21		1488 21
Baltimore,	48	8	2303	23573	3546	332 19		388 19
Barnard,	586	89	24506	287600	68700	3563 90		4238 90
Bethel,	840	93	24823	368481	80234	4488 05		5121 05
Bridgewater,	523	78	28363	239189	68995	3081 75		3681 75
Cavendish,	700	83	24733	400428	144587	5140 15		6223 15
Chester,	1020	153	33917	627626	259646	8872 72		10044 72
Hartford,	1302	123	25369	682036	177060	8590 96		9975 96
Hartland,	858	131	27027	622592	103387	7259 19		8048 19
Ludlow,	856	130	19383	418151	100341	5181 95	78,	6091 95
Norwich,	678	73	25212	345983	57477	4034 60	.	4785 60
Plymouth,	456	72	23952	203196	26561	2297 59		2625 59
Pomfret,	504	86	22404	307005	79958	3869 63		4459 63
Reading,	454	68	25251	248376	80361	3287 37		3809 37
Rochester,	690	73	30602	273318	60009	3383 21		4095 21
Royalton,	776	72	23523	375993	91680	4676 73		5524 73
Sharon,	454	83	23471	257598	30720	2883 18		3419 18
Springfield,	1476	112	29419	923900	483334	14072 34		15660 34
Stockbridge,	500	70	28078	193914	30715	2246 29		2816 29
Weathersfield,	634	103	25174	448551	92262	5408 13		6132 13
Weston,	414	63	19484	158534	55417	2143 51		2620 51
West Windsor,	326	38	14131	231440	69857	3092 97		3458 97
Windsor,	784	85	11062	504199	174797	6789 96	72,	7586 96
Woodstock,	1328	141	25153	1033830	376045	14068 65	180,	15357 65
Totals,	16198	2055	559860	9484863	2738030	120228 23	330,	138152 23

GORES AND UNORGANIZED TOWNS.

TOWNS.	Polls.	Dogs.	Real Estate.		Personal Property.	1 per cent.	Deductions.	List for State Taxes.
	dolls.	dolls.	acres.	dolls.	dol.s.	dolls. cts.	dolls.	dolls. cts.
Averill,			20468	16760		167 60		167 60
*Avery's Gore,			See Buel's Gore.					
†Avery's Gore,			10625	6000		60 00		60 00
‡Avery's Gore,	4		7310	9125		91 25		95 25
Buel's Gore,	13		3609	7075		70 75		82 75
Ferdinand,	10		27164	32115		321 15		331 15
Goshen Gore,			See Harris' Gore.					
Harris' Gore,	8	1	8846	24175		241 75		250 75
Lewis,			21384	32250		322 50		322 50
Norton,	96		20520	42630		2600	446 30		542 36
Warner's Grant,			2000	3000		30 00		30 00
Warren's Gore,			5896½	10235		102 55		102 55
Totals,	130	1	127623	183385	2000	1853 85		1984 85

*Chittenden County. †Essex County. ‡Franklin County.

GRAND LIST, 1874—AGGREGATE.

Addison,	9472	1621	422932	6571145	1381414	79525 59	138,	90480 59
Bennington,	9008	1246	360866	4677373	852226	55295 99		65549 99
Caledonia,	10415	931	371583	6067913	1966253	80341 66	300,	91388 66
Chittenden,	11956	1586	300226	8616812	1680124	102969 36	354,	116157 36
Essex,	3058	363	255739	1511440	424946	19393 86		22814 86
Franklin,	11072	1757	351310	6689847	980410	76703 57	312,	80219 57
Grand Isle,	1478	262	47843	944226	171177	11154 03		12894 03
Lamoille,	5843	706	246664	2636985	374563	30115 48		36363 48
Orange,	10436	1471	389883	5275092	1297244	65723 36	80,	77550 36
Orleans,	8850	1085	379724	4615186	909698	55243 84		56193 84
Rutland,	16894	2687	522574	10013650	3268955	132822 85	440,	151963 85
Washington,	11626	1444	383541	6078563	1150100	75286 63	844,	87513 63
Windham,	12696	1724	453489	6353007	1833312	83883 19	711,	97389 19
Windsor,	16198	2055	550830	9284893	2738030	120229 23	330,	138152 23
Gores, &c.,	130	1	127622	183385	2000	1353 85		1984 85
Totals,	139142	19939	5170683	79724217	19330432	990540 49	3512'	1145115 49

STATE OF VERMONT.

OFFICE OF SECRETARY OF STATE, }
Northfield, Sept. 14th, 1874. }

I hereby certify that the foregoing is a true list of the polls and personal estate, as appears from the abstracts of the grand list of 1874, on file in this office, and of the real estate of the State of Vermont, as averaged and equalized by the State Equalizing Board.

GEORGE NICHOLS, *Secretary of State.*

GENERAL INDEX.

A.

B.

C.

D.

G.

J.

K.

L.

M.

N.

O.

P.

R.

S.

T.

U.

V.

W.

ACTS AND RESOLVES

PASSED BY THE

GENERAL ASSEMBLY

OF THE

STATE OF VERMONT,

AT THE

SPECIAL SESSION,

CONVENED PURSUANT TO A

PROCLAMATION OF THE GOVERNOR,

JANUARY 13, A. D. 1875.

ACTS AND RESOLVES.

SPECIAL SESSION, A. D. 1875.

No. 1.—AN ACT RELATING TO THE VERMONT REFORM SCHOOL.

It is hereby enacted by the General Assembly of the State of Vermont :

SEC. 1. A sum of money not exceeding thirty thousand dollars is hereby appropriated for the purpose of erecting and fitting up buildings for the Vermont Reform School, and all the necessary fittings, fixtures and furniture for the same, and for the purchase of lands for the use of said school ; and said bills and expenses incurred shall be approved by at least two of the trustees of the school, and audited by the auditor of accounts, who shall draw his order for said expenses upon the state treasurer.

32

SEC. 2.   The governor is hereby authorized to purchase for the use of said school, the grounds and buildings known as the Champlain Arsenal property, at a cost not to exceed eleven thousand dollars, and the Vermont Reform School shall hereafter be located at Vergennes.   The governor is also directed to purchase such additional lands at Vergennes, as he may deem necessary for the purposes of the school, at a further cost not to exceed eight thousand dollars,—said sum to form a part of the appropriation mentioned in section one.

SEC. 3.   The necessary buildings and fixtures at Vergennes, for the use of said school, shall be erected under the supervision of the governor, and trustees of the Vermont Reform School.

SEC. 4.   The trustees of the Vermont Reform School are hereby authorized to sell the lands belonging to the state at Waterbury, and such other property as cannot be profitably used at Vergennes, and the proceeds thereof shall be covered into the treasury of the state.

SEC. 5.   This act, so far as it shall be construed to relate to the place of confinement of the inmates of the Vermont Reform School, shall take effect on the first day of December, A. D. 1875, and for all other purposes it shall take effect from its passage.

Approved, January 15, 1875.

No. 2.—AN ACT RELATING TO THE VERMONT RE-FORM SCHOOL.

SECTION	SECTION
1. Trustees and superintendent shall remove the pupils to the school buildings in Vergennes as soon as may be after the completion of said buildings: such transfer to be lawful and regular.	2. Proceeds of sale of property at Waterbury, available for the benefit of the school at Vergennes. 3. To take effect.

It is hereby enacted by the General Assembly of the State of Vermont :

SEC. 1.   As soon as practicable after the completion of the Vermont Reform School buildings at Vergennes, as authorized by an act approved January 15, A. D. 1875, entitled "An act relating to the Vermont Reform School," it shall be the duty of the trustees and superintendent thereof to cause the pupils therein to be conveyed to and committed within the buildings so completed as aforesaid, and such transfer and commitment shall in all respects be deemed lawful and regular, and a legal continuance of their sentences of imprisonment respectively, the same as though they had been kept in said school at Waterbury.

SEC. 2.   The proceeds of the sale of the real estate and property at Waterbury, authorized to be sold by the terms of the act aforesaid, shall be available for the benefit of said reform school, and may be drawn from the state treasury upon the order of said trustees, and used in paying the expenses of finishing and furnishing said school buildings.

SEC. 3.   This act shall take effect from its passage.

Approved, January 15, 1875.

No. 3.—AN ACT PROVIDING FOR THE ADMISSION OF GIRLS TO THE VERMONT REFORM SCHOOL.

SECTION	SECTION
1. Girls not less than ten admitted to Vermont Reform School; jurisdiction of courts.	3. Five thousand dollars appropriated for the objects specified in this bill.
2. Duties of trustees relating to arrangement of buildings.	

It is hereby enacted by the General Assembly of the State of Vermont:

SEC. 1. Girls not less than ten years of age, nor more than fifteen, shall be admitted to the Vermont Reform School upon the same terms and for the same crimes and offenses that boys are now admitted. And the several courts within this state shall have the same powers to sentence or commit girls to the Vermont Reform School, that they now have or may hereafter have by the laws of this state to sentence or commit boys.

SEC. 2. The trustees of said school shall arrange buildings for the complete separation of the sexes, except for educational and religious instruction, and such recreation as may be allowed by the trustees and superintendent, in their discretion.

SEC. 3. That a sum not exceeding five thousand dollars be appropriated to carry the objects of this bill into effect.

Approved, January 15, 1875.

No. 4.—AN ACT RELATING TO CONVICTIONS AND SENTENCES TO THE VERMONT REFORM SCHOOL.

It is hereby enacted by the General Assembly of the State of Vermont:

SEC. 1. No boy under the age of ten years shall be sentenced to the Reform School for any offense which by the general law is punishable by fine only; provided, that when any boy under that age shall be sentenced by any court to pay a fine, or a fine and costs, and shall be committed for the non-payment thereof, such commitment shall be to the Reform School instead of the county jail, and the mittimus shall be drawn accordingly.

SEC. 2. This act shall take effect from its passage.

Approved, January 15, 1875.

No. 5.—AN ACT RELATING TO THE JURISDICTION AND AUTHORITY OF THE JUDGES OF THE SUPREME COURT OVER BOYS CONFINED AT THE VERMONT REFORM SCHOOL.

It is hereby enacted by the General Assembly of the State of Vermont:

SEC. 1. The kindred or friends of any boy confined at the Vermont Reform School, or the selectmen or overseer of the poor of any town, or mayor or aldermen of any city, from which such boy is sent to said school, may by petition and summons annexed, signed by any judge of the supreme court, cause such boy to be brought before said judge, who shall have full jurisdiction on all matters and questions relating to such boy's confinement at said school, and may, upon such petition and hearing, discharge such boy from said school, or remand him back to said school, or make such order or orders in the case as to said judge shall seem just and reasonable ; and the record upon such petition, made and signed by the judge hearing said case, shall be final and conclusive in such case.

SEC. 2. This act shall take effect from its passage.

Approved, January 15, 1875.

No. 6.—AN ACT IN AMENDMENT OF AN ACT AP-PROVED NOVEMBER 19, 1866, ENTITLED "AN ACT FOR THE REGULATION AND GOVERNMENT OF THE VERMONT REFORM SCHOOL," AND IN AMENDMENT OF AN ACT IN ADDITION THERE-TO, APPROVED NOVEMBER 21, 1867.

It is hereby enacted by the General Assembly of the State of Vermont :

SEC. 1. Section one of an act approved November 19, 1866, entitled " An act for the regulation and government of the Vermont Reform School," is hereby amended by striking out the word " Waterbury," and inserting in lieu thereof the word *Vergennes.* Sections one and two of an act in addition thereto, approved November 21, 1867, are hereby amended by striking out the word " Waterbury," and inserting in lieu thereof the word *Vergennes;* and section two of the same act is amended by striking out the word " Washington," where it occurs in said section, and inserting in lieu thereof the word *Addison.*

SEC. 2. This act shall take effect December 1, A. D. 1875.

Approved, January 15, 1875.

No. 7—AN ACT APPROPRIATING MONEY TO COVER THE EXTRA EXPENSE OCCASIONED BY THE DESTRUCTION OF THE VERMONT REFORM SCHOOL BUILDING BY FIRE.

SECTION
1. Extraordinary expenses of Reform School to be paid out of moneys appropriated to defray ordinary expenses thereof.

SECTION
2. Accounts to be paid as ordinary expenses are paid.
3. To take effect.

It is hereby enacted by the General Assembly of the State of Vermont:

SEC. 1. The trustees of the Vermont Reform School are hereby authorized and directed to pay the extraordinary expenses occasioned by the destruction of the Vermont Reform School building by fire, out of any moneys now remaining in the treasury, of the appropriation heretofore made to defray the ordinary expenses of said school.

SEC. 2. All bills and accounts coming within the provisions of this act shall be audited and paid in the manner now provided by law for the payment of the ordinary expenses of the Vermont Reform School.

SEC. 3. This act shall take effect from its passage.

Approved, January 15, 1875.

No. 8.—AN ACT PROVIDING FOR NECESSARY IMPROVEMENTS IN THE STATE PRISON.

It is hereby enacted by the General Assembly of the State of Vermont :

SEC. 1. A sum of money not exceeding twelve thousand five hundred dollars is hereby appropriated, to be expended under the direction of the directors of the State Prison, in the enlargement of the prison work shops, the extension of the hall, and the erection of more cells for the lodgment and safe keeping of convicts, and in providing more suitable accommodations for the female prisoners ; and the auditor of accounts is directed to audit the accounts of the directors of the State Prison for the expenditure herein provided, and draw orders therefor on the state treasurer, who shall pay the same as they may be presented.

SEC. 2. This act shall take effect from its passage.

Approved, January 15, 1875.

No. 9.—AN ACT TO AUTHORIZE THE JUDGE OF PROBATE AND REGISTER OF HIS COURT, WITHIN AND FOR THE DISTRICT OF BENNINGTON TO COMPLETE THE PROBATE RECORDS OF SAID DISTRICT.

It is hereby enacted by the General Assembly of the State of Vermont:

SEC. 1 The judge of probate and the register of his court, within and for the District of Bennington, are hereby authorized, and it is made their duty, during the present term of office of said judge, to record in convenient and suitable books for that purpose, all unrecorded acts, orders, decrees and proceedings whatsoever, lawful to be recorded, of the predecessors in office of said judge, so far as may be done from the minutes and files belonging to the probate court within said district

SEC. 2. Said judge or register shall certify and attest at the close of each record so made by him as aforesaid, that the same is a true record from the original minutes and files in the probate office of said district, and shall affix the date of making such record.

SEC. 3. All copies of such records, duly attested by the probate judge or register of said district, shall be received in evidence in all the courts of law and equity in this state, the same as though said records had been

duly made and attested by the several judges and registers of probate whose duty it was to have made and attested said records.

SEC. 4. The aforesaid judge of probate shall receive
as compensation for the making and attesting said records
as aforesaid, the sum of ten cents per folio, to be paid in
the same manner as is now provided by law for the payment of the salaries of judges of probate; the aforesaid
judge having first rendered his account therefor to the
auditor of accounts, duly verified by the oath of himself
and the register of his court.

SEC. 5. This act shall take effect from its passage.

Approved, January 15, 1875.

No. 10.—AN ACT TO PAY CERTAIN OFFICERS OF THE GENERAL ASSEMBLY THE SUMS THEREIN MENTIONED.

It is hereby enacted by the General Assembly of the State of Vermont:

SEC. 1. The auditor of accounts is hereby directed to
draw orders on the treasurer in favor of the clerk of the
house and secretary of the senate for the sums of fifty
dollars each; also orders in favor of the assistant secretary of the senate, assistant clerks of the house, and reporters of the senate and house of representatives, for

the sums of thirty dollars each, as compensation for services for the extra session of 1875.

SEC. 2. This act shall take effect from its passage.

Approved, January 15, 1875.

No. 11.—JOINT RESOLUTION DIRECTING THE PRESIDENT OF THE SENATE AND SPEAKER OF THE HOUSE TO MAKE ARRANGEMENTS WITH THE CENTRAL VERMONT RAILROAD TO TRANSPORT THE MEMBERS OF THE LEGISLATURE TO VERGENNES.

Resolved by the Senate and House of Representatives:

That the president of the senate and speaker of the house are directed to make arrangements with the managers of the Central Vermont Railroad to transport the members of both branches of the legislature to and from Vergennes, on the 14th instant, for the purpose of allowing said members to inspect property at that place with a view to decide upon a site for the Vermont Reform School. And that the trustees and superintendent of the Vermont Reform School be requested to join the general assembly in this inspection.

LYMAN G. HINCKLEY,
President of the Senate.

J. GROUT,
Speaker of the House of Representatives.

No. 12.—JOINT RESOLUTION TO PAY JOSEPH SCOTT.

Resolved by the Senate and House of Representatives:

WHEREAS, Joseph Scott, the member of the house of representatives from the town of Craftsbury, now in attendance upon this extra session of the general assembly, has fallen ill, and is now confined to his room; therefore,

The treasurer of the state is hereby directed to pay said Scott his per diem until such time as he may so far recover as to be able to leave for home.

LYMAN G. HINCKLEY,
President of the Senate.

J. GROUT,
Speaker of the House of Representatives.

STATE OF VERMONT.

OFFICE OF SECRETARY OF STATE, }
Montpelier, January 16, 1875. }

I hereby certify that the foregoing twelve numbers are true copies of the Acts and Resolves passed by the General Assembly at a Special Session convened, pursuant to a Proclamation of the Governor, January 13, A. D. 1875.

GEORGE NICHOLS, *Secretary of State.*